P9-DGR-381

ZEUS

By the same author

The Summer of My Greek Tavérna: A Memoir

Greece: An Illustrated History

The Essential Greek Handbook

Greek-English Dictionary

Patmos: A History and Guide

The Greek Food and Drink Book

Armstrong: A Novel

ZEUS

A Journey Through Greece in the Footsteps of a God

TOM STONE

BLOOMSBURY

Published by Bloomsbury USA, New York
Distributed to the trade by Macmillan

All papers used by Bloomsbury USA are natural, recyclable products made from wood grown in well-managed forests. The manufacturing processes conform to the environmental regulations of the country of origin.

LIBRARY OF CONGRESS CATALOGING-IN-PUBLICATION DATA

Stone, Tom.
Zeus : a journey across Greece in the footsteps of a god / Tom Stone.
Includes bibliographical references and index.
p. cm.
ISBN-13: 978-1-58234-518-5
ISBN-10: 1-58234-518-X
1. Zeus (Greek deity). 2. Mythology, Greek. 3. Gods, Greek.
4. Greece—Religion. 5. Greece—History. I. Title.

BL820.J8S76 2008
292.2'113—dc22
2007044077

First U.S. Edition 2008

1 3 5 7 9 10 8 6 4 2

Typeset by Westchester Book Group
Printed in the United States of America by Quebecor World Fairfield

For Fárzaneh

. . . to move from place to place in Greece is to become aware of the stirring, fateful drama of the race as it circles from paradise to paradise. Each halt is a stepping-stone along a path marked out by the gods. They are stations of rest, of prayer, of meditation, of deed, of sacrifice, of transfiguration. At no point along the way is it marked FINIS.

HENRY MILLER, *The Colossus of Maroussi*

Divinity at its very source is human.

JANE HARRISON, *Themis*

CONTENTS

BALKAN MTS.
Black Sea
Adriatic Sea
Bosporus
Constantinople
(Istanbul)
Evros River
Sea of
Marmara
Thessaloníki
Samothrace
Mt. Áthos
Dion
Mt. Ólympus
Hellespont
PHRYGIA
Troy
Thessaly
HITTITE EMPIRE
Dodóna
Mt. Pelion
Aegean Sea
Asia Minor
Iónian Sea
VIOTÍA
Delphi
Évia
LYDIA
Thebes
Ithaca
Corinth
Athens
Samos
Olympía
Mycenae
Piraeus
Argos
Tíryns
Miletus
CARIA
Náfplion
Peloponnese
Sparta
Santoríni
Rhodes
Iráklion
Crete
Knossós
Mt. Ida
Górtyn
0
125 Miles
0
125 KM
Mediterranean Sea

CHRONOLOGY

NEOLITHIC AGE

c. 7000 B.C.	Zeus is worshipped as amorphous Sky God by Greek-speaking tribes in Russian steppes and south of the Caucasus.
c. 6500 B.C.	Goddess-worshipping Neolithic farmers from Mesopotamia inhabit Greek mainland, islands, and Crete.
c. 2500 B.C.	Beginnings of Minoan civilization on Crete and Santoríni.

BRONZE AGE

c. 2000 B.C.	First Minoan palaces on Crete. Minoan ships control eastern Mediterranean.
c. 1680 B.C.	Zeus worshippers from Caucasus invade mainland Greece, establish strongholds at Tíryns, Mycenae, Pylos, and elsewhere.
	Beginnings of Mycenaean civilization.
c. 1640 B.C.	Massive explosion of "Holy Volcano" on Santoríni severely weakens Minoan hegemony.
c. 1640–1480 B.C.	Minoans and Mycenaeans establish extensive trade relations.
c. 1480 B.C.	Mycenaeans invade and occupy Crete, dominating all Greece.

	Zeus is "born" in anthropomorphic form in a cave atop Crete's highest mountain. Spends childhood on Crete. Travels to mainland to overthrow his father, Krónos, and other Titans. Establishes rule on Mt. Ólympus. Fathers numerous deities as well as the royal lines and heroes of Crete, Mycenae, Argos, Thebes, Macedonia, and Troy.
	Prométheus steals fire for mankind. Zeus imprisons him in the Caucasus, punishes mankind with Pandóra and Great Flood, promises further retribution.
	Followers of Zeus and the Great Goddess coexist, often tempestuously, on the mainland and the islands.
c. 1225 B.C.	The Trojan War between the united Greek forces and Troy and its allies. Zeus, said to have started the war to punish the Greeks, sides with the Trojans. The Greeks win but are badly weakened.
c. 1200 B.C.	Greek-speaking tribes from north and northeast, collectively known as Dorians, invade Greece, reducing Mycenaean hegemony to rubble.

IRON AGE ("DARK" AGE)

c. 1200–776 B.C.	An unsettled period of migration and political realignment as all knowledge of writing, of the past, and of the building of fortified citadels is lost. Gradual replacement of former kingships with rule of *áristi* (best men) in agriculture-based city-states.
	Zeus and his fellow Olympians are given nearly absolute rule at all major Great Goddess–worshipping sites throughout Greece, particularly at Dodóna, Delphí, and Olympía.
c. 900 B.C.	Writing resumes as the Phoenician-based alphabet is adapted to spoken Greek.
c. 800 B.C.	Building of the first temples to house all gods and goddesses but Zeus.

c. 776 B.C.	Recorded history is said to begin with the first inscribed date of the Games at Olympía, honoring Zeus.
c. 750 B.C.	Homer's *Iliad* and *Odyssey* are written down.
c. 700 B.C.	Hesiod's *Theogony* and *Works and Days.*
	End of Greece's Dark Age.

ARCHAIC AGE

c. 800–500 B.C.	Gradual evolution of the city-states. Increasing territorial disputes. Tyrants replace aristocratic rule in some states, including Athens. Zeus assumes dominant role as protector of all aspects of Greek life, public and private.
594 B.C.	Athenian leader Solon introduces radical social and political changes, foreshadowing democracy.
582 B.C.	Thales establishes first school of philosophy at Miletus, on the Aegean coast of Turkey, mainly concerned with the knowable (i.e., "scientific") causes and workings of the cosmos.
509 B.C.	Athenian leader Cleisthenes begins reform of constitution, grants equal political rights to all citizens, and abolishes aristocratic tribal classifications. Beginnings of the world's first democracy.

CLASSICAL AGE

490 B.C.	Persians invade Greece, are defeated by Athenian-led Greeks at the Battle of Marathon.
480 B.C.	Persians reinvade. United Greek city-states again repel invasions, destroying Persian fleet at Battle of Salamís.
	Zeus is given much credit for the Greeks' near-miraculous victory, as several storms, earthquakes, and pronouncements of Delphí's oracle (revealing the will of the god) prove pivotal in victory.

466 B.C.	Gigantic Temple of Zeus, one of the Seven Wonders of the World, is begun at Olympía.
460 B.C.	Provoked by Athens's imperial ambitions, Sparta and its Peloponnesian League allies declare war.
456 B.C.	Temple of Zeus is completed.
445 B.C.	Athens and Sparta agree on thirty-year peace.
432 B.C.	Sparta resumes war after blatant breaches of treaty by Athens.
c. 425 B.C.	Colossal gold and ivory statue of Zeus is installed in temple at Olympía.
404 B.C.	Athens capitulates unconditionally to Spartans.
399 B.C.	Socrates, convicted of corrupting the young with his talk of being guided by a "voice," or *daímon*, in his head, is condemned to death. Rather than flee, he follows his *daímon* and poisons himself with hemlock.

POST-CLASSICAL AGE

404–371 B.C.	Sparta is dominant in Greece.
373 B.C.	Temple of Apóllon, housing Delphí's oracle, is destroyed by earthquakes, fire, and floods.
360–346 B.C.	Third Sacred War to guard Delphí's autonomy allows Macedonian king Philip II to join the once-exclusive league protecting the sanctuary.
338 B.C.	Battle of Chaeronea. Philip and son, the eighteen-year-old Alexander, defeat Athens and Thebes to control all Greece; install gold and ivory statues of royal Macedonian line opposite Zeus's temple at Olympía.
336 B.C.	Philip is assassinated; Alexander the Great becomes king.
334–323 B.C.	Alexander conquers most of Asia Minor and Egypt; proclaims himself a son of Zeus after visiting the oracle of Zeus Ammon in the Libyan desert.
323 B.C.	Alexander dies.

HELLENISTIC AGE

323–280 B.C.	Wars of Alexander's successors over control of his empire.
279 B.C.	Gauls invade Greece. Zeus, in defense of Delphí, destroys their army with earthquakes and a blizzard. It is the god's last stand.

THE ROMAN OCCUPATION

197–146 B.C.	Roman conquest of Greece, taking Delphí in 191 and Olympía in 146 B.C.
c. 180 B.C.	Great Altar of Zeus is built at Pergamon in Asia Minor. Described in Revelations as the site of "Satan's seat" (Rev. 2:12–13). Later used as a model for one of Hitler's rostrums.
165 B.C.	Revolt of the Maccabees after Alexander's successor, Antiochus IV, installs an altar to Zeus in the Temple of Jerusalem. Today, the Maccabees' rededication of the temple is celebrated as Hanukkah.
27 B.C.	Julius Caesar's adopted son, Octavian, becomes emperor and is given the name Augustus. Beginning of the Pax Romana (Roman Peace).
A.D. 14	Death of Augustus. Shortly afterward, he becomes deified. At Olympía, a statue of Augustus as Zeus, holding a thunderbolt in his right hand, is installed in the former temple of the Great Mother, now dedicated to the Roman emperors.
37–41	Reign of Caligula. Tries to have Zeus's statue at Olympía transported to Rome, but the statue utters such a roar of laughter that the workmen run off.
117–138	Hadrian is emperor. Finishes great Temple of Zeus, the Olympieum, in Athens in 131.
313	Emperors Constantine and Licinius legitimize Christianity.
361–363	Julian is emperor. Attempts to restore primacy of

	"pagan" faiths, is visited by Zeus, but is subsequently killed in battle with Persians.
380	Theodosius I is crowned emperor, has himself baptized as a Christian, and begins persecution of pagans.
391	The cult of Zeus is banned.
c. 394	Zeus's colossal gold and ivory statue is dismantled and carried to Constantinople.

AUTHOR'S NOTE

Only shards and echoes remain of the original tales that the Greeks fashioned about the life and times of their supreme deity. There was little writing to speak of in those days, just a rough, wedge-shaped script that had no literary use, and the stories that circulated around the hearth fires of his worshippers went completely unrecorded.

In fact, some seven hundred years would pass between Zeus's nativity and the earliest written accounts we have of him and his fellow Olympians. Initially, these were only those scattered glimpses woven by Homer into the much greater tapestries of his *Iliad* and *Odyssey*—but the Zeus that we encounter there was well into his prime, having previously battled to sole possession of the throne on Mt. Ólympus and fathered a multitude of offspring to fill the offices of his regime. In addition, in Homer's works, the Great Thunderer was already locked into that notorious, knock-down, drag-out marriage with his sister and second wife, Héra.

For information about Zeus's birth and early years, it is necessary to go to the writings of a peasant farmer from the Greek mainland named Hesiod. Hesiod flourished about fifty years after Homer, c. 700 B.C., and his musings have survived in two long poems: *Hesiod's Theogony*, a genealogy of the gods from the creation of the cosmos until the fathering by Zeus of the semidivine hero Hérakles; and *Works and Days*, for the most part a treatise on living a good and honest life, but incorporating, as object lessons, fascinating digressions on the Five Ages of the World and Zeus's doings with Prométheus and Pandóra.

While Homer's and Hesiod's works comprised what might be called the ancient Greeks' Book of Genesis, there was never a formally accepted, hidebound holy book as such. Certain cults had liturgies of sorts, but these were entirely local, as were many of the tales that coalesced around a given region's favored god or goddess. Neither Greece's geography, with its scattered islands and hilltop redoubts, nor the character of its proudly independent people have ever been conducive to a national consensus about anything.

In the centuries that followed, countless other mythographers retold these stories and grafted their local variants onto them, while making passing references to deities that would have been easily understood by their public but are often mystifying to us. The myths that we know are the survivors of a long period of competition with and evolution out of local versions constantly changing to suit the aims of the teller and his audience. Thus, it is impossible to arrive at a definitive version of any of the myths. We can only guess at their original content through a dark and badly fragmented glass. Today, a writer on the subject must pick and choose what appeals to him and trust his instincts—the whisperings of the Muses in his mind—to retell the tales in a way that will find approval not only with his readers but, of course, with the gods (and scholars) as well.

A NOTE ON THE TRANSLATIONS

Unless otherwise indicated, the translations of the Greek texts are, for better or for worse, mine. For the most part, I have kept the names of the deities and places in their most familiar forms, for example, Zeus instead of Zéfs. Those that I have transliterated directly from Greek are ones that I feel would benefit by a return to their original form, particularly in terms of how they should be pronounced, for example, Évia instead of Euboea and Evrópi instead of Europe or Europa. In these transliterations, the vowels are pronounced as follows: *a* as "ah"; *e* as "eh"; *i* as "ee"; *o* as "oh"; *u* as it would be in English. I have placed an accent mark (´) over those vowels whose syllables should be stressed. Unaccented names have been left as is because the Western way of pronouncing is either correct or too entrenched to suffer adjustments.

The quotations from the Bible are, unless otherwise indicated, from the King James translation.

FOREWORD

Anyone who has ever ventured into the world of Greek myth knows how quickly you can become lost in its labyrinth of tales, with their hordes of gods and goddesses, heroes and heroines, demigods, nymphs, satyrs, monsters, and the occasional, often badly treated mortal. Most mythographers deal with this by retelling the stories as separate units: Theseus and the Minotaur, Léda and the Swan, Kadmos and Harmonía, et cetera. In this book, I have ventured to order the tales into a coherent whole by focusing on their primary cause, Zeus, and recounting them as they happened during the course of both the god's lusty, tempest-tossed reign and the history of the people who worshipped (and created) him according to their ever-changing needs.

For most of his "life," Zeus was not thought of as dwelling disembodied in some distant ethereal realm. Nor did his worshippers believe that he had created the universe and all its living creatures. Instead, he was said to have been sired by one of the gods who came before him, was born on Earth in human form, and grew into adulthood in sites that can be visited today, much as pilgrimages can be made to Bethlehem and Golgotha. Thus, it is possible to chart the god's journey—the stations of his cross, as it were—through real places and actual, near-historical times, from his rough-and-ready beginnings in the steppes of Russia to the heights of his glory in Classical and Hellenistic Greece, and thence, to his last, mortifying days as a pagan trophy of the newly Christianized Roman Empire in Constantinople.

In writing this book, I have drawn parts from the odds and ends of knowledge I had picked up during the twenty-two years when I lived and worked in Greece, mostly as an English teacher, often in the theater, and, for one memorable summer, as a restaurateur (of sorts). The greater portion of what I've written, however, is the result of research that I did before, during, and after this period—my enchantment with the Greek myths extending back to my childhood and my fascination with Greek reality ongoing, even from as far away as Los Angeles. Of equal importance are the insights gained during a trip that I recently made to Greece with my new Persian wife, Fárzaneh, to tour the major sites associated with Zeus (many of which I had never visited before) and get a firsthand feel for the Great Thunderer in his natural settings—in, as it were, the flesh.

If I sometimes, perhaps confusingly, treat Zeus and the other immortals as though they had actually been alive, I beg the reader's forgiveness. When you live as long as I did in Greece, or are perhaps just passing through on a visit, you, too, may get the somewhat spooky sensation—"a shadow of a magnitude," Keats called it—that the gods and goddesses are all still there, poised to manifest themselves at any moment in unexpected ways, to remind us that behind the comforting facades of high-rise resorts and happy billboards, there is still the mystery, the terror, and the magic. And still a chance, if we are in the right place at the right time, for a god to descend and, in some transcendent moment, effect profound changes in our lives. Anyone who has wandered by the Aegean on a moonlit night, or sat on a mountainside rock in the vast, cicada-filled silence of a hot Greek afternoon in a universe seemingly emptied of all other humanity, will, I think, understand exactly what I mean . . .

PART ONE

ADVENT

1

PERICLES

My wife and I arrived in Athens in early April, at the beginning of the Greek Orthodox Holy Week, and were extremely fortunate to chance upon a travel agent who could not only get us on a ship to the island of Santoríni, but from there to Crete in time for the Easter weekend. I explained how important this was, since the massive volcanic eruption that had torn out the center of Santoríni some 4,500 years ago had also announced the coming birth, on Crete, of Zeus in human form.

The agent, a squat, balding man in his fifties with the improbable name of Pericles, looked up from the scattering of brochures on his desk. "Birth? Zeus? Born, you mean, like a baby?"

"Yes."

"Zeus."

"That's what they say."

Pericles raised a skeptical eyebrow, cocked his head sideways, and regarded me over his glasses with an amused glint in his eyes. His namesake had been the fifth-century-B.C. Athenian politician whose achievements included the building of the Parthenon and the other magnificent monuments of the city's Golden Age. Our Pericles, however, his eyes Sunday-morning bleary and an unshaven stubble grizzling his cheeks and chin, looked less like that Classical forefather than like a wily, aging Odysseus adrift on the high seas of life, still working his long, hard way home.

An hour or so before, when my wife and I were making our first foray into the streets of Athens after checking into our hotel, he had hailed us from the doorway of his travel agency. It was a little before seven a.m., and we were still fumbling through the fog of a sixteen-hour journey from Los Angeles, so we had not had the quickness of mind to simply ignore his greeting and walk on. In fact, Fárzaneh, having never been in the country before and innocent of the ways of the Greeks, had actually stopped and smiled and nodded hello.

Our hotel, an inexpensive, homey hodgepodge of shoebox rooms with minuscule toilets and showers jerry-built into their nooks and crannies, was in the Plaka district of Athens. Plaka, which presses up against the sharply rising cliffs of the Acropolis, is a wonderfully picturesque warren of nineteenth-century shops and buildings said to be the oldest continuously inhabited area of the city—most probably because it is, with so many tiny streets forever wandering back upon themselves, a natural tourist trap. It's not only hard to find your way out, but as you walk around, you have to be prepared to resist a constant series of come-ons from merchants hailing you from their doorways.

But Pericles was charm incarnate: "Good morning, madam," he had said in Greek, mistaking Fárzaneh, with the Persian cast of her looks, for one of his own. She has chocolate-brown eyes, dark auburn-tinted hair, a natural touch of red to her lips, and a small beauty mark perched just above the right side of her mouth. She is also barely five feet tall, which made her just a hair shorter than Pericles.

I, on the other hand, am a round-faced, graying blond and such a clean-cut American WASP that I can go without shaving for two days without raising a five-o'clock shadow. So when Pericles realized that Fárzaneh wasn't understanding his Greek, he turned to me and said, in English, "You need some help? I am Pericles. What can I do for you two? Come on in my office, sit down, relax."

In Greek, I tersely replied, "We are going for coffee."

He didn't skip a beat, continuing his pitch in English: "I'm making some. What kind do you want? Greek? American? Come on in. You need some information? Boat schedules? Plane schedules? Doesn't cost you a thing. Here, in Pericles's office, is information for free!"

So we had let ourselves be guided inside and had found, much to our surprise, that the information was indeed free. There was lots of it, too, with hardly a hint of sales pressure. Pericles appeared to enjoy foreign company even more than he did money, and even if this wasn't entirely true, he certainly went about his business with the convincing chumminess of a born pro.

He must have intuited, too, that this was exactly what I needed. Having not really been in the country, except for a hasty week or two, in over a decade, I was feeling more than a little lost. So, while savoring a second cup of thick Greek coffee—fragrant with memories of summer seaside mornings and hot, herb-scented air—and gazing though Pericles' travel-postered windows at the mounting chaos of the Athenian early morning traffic, I could feel my initial resistance to his overtures, much of which was prompted by pride in my own self-sufficiency, beginning to crumble.

Pericles, meanwhile, had jumped on the bandwagon of our proposed journey after Zeus. Within seconds, he had sketched out several itineraries that could get us to every major site associated with the god (from Crete in the south to Mt. Ólympus in the north) in just the amount of time (three action-packed weeks) that we had available before returning to our jobs in L.A. And his price for what he called "a special package deal I make just for you and lovely Fárzaneh" seemed highly reasonable, too, with car rentals and ship and hotel accommodations all included.

Sealing the bargain had been Pericles' reaction when I told him Fárzaneh was Persian. It was as if I had suddenly presented him with a bouquet of bright red roses. Instantly, he began spouting out phrases in Farsi, Fárzaneh's native tongue: "Madame!" "You're welcome!" "Beautiful!" "Persee-a!" and finally, "Soraya!" the name of the former shah's gorgeous second wife.

Fárzaneh's dimpled smile blossomed. For years she had dreamed of visiting Greece. But having been brought up on tales of the two countries' ancient enmities and of the still-reviled Iskander (Persia's name for Alexander the Great) sacking and burning the magnificent capital of Persepolis, just thirty miles from her childhood home, she had understandably been a bit nervous about landing in the midst of all these bloodthirsty savages.

Instead, here was Pericles greeting her as if she were a long-lost relative. "It's like I was back home in Iran," she said later. "Iranians don't ever get treated that way anywhere else in the West, believe me. He made me so happy!"

"So you're telling me," continued Pericles later, "that Zeus, the god, was born—and then died, too? And that he also came back to life?"

I nodded.

"You mean, like Jesus?"

"Well—in a way. And not only that," I continued, "but first, before they buried his remains, they ate of his flesh."

Pericles stared at me, clearly beginning to wonder about my sanity as well as my professional qualifications.

"Who?"

"The men his father had sent to kill him."

He stared at me. And then grinned. "Well, there's one thing I know you can say for sure about Zeus."

"What's that?" asked Fárzaneh.

Pericles gave her an appreciative smile—part gentleman, part old-fashioned wolf.

"He definitely had a soft spot for the ladies."

2

THE COMING OF THE GREEKS

Soft countries breed soft men. It is not the property of any one soil to produce fine fruits and good soldiers too.

CYRUS THE GREAT, KING OF PERSIA (C. 585–529 B.C.)*

The truth was that for the first millennium or so of his existence, Zeus wouldn't have had the wherewithal, anyway, to be fond of any of the ladies, mortal or immortal, in any manner imaginable. Because, in the beginning, he had been without form of any kind, hovering instead over the face of the earth and its waters as a primal, amorphous power—the God of the Bright Sky—which manifested itself to his awed and cowering flock solely as the great, thunderous flashes of fire that rent the heavens, the snow that brought hard death to nearly all living things, and the rain that gave them life again.

In fact, Zeus of the Bright Sky would not acquire a body until many hundreds of years and a journey of a thousand miles later, when his worshippers, having conquered a far-off kingdom in the southern Aegean Sea, would decide to have him born unto them in human form. While this tremendous journey is not a part of his corpus of myths, it is nevertheless crucial to an understanding of the na-

---

* For this and other sources see Notes, pp. 240–291.

ture not only of the god but of his followers—of how they came to be what they so remarkably were.

The people who first imagined Zeus as their god were nomadic hunters hacking out a hardscrabble life in the Russian steppes, that wide and nearly treeless expanse of land above the Black Sea and the Caucasus Mountains. Each of the tribes that wandered there had slightly different names for him, but all referred to the brightness of the sky, both in the daytime and in the sudden illuminations of lightning at night. Some called him Dyaus, others, Dies, Dios, Deus and Deu pater. Those who eventually migrated to Greece called him Zeus. His companion, Earth, they named "the Broad One" and saw her as lying beneath him, as a woman might.

In about 7000 B.C., someone discovered that they could domesticate many of the animals they'd been hunting, keep them in pens, and slaughter them at will. Another two millennia would pass, however, before they stopped eating their horses and learned how to ride them. With that knowledge—and with the development of the wheel—Zeus's worshippers, a restless people to begin with, began to move farther afield, in search of warmer territory and greener pastures.

South of the Caucasus, they came upon lush river valleys and verdant highland pastures. Protected by the mountains from much of the harsher northern weather, they stopped their wanderings and settled down. Agriculture developed, communities formed, tribes merged, populations grew, leaders arose and established themselves as kings, and different languages began to take shape. Those who called their god of gods Zeus took for themselves a large stretch of land in the foothills of the mountains. Here they came upon wild grapes for the first time and quickly realized the heady joys of letting the juices ferment into wine. And then there was the gold. They discovered it while washing the fleeces of newly slaughtered lambs in the mountain rivers. The fleeces came out of the water heavy—golden—with flakes and granules of the stuff. Tin, silver, lead, and copper were also available. Someone stumbled upon the fact that if they were melted together in the right proportions, they would become bronze. And bronze made the strongest weapons ever seen—more and more of a necessity as the populations of neighboring tribes grew and battles over gold and the available land became a part of their daily life.

Meanwhile, from their houses and walled citadels, Zeus's worshippers could see the great sea spreading out to the west, consuming Helios, the sun, every evening. At first, they kept away from it. The sea was like a brother to Zeus, mirroring the sky's radiance, yes, but also its rages. At the same time, in its vastness and the fruitfulness of its harvests, it also reminded them of the steppes with its equally wide vistas and promise of both dangers and wondrous enchantments lying just beyond the horizon.

Slowly, they began to take to the sea's waters, to build bigger and better boats, and to make their way along its shores westward—toward the promises they knew awaited somewhere, someday, just beyond the next wave, the next inlet.

As these people possessed no form of writing, what they called themselves is unknown. Centuries later, when the Archaic and Classical Greeks began to write down their stories, they gave them a variety of names. Homer, whose *Iliad* and *Odyssey* were composed in about 750 B.C., referred to them, interchangeably, as Danaans, Achaeans, and Argives. Herodotus, the father of Greek historians, spoke of them as Macedons and Dorians. Thucydides, the late fifth-century-B.C. soldier-author who wrote about the tragic wars between Athens and Sparta, said they were the progeny of a man called Hellen. Hellen was believed to be the son of Deucalion, the Greek Noah who, along with his wife and animals, had survived the Great Flood that Zeus had brought about to destroy mankind for its impieties. So Thucydides called their descendants Hellenes, and this is the name they take for themselves even today, pronouncing it "Élliness." The people of the West would adopt a later, Roman appellation, calling them Greeks.

* * *

Exactly when and how these proto-Greeks first migrated to Greece may never be known. For years, most experts in the fields of history, archaeology, and linguistics agreed that the Greeks initially arrived in what is now thought of as their homeland through the difficult-to-traverse Balkan mountain range in about 2000 B.C. Recent discoveries, however, have made a date in the mid-1600s much more likely and the Black Sea the more probable route. Underwater archaeologists studying the wrecks of cargo vessels along its southern shores have shown that since c. 1700 B.C., there had been an increasing amount of trade going on in this area, and that goods were being carried to and from the mineral-rich Caucasus out of the Black Sea into the Aegean and from there to the Levant, with the coastal fortress of Troy controlling the flow.

Additional research has persuasively argued that at about this same time, the proto-Greeks traveled from the Caucasus to mount a seaborne invasion of the Greek mainland, landing in Thessaly and quickly establishing their hegemony along the coast all the way to the western shores of the Peloponnese.

If this was so, we can imagine that their initial incursion took place in about 1680 B.C., on one of those lovely autumn afternoons between the subsiding of the fierce summer winds blowing out of the Black Sea and the beginning of winter's treacherous squalls. It was an exciting prospect. News of this new world had probably been brought back to the Caucasus by Greek traders, whose glowing accounts of a golden, sun-drenched paradise had prompted further explorations. The traders' description proved to be only slightly exaggerated. The coast of this nearly virgin territory was blessed with beautiful natural harbors and mountains so densely forested that you could build a thousand ships and still have timber enough for thousands more. Moreover, inland there was an enormous expanse of flat, fertile farmland nearly as big as the sea itself.

Of course, people were already living there—thousands of them, in fact, clustered in small communities and farming settlements all across the plain—but this did not seem to be a problem. They seemed to have no weapons worthy of the name, hardly any bronze at all, and no horses or chariots either. Not only that, but their settlements were barely fortified, encircled by low mounds of earth and flimsy stockades that could be breached by seasoned Hellenic fighters in a single assault. The invasion force that the proto-Greeks assembled bordered on overkill, their ships packed not only with bronze-armored warriors but with horses and highly maneuverable chariots so lightweight that one man could lift them.

The initial battle—and all of the subsequent ones in the Greeks' march along the coast—was over in a matter of minutes. While the natives had probably fought off roving bands of raiders before, they would have never encountered warriors coming at them on horseback and chariots, nor would they have seen longbows whose arrows could fly 150 yards and still hit their target with full force, and long, bronze-hard swords capable of slicing through a body as if it were a stalk of wheat.

After the battle, the Greeks put the natives to work building a wooden stockade on the most suitable hilltop inland from the harbor; later, they would replace the wood with massive stone walls, of the kind they had used back in the Caucasus. Meanwhile, they watched with some amusement as the natives prostrated themselves before tiny clay and wooden figures which they claimed were their goddess—an earth mother, whom they first called Gē, the Greek word for "earth," and later, Gaía.

To the Greeks, this must have seemed the height of impiety—to think that any deity, even a female one, could be reduced to such a size and such a shape, that the power of the Great Thunderer could be contained within the form of a man! A much more appropriate object of worship, they thought, was the enormous, cloud-shrouded massif to the north, its storm-catching summit often crackling with lightning, echoes of distant thunder rolling across the plain. When they asked the natives its name, the natives, who hadn't thought to call it anything, replied with their word for all mountains.

"Ólympos," they said. "It is ólympos."

The Greeks also learned that the reason that the natives were prostrating themselves before these little statues so fervently and so often was to pray for rain. It had been a terrible summer, hot and dry, and their crops were dying. But the skies remained a pristine blue, with the only clouds in sight—that great group massed around the top of the great mountain to the north—seemingly forever stationary. Meanwhile, now that the Greeks had established a base, there were many more members of their tribes, including women and children, arriving in the area, and the wells were drying up. Drinking water was running short.

Clearly, the prayers that the natives were offering were not enough. What was needed was weather magic of the kind that the Greeks had practiced back in the Caucasus. While they could have used one of the natives' girls, they knew in their hearts that it had to be a member of their own tribe. After all, a sacrifice was a sacrifice.

Behind the harbor rose a good-sized, heavily forested mountain whose summit could be reached without too much difficulty. The girl they chose—with honey-colored hair and eyes as blue as cornflowers—came from one of their lesser families. There was no point in sacrificing the child of a king for rain. A war, perhaps, but not rain.

For the procession up the hill, the priests tied the girl to an ass and flung over her one of the fleeces that the tribes had used for sifting gold out of the streams back home. A ram's fleece. Very special. It still had a yellowish cast to it, as if the gold, after all those years of use, had permeated the wool. It was hot and heavy to wear and stank in the heat of the day. By the time the girl reached the summit, she must have been eager to be rid of the world, which had shrunk to the weight and odor of this golden fleece.

The priests also wore fleeces, and, after they cut the girl's throat and left her body for the wolves, they piled their fleeces on the back of the ass for the trip back down, giving the poor animal a good whack and letting it find its own way home, taking the stink of blood and sweat with it.

Within a week of the girl's sacrifice, the clouds above Ólympus had broken up and spread south. Soon, a steady rain fell upon the plains and mountainsides, producing just enough downfall to fill the wells and cisterns but not ruin the crops. The natives, who had been appalled at the sacrifice, were overjoyed. Embers of hatred and fear still smoldered in their eyes, but there was also, now, a flicker of respect.

With winter coming, the Greeks decided to move south, some overland, the others by ship along the coast, leaving one of the chieftains and his tribe behind to secure Thessaly as a base.

In this way, settlement by settlement, the Greeks gradually took control of most of the mainland—which is to say, its harbors and strategic hilltop sites—from modern-day Thessaly south along the coasts of Euboea (Évia) and Boeotia (Veeótia), Attica, the Argolid, and the entire eastern and western coasts of the Peloponnese. For the most part they spared the lives of the natives, leaving them to their mud-caked hovels and work in the fields. Occasionally, when they found a strategic bit of high ground already occupied, they burned the buildings that were there and built their thick-walled citadels on top.*

Along the way, as the Greeks picked up more of the indigenous

* In these places, the only things the Greeks left standing were the names, most of which, with their *–ai*, *-nth*, *-os*, *-us*, and *-ss* endings, have come down to us today in modern Greek: Athínai (Athens), Kórinthos (Corinth), Mikínai (Mycenae), Pelopónissos (the Peloponnese), et cetera, a litany of the sounds of a lost Neolithic language and its people.

language, they became fascinated by the tales that the natives had to tell of their gods and goddesses and of how the world was created. While the Greeks had their own pantheon of deities—Zeus; Mother Earth, the Broad One; Helios, the Sun God; Aurora, Goddess of the Dawn; and Zeus's twin brother, the Sea and Earth Shaker—these were forces of nature, doing what they had always done year in and year out. The natives, on the other hand, had *stories* to tell, and in their stories, these forces came alive in the most dramatic fashion, as if they were beings themselves. Not people, of course, but close enough for you to almost picture them. And understand how they felt . . .

At first (said the natives' tale tellers) there was only Chaos, a swirling cloud of nothingness. In time, out of this cloud, came the goddess who would give shape to it all. She had the body of a woman and the tail of a fish. Her name was Evrynómi—the wide-wandering Great Mother.

Alone in the world, Evrynómi brought forth the sky and the sea and the wind, and out of the wind made herself a lover, a giant serpent called Ophíon. Ophíon, finding the goddess irresistible, wound himself around her (as she wished him to do), and out of their union came the Universal Egg. From this was born the sun and moon and stars and all the things on the earth, including its plants and animals.

For a while, Evrynómi ruled in harmony with Ophíon from the highest mountain in the world. But when the serpent began boasting that it was really he who had created everything, she kicked him out, sending him down to dwell forever in the depths of the earth as a tiny, toothless worm.

Next, the goddess created gigantic divinities called Titans to rule over the six planets, and from the earth, she brought forth the first man, Pelasgus, and gave him companions, male and female, to work the soil from which he had sprung. The natives were descendants, they said, of these people, the first to occupy the land, not their land, but everyone's, given to them all by the goddess. They called themselves Pelasgians.

The Greeks were wary enough not to dispute this account out loud. You could never be sure what the gods or goddesses had done in the distant past. Or would do. Or who they were, exactly. So there was no point in affronting any of them, male or female, just in case. At the same time, the Greeks must have felt a twinge of envy. It would be wonderful to have similar stories about Zeus, telling how he had come to rule over the cosmos. But, of course, they didn't know. How could you? He simply was what he was. They had long forgotten, of course, that they had been his creators, that this terrifying entity was purely a product of their imaginations, its loftiest vistas—and darkest corners. Nothing more than that. But nothing less, either.

By about 1650 B.C., the Greeks, having conquered the mainland, were now turning their thoughts to the islands of the Aegean, in particular to what the natives called the Great Island, which lay some six days' voyage to the south. It was a wondrous place, said the natives, a paradise—rich in agricultural produce, pottery, and minerals—and its people, with their great trading fleet plying the sea as far as Egypt and Syria, were wealthy beyond imagining.

The Greeks asked how big an army and what kind of fortifications this island had. None, replied the natives. Such things were not necessary. They were protected by the Great Goddess and her priest-king, Minos. This king had presided over the island for as long as anyone could remember.* Thousands of years, probably, constantly being reborn to the throne. But only because the goddess had wished

* Minos's subjects, today known as Minoans, were not given that name until 1900, when the British archaeologist who uncovered the great palace of Knossós, Sir Arthur Evans, dubbed them as such.

it so. Hers was the real power. If the Greeks sailed south, they could see the evidence for themselves. Less than a day's voyage north of Minos's kingdom was her dwelling place: a great mountain whose interior was filled with liquid fire, fire miraculously spouting forth from the waters of the sea.

3

THE MINOANS

Crete is something else. Crete is a cradle,
an instrument, a vibrating test tube in which
a volcanic experiment has been performed.

HENRY MILLER, *The Colossus of Maroussi*

The natives' story was not all that far from the truth. The people of this island (and their various rulers) had, in fact, been there for thousands of years, having arrived in the region at about the same time, c. 6500 B.C., as the mainland natives and the peoples who populated the central islands. Like them, the Minoans were worshippers of the Great Goddess, a faith which they had brought with them from their homeland in the Middle East, most probably the fertile crescent of Mesopotamia.*

To the followers of this faith (which had held unchallenged supremacy in Europe and the Middle East for nearly twenty thousand years), the entire cosmos—earth, sky, waters, and the plants and animals within and upon them—was a single entity enveloped by the life-giving and -receiving Great Mother, she who created, nurtured, and took into her bosom all living things, just as, on a much smaller scale, the females of every species daily performed mirroring aspects of the

* Once famous as the site of the Garden of Eden, it has now become better known as Iraq.

same miracle. The statues that were offered to her, or fashioned to be worshipped in her stead, were the same tiny but enormously voluptuous female figurines that the Greeks had made such cautious fun of upon their arrival in the area. Wide-hipped, sometimes large-vulvaed, and full-breasted, these effigies were the essence of Earth in all its endless fecundity. Some of them, however, were tellingly blind. The goddess, who could at one moment bestow wondrous bounties upon her creation and the next, visit it with all manner of afflictions—earthquakes, plagues, storms, floods, and droughts, all without apparent provocation—was utterly indifferent to individuals, blind to their tiny needs and little sorrows. She cherished only Life itself.

But the Minoans were nevertheless highly grateful for her favors. It was thanks to the goddess that they had become so prosperous. For the thousands of years that her mountain had guarded Crete, they had known nothing but peace. Only once, in about 3000 B.C., had there been a slight disruption—when several boatloads of armed foreigners had suddenly appeared on the horizon. But these intruders turned out to be not only peaceful but the possessors of a wonderful new technique of melting tin with copper to make bronze, a metal perfect for fashioning tools, hunting weapons, and cooking utensils. Thus, the Cretans came to regard the appearance of these strangers, too, as a gift from the Great Mother. Later, it would be said that they had also brought with them the arts of magic, shepherding, and honey gathering, and they would pass into legend as the Idaían Dactyls, *daímones* (minor gods) who were attendants of the Great Mother. Afterward, when the birth of Zeus had come to pass, they would be transformed into the young warriors, or Koúrites, sent by Gaía to guard the Divine Child. But, as we shall see, being neither Greek nor Minoan, they may also have been the ones who murdered and ate him.

The ancestors of the Minoans had first made their way to Crete by island-hopping to it from the coast of southwestern Turkey on rafts and dugout canoes. When they came in sight of the Great Island, with its white-capped mountainous interior and endless, luminous shoreline, they must have thought they had stumbled upon paradise. Thickly wooded with cedar and cypress forests, its mountainsides, valleys, and marshes rife with birds and small game, Crete was (and in many ways still is) a rough-hewn, craggy-peaked Garden of Eden. Water was abundant, and fertile alluvial plains undulated down from the mountain ranges northward to the seashores, where numerous coves teemed with fish and there were enough natural harbors to shelter small groups of fishing and trading boats.

The island's only drawback was its susceptibility to earthquakes. Crete sits almost exactly on top of the collision point between the tectonic plates of Africa and Eurasia, where slippage of one beneath the other causes both earthquakes and, occasionally, the shooting up of lava from the depths. But the Cretans, tempered by millennia of coming to terms with the goddess and her temperamental outbursts, were hardly fazed. No matter how many times the Great Mother devastated their communities, they immediately raised them up again, sometimes right on top of the previous structures.

Because of the abundance of the island's natural (as well as manmade) resources, and the protection afforded by the treacherous seas which surrounded it, the Cretans, in their splendid isolation, were able to develop one of the most magnificent and influential civilizations the world had ever known. Around 2000 B.C., the first great Cretan palaces were built, and by the time the Greeks appeared on the horizon, c. 1650, their fleet was acknowledged—even by the Egyptians—to be the dominant force in the eastern Mediterranean. Remarkably, the Minoans had achieved this dominance without the use of force. Among the ninety cities that Homer said were on Crete, not one had defensive fortifications. While much of this was due to the size of the island's fleet and its protected position in the Mediterranean, a lot of credit—on many levels—must be given to the unifying faith of the

Great Goddess and the intimidating effect of her fiery dwelling place on what is known today as the island of Santoríni.

It is nearly impossible to imagine the impact of this burning mountain on the people of the time. The Great Goddess had already been venerated as Mistress of the Mountains for thousands of years, with fire being worshipped as her earthly embodiment. So for her followers to come across these two elements combined in one seemingly unique site* would have been akin to a divine revelation, with the mountain and its crater quickly becoming revered as the very entrance to the goddess's molten realm, the heart and soul of her universe.

In about 1800 B.C., the Cretans established what seems to have been a religious center (today called Akrotíri) on the southern shores of Santoríni, some ninety miles almost due north of the Minoan capital of Knossós. Archaeologists who have dug about half of it out of its thick covering of volcanic ash estimate the size at five acres, a bit greater than the area covered by a football field. What has been unearthed so far shows a settlement imbued with enormous wealth and with a living, breathing reverence for the goddess. Its inhabitants lived much in the same luxurious manner as the priestly castes within the various palace sanctuaries, such as Knossós on Crete. They had two- and three-story houses, with indoor plumbing (including baths, toilets, and, perhaps, hot running water from thermal springs) leading out into a system of drains beneath the streets. On the upper floors, beautiful, richly detailed frescoes adorned the walls. One depicts a fleet of merchant ships, some so large that it took twenty to forty oarsmen to propel them. But scenes of nature—the goddess's surface realm—predominate: In a profusion of gracefully limned flowers and plants, antelopes, dolphins, monkeys, lions, swallows,

---

* There were no other active volcanoes within two thousand miles, the Italian triumvirate of Stromboli, Etna, and Vesuvius being quiescent at the time.

deer, wildcats, and a griffin populate the walls, while the humans that are portrayed are always engaged in paying ritual homage to the locus of their lives: the Great Mother.

Behind the city, only a few miles to the north and doubtless visible from every house, there rose the Holy Mountain, home of the divine and implacable force that was pulsating the cosmos. But in spite of its rumblings and intermittent spitting of fire, rocks, and ashes, the volcano's presence must have been of great comfort to both the people of Santoríni and of the Minoan Empire as a whole. After all, in what other civilization of the world had the Great Goddess so visibly and palpably elected to abide? They were, without a doubt, the Chosen People.

Of course, neither the Minoans nor the Greeks would have had any inkling of its destructive powers, Santoríni's volcano having not had a major eruption in about twenty thousand years. But even an awareness of such a possibility would probably not have deterred the former from living there (witness those of us who reside in L.A., not to mention on the slopes of Etna). Nor would it have stopped the Greeks from continuing to contemplate—or perhaps even prepare for—an invasion of Crete. If they could take this Great Island, with its mineral and agricultural riches and mighty trading fleet, they would have themselves a ready-made empire and control of the entire Aegean. The prize was much too tempting to worry about any sort of danger. Besides, the Greeks held death—particularly death in battle or a hunt—to be the most sacred act of all, and the most worthy. Therefore, it is entirely possible that when the volcano exploded, the Greeks were actually out on their southernmost beaches, ships in the shallows, chariots and weapons assembled, putting their final touches to an armada.

The eruption mostly likely happened on a brisk and beautiful autumn morning in about 1640 B.C., that period of the year when the haze of summer has just evaporated and, for the first time since the previous spring, you can see the rocks and trees on islands forty miles away. While the Minoans seem to have gotten off Santoríni in time,* the Greeks, comfortably settled on their mainland beaches, may have had little or no warning. Hurtling suddenly out of the south, there would have come a series of wind blasts violent enough to knock people and even animals off their feet. Chasing after the wind was the sound of something like thunderclaps, a terrifying crackling and thudding as if the earth itself were breaking apart. For two days, the racket continued. On the third afternoon, this was followed by a tremendous roar, like that of a thousand bulls bellowing at once. At the same time, an immense blast of air hit the shore, this time tossing the beached ships up into the air as if they were little more than hollow gourds. And you could see, miles away, billowing up from beneath the southern horizon as if shot from the bowels of the earth, a thick, roiling, grayish black trunk of smoke, flashing with fire, which rapidly reached the heavens and mushroomed out to consume the sun, covering the earth with darkness, with the chill of winter and of death.

Then came the wave.

---

* No bodies were discovered trapped beneath the ash, as they had been in Pompeii.

4

FEARSOME ECHOES

There have been, and will be again, many destructions of mankind arising out of many causes; the greatest have been brought about by agencies of fire and water.

PLATO, *Timaeus* (c. 360 B.C.)

Even in an age as conversant with mass destruction as ours, the enormity of the blast that tore apart the island of Santoríni remains nearly beyond comprehension. Vulcanologists estimate that the energy released by the eruption was four to eight times as great as that of Krakatoa's, which took place in the Indian Ocean in 1883 and was the largest volcanic explosion in recorded history. The Santoríni detonation would thus have been the equivalent of at least 600 megatons of TNT, or several million times the force (15,000 tons) generated by the atomic bomb that obliterated Hiroshima.

Krakatoa's explosion was so powerful that it could be heard three thousand miles away. Its shock wave traveled seven times around the world. Meanwhile, the huge cloud of ash and pulverized rock ejected by the eruption reached a height of fifty miles, nearly ten times that of Mt. Everest. Within minutes, it had blotted out the sun, and for three full days, a thick, heavy darkness shrouded the surrounding region. Immediately afterward, a succession of four tsunamis, or sea waves, some as high as a fourteen-story building, plowed through nearby coastal communities in Java and Sumatra at speeds of up to sixty miles per hour, wiping out entire towns and killing some thirty-six thousand people.

The tsunamis that followed the much more massive Santoríni eruption would have roared into Crete (only 50 miles to the south) and the coastline of the Argolid (130 miles to the north) at speeds approaching one hundred miles per hour and destroyed any supplies, chariots, horses, and ships beached or anchored anywhere near its shores. For weeks afterward, the sea would have been scummed with debris, the sun dimmed to a wintry gray, and the sky at dusk an ominous bloodred. Meanwhile, every trace of life on Santoríni was completely wiped out, shrouded in layers of ash and pumice as deep as 165 feet. As Farzaneh and I would discover in making this the first stop on our journey after Zeus, it is a devastation which still haunts the island today, despite its current sheen as one of Greece's premier tourist destinations.

My initial visit to Santorini had been in 1969, but I had never forgotten arriving in its harbor, in the immense caldera created by the eruption, and I was hoping to treat Fárzaneh to the same breathtaking experience: the jagged cliff face towering nearly a thousand feet above the ship; houses clinging insanely around its rim as if the people who had built them had somehow been drawn, as blindly as lemmings, to an inevitable plunge into the sea; and, last but not least, in the caldera's center, the sinister tips of a new volcano spreading its dark spidery shape out over the sea's surface, wisps of sulfuric fumes occasionally drifting skyward, a reminder that at any moment, it could once again fire up and swamp you in Hell.

This time, however, when Fárzaneh and I emerged on deck, it was only five a.m. and the sky was still pitch-black. The only indication of the caldera's enormity was a string of what must have been the street lights of Firá, the island's capital, high up on the rim, shimmering like tiny stars in the immense and chilly darkness.

An hour or so later, after we had checked into our hotel, showered, and walked up through the city of Firá to the caldera's edge, the sun had risen and the island and its waters were bathed in that beneficent and incomparable Greek light that is often at its clearest in April. The sea and the sky were a nearly identical, crystalline blue, and the heavens dotted with tiny islands of cumulus clouds, as puffy and white as the fleece of a baby lamb.

The Santoríni that I remembered from thirty-five years before had almost entirely vanished. In fact, if the great open wound of the caldera had not insisted on so dominating the senses, the rest of the island—in its blue-domed, picture-postcard perfection—would have been nearly unrecognizable.

Back in 1969, its population decimated by a terrified exodus after an eruption of the new volcano in 1950 and a devastating series of earthquakes in 1956, Santoríni had been a desolate, windblown atoll all but devoid of the usual tourist amenities and, in fact, of tourists themselves. Firá was nearly a ghost town, its many abandoned houses, some of them split in half, barely clinging to the edge of the caldera, with nothing below them but that sheer one-thousand-foot drop to the sea.

The natives of the island seemed in a permanent Doomsday state of mind. Most of their more sensible and/or enterprising neighbors had fled to make a new life elsewhere. The ones left behind, trying their best to put a more hospitable face on things for my benefit, nevertheless went about their daily tasks enveloped in a pall of gloom. Who could blame them? Living there, looking down into the pit of the caldera with that still-smoking volcano, its clouds of sulfurous gases puffing skyward with alarming regularity, was like being perched on the fence of a graveyard. As soon as I could, I fled.

But now, thirty-five years later, here Santoríni was, gloriously reborn as Greece's premier poster child and featured on seemingly every tourist calendar in existence. Below us, a huge cruise ship steamed into the placid blue-blue waters of the lagoon, looking, from 1,500 feet away, like a toy boat in a bathtub. Seagulls careened above our heads, and the clouds scudded along with them in a brisk April breeze. Even the volcano was cooperating, having ceased all signs of activity, with not the slightest hint of smoke emerging from its center. Instead, its emerging cone was now a tourist destination, a black sponge of distant rocks about as threatening as San Francisco's empty-chambered Alcatraz. And along the caldera's rim, a colorful, undulating necklace of boutiques, bars, restaurants, hotels, coffee shops, nightclubs, jewelers, galleries, and beautiful private villas, many of them built over structures that had collapsed in the previous catastrophe, hung right on the edge, as if to get the best possible view of the sheer drop that awaited them. Was this, I wondered, just a case of willful ignorance peppered with the thrill of staring Death in the face? Or was it also in part a vestigial memory of the volcano's sacredness, a yearning for a close encounter with God—face-to-face with the fire in the mountain?

After a dizzying brunch on a balcony overhanging the abyss, Fárzaneh and I took our rented car and drove nine miles along and around the caldera to the south coast to see what had been excavated of the large Bronze Age city buried there by the great eruption of 1640 B.C. The road wound past acres of vineyards, their gnarled, darkened winter stumps just beginning to freshen with tiny sprouts of light-green grape leaves. But there were hardly any trees. While the layer of pumice and ash that covers this part of the island holds water longer than regular soil, it cannot support an extravagance of deeply rooted life.

The same shroud also covers most of ancient Akrotíri, which lies amid the undulating countryside outside the modern village of the same name, where the land slopes down to the Sea of Crete. From here, which is where the Bronze Age harbor must have been, the Minoan capital of Knossós is directly south, just over the horizon.

An enormous steel-girdered shed covers the site, raised by

archaeologists to shield its fragile contents, so long buried under protective layers of ash and pumice, from the weather, which would quickly erode much of it out of existence.

Descending into the digs was like entering an antechamber to Hell. Already the sun had been beating down on the roof for several hours, and even in April the interior was starting to feel like an oven. In midsummer, at midday, it must be unbearable. In the light filtering down through panels of translucent corrugated plastic set into the roof, the brownish ochre cast of everything inside—the walls, the dirt, the pottery, and the wooden planks and beams that add support and walkways to the dig—is intensified, increasing one's discomfort. Everything looks as though it has been dusted over or fashioned out of cakes of sulfur, otherwise known as brimstone, used by God to destroy the cities of Sodom and Gomorrah and, in the Book of Job, to lay waste the land of the wicked. When you visit the excavated ruins at Pompeii and Herculaneum, you are at least out under the open sky, with grass, bushes, and weeds growing everywhere. In the digs at Akrotíri, once the vibrant heart of devotion to the Great Goddess and her Holy Mountain, you enter a dead zone, a sulfur-colored silence where hope has clearly been abandoned.

Experts disagree about how much was left of the volcano after the initial eruption. Some say that only the top part was shorn off, with the rest collapsing much later; others that nothing remained but the caldera we see today. Whichever, the Greeks, with most of their fleet destroyed and smoke continuing to belch ominously from the mountain's remains, would have been understandably leery about going anywhere near either Santoríni or, by extension, Crete. Clearly, a deity had spoken, but which one—Zeus or the Great Goddess? And why? No one could be sure. Within the deep collective memory of both the Greeks and the Minoans, nothing as catastrophic as this had ever before occurred.

A thousand years later, after word of mouth had passed the story down from generation to generation, successors to these original Greeks would attribute the catastrophe entirely and unequivocally to Zeus, to the Great Thunderer's desire to punish that generation for its sins. The tale of the Noah-like flood of Deucalion which Zeus unleashed upon mankind may have been one such recollection, as would Euripides' description of the terrible wave that destroyed the impious Hippolytus, the depiction as vivid as if the playwright himself had been there to witness it.

There came a sound awful to hear,
As if Zeus's hollow thunder were booming within the earth, . . .
And a tremendous wave towered to the skies, engulfing the headland . . .
Swelling and frothing with foam, it broke upon the shore . . .
And from that mighty wall of waters there issued
A monstrous bull whose bellowing filled the land
With fearsome echoes.

Then there was the haunting legend of Atlantis, that magnificent civilization whose homeland, a continent-sized island, was so ravaged by violent volcanic paroxysms that, in a single day and night, it disappeared forever beneath the sea. The story comes to us through Plato, who had Socrates claim it was passed down to him from a distant generation of Egyptian priests. In this telling, it is clearly the Minoans who were at fault.

> Zeus, the god of gods, who rules according to law, and is able to see into such things, perceiving that an honourable race was in a woeful plight, and wanting to inflict punishment on them, that they might be chastened and improve, collected all the gods into their most holy habitation, which, being placed in the center of the world, beholds all created things. And when he had called them together, he spake as follows—

But here, the dialogue breaks off, Zeus's reasons forever lost to us—as obscure as they must have seemed to the Greeks and the Minoans on that apocalyptic autumn day.

Almost two hundred years would pass before the trauma of this event would be sufficiently forgotten for the Greeks to once again heed the siren calls of an invasion. The Minoans, on the other hand, must have had their faith in the goddess severely shaken. After so many millennia of peace and prosperity, to have been so cruelly attacked by the very force you daily worshipped and gave thanks to, abandoned by the Mother who had heretofore given you all her bounty and to whom your reverence had been so exemplary, must have been traumatizing to an extreme. But things weren't as bad as they seemed. Although most of Crete's crops had been destroyed, the capital of Knossós and its harbor had emerged miraculously unscathed. Prevailing winds had pushed the blast's thick cloud of pumice over to the eastern end of the island, while the tsunamis seemed to have been split by the tiny offshore island of Dia just before it reached Knossós's harbor, near what is today the island's capital of Iráklion. So there was a silver lining to the cloud. Perhaps the goddess did care, after all . . .

Catastrophes such as these often make fascinating bedfellows. With the Minoans needing food, and the Greeks, though badly weakened, still controlling the rich agricultural plains of the mainland, serious trade between the two empires would have begun to flourish. With this, a new balance of power became established in the Aegean—one that would, over the next century and a half, bring unparalleled prosperity to both parties. However, it would be the Greeks who would get the best of the deal. And this most probably kept them (and the will of their god) pacified.

During this period, c. 1640–1480 B.C., the Minoans introduced the Greeks to the best available trading routes to the east, connecting them with ports in Asia Minor, Cyprus, parts of the Middle East, and Egypt. In the process, they instructed the Greeks in the art of keeping inventories by teaching them to write, adapting spoken Greek to the partly pictographic, partly linear script that the Minoans had been using for eons.* Meanwhile, in the Greeks' centers of power at places such as Mycenae and Tíryns on the Argolid peninsula, Pylos in the Peloponnese, and Orchomenos and Thebes in central Greece, Cretan artists and craftsmen turned what were basically badly built, dirt-floored hovels into lushly decorated palaces, and their frescoes, pottery, and metalwork (including armor and weapons) into high art.

At the same time, however, the Minoans were also hard at work rebuilding their own damaged cities and palaces, fashioning them with even greater splendor than before, and, in particular, turning Knossós into the extraordinary edifice whose remains we see today. It was as if the Minoans needed to prove (to both the world and themselves) that rather than having been abandoned by the Great Mother, they were, in fact, more than ever in her good and powerful graces.

No one knows exactly when the Greeks, most likely their trading representatives, first set foot on Crete, but if they came during or after the Minoans' rebuilding efforts, they would have been suitably awed. Certainly, they would have never seen—nor perhaps even been capable of imagining—anything like Knossós's massive, multilevel complex of rooms and courtyards. In c. 1600 B.C., the settlement covered about 185 acres and is estimated to have held anywhere from 15,000 to 100,000 inhabitants. The palace itself stood near the center, atop a mound built upon the ruins of ten other earthquake-toppled structures raised on the same spot over the previous five thousand years. Unlike the abodes of the Greek kings, which were defensive in nature and set upon the highest possible grounds, far above the dwellings of their subjects, Knossós was an organic part of the city it ruled, with its huge central courtyard easily accessible from numerous points in the surrounding community.

---

* The original Minoan script, still not deciphered, is known as Linear A. The successfully deciphered Greek adaptation is called Linear B.

From this courtyard, the palace spread out on all sides along a maze of corridors, stairways, alcoves, antechambers, and interconnecting rooms that covered four levels. But instead of protecting its inhabitants from the outside world, as Greek dwellings were designed to do, Knossós embraced every aspect of its surroundings: light and air flooding through the countless windows, doors, and overhead openings; water bubbling and cascading its way through the palace's pipes and drains from a source in a mountain several miles away; ordinary citizens freely passing into the central courtyard from the surrounding settlement; and birds of all sorts wheeling in and out of the light wells and windows and fluttering to a stop on ledges against the color-washed walls as if the palace were their nesting place, their home. Inside Knossós, even in the midst of winter, it must have seemed like spring.

Signs of the goddess's sacred presence—in particular, the bull and the double ax—were everywhere, adorning the palace with her divinity. To the Greeks bulls, of all animals, were the most like their Sky God—smoldering clouds of gusting, explosive power—and, since time immemorial, they had been sacrificing them and eating their flesh to partake of this terrible potency. In contrast, the Minoans played with their bulls during their ritual games and dances, somersaulting over their horns and then pivoting off the back to land with graceful ease on their feet, their assurance in the presence of such danger as great a demonstration as any of the protection given them by the Great Mother. Then they would sacrifice them, felling the great beasts with a single blow of the double ax—the sacred implement of the goddess's cult. As the instrument that brought down the sacrificial bull, it was venerated as the embodiment of the goddess's power. But the ax was not the killing tool. This was the knife that slit the monster's throat as it lay upon the altar. The ax was an instrument of life, its double blades mirroring the double wings of the butterfly. As the butterfly so gloriously resurrected itself out of the coffin of its cocoon, so the blow of the double ax, in rendering the bull unconscious and allowing it to be placed upon the altar, began the ceremony that would, through the agency of the Great Mother, bring renewed life to the world.

Thus, in the great central square of Knossós, two pairs of sculpted, stuccoed, clay horns sat upon separate platforms, and in the middle of each pair, between the horns, arose a double ax, upright and predominant, the goddess's stone butterfly, her supremacy, her dominion over death, incarnate.

There were so many axes throughout the complex that the Cretans, using their ancient word for ax—*lábrys*—called Knossós the *Labyrinthos* (the Place of the Axes), less a residence for their ruler than a shrine to the goddess he served. This ruler, who was said to be their priest-king, dwelled somewhere within the labyrinth's core. It seems entirely possible that the Greeks rarely—if ever—caught a glimpse of him. In the myths and legends that they would pass down to us, he appears as a shadowy, highly enigmatic figure whose name, Minos, was apparently not even his own, but that of each of the rulers who took this office. There is also evidence that every seven years, when the goddess's full moon appeared to dispel the darkness of the longest night of the year, he would appear to his subjects as a bull, which would be sacrificed to the Great Mother to ensure the survival of the community until the full moon and the winter solstice once again coincided, seven years later.

What impressed the Greeks the most, however, was the way Knossós and its fleet had managed to survive the great catastrophe. All over the Aegean, the shores and shallows were littered with the splintered skeletons of ships caught by the tsunamis, its seaside communities equally torn to pieces. Yet here was Knossós—and its fleet—miraculously untouched. Was this really due, as the Minoans claimed, to the protection of their goddess? Was there actually something more to their rituals than met the eye—ancient secrets going back to the beginnings of time which could bring to the Greeks all the splendor that now adorned Crete, if only they could possess them? Judging from the metamorphosis that their amorphous God of the Bright Sky would soon undergo, the Greeks may have been gradually drawn by the Minoan observances into wanting their Zeus to have attributes similar to those of the Great Goddess—to have a graspable image, one which could always be looked to for comfort and support. In addition, the new generations of Greeks could appreciate the way the Minoans' rich trappings lent an impressive glory not only to their deities but to themselves. How fitting it would be, then, if Zeus, too, could dwell in this manner among his worshippers. In their image. And they in his.

Scholars remain mystified by the specific reasons for the Greeks' apparently sudden decision to attack Crete. It is possible that up-and-coming Greek hotspurs, restless from years of perceived lassitude on the part of their forebearers, would have found it relatively easy to drum up support for once again attempting to establish absolute Greek hegemony in the Aegean. There may also have been unrest on Crete itself, resentment against the aid that the authorities at Knossós had been giving the upstart Greeks, helping them establish trade routes to Egypt and the East, sending artisans to rebuild and decorate their palaces, even teaching them to write and keep inventories. This could have caused discontent and even rebellion by the citizens and rulers of the other palatial centers at Phaistos, Malia, and Zakro, already disillusioned by the religious unease and economic difficulties wrought by the eruption of the Great Mother's Holy Volcano. In turn, Knossós may have called on the Greeks for help in quelling any disturbances and so may have inadvertently opened the door for a full-scale invasion.

Then there were the disturbances of Mother Earth herself. The renewed seismic activity that had been recently radiating out from the Santoríni volcano could have caused a sudden collapse of what was left of its already-fragile cone, the magma chamber all but emptied by the terrible eruption of 1640. If so, this new tsunami might, this time, have caught most of the Minoan fleet at anchor and destroyed it, thus completing the demoralization of the Cretans, whose spirit (and faith in the Great Goddess) had already been deeply scarred by the previous catastrophe. In addition, if there had been any hesitation on the part of the Greeks about invading Crete, such an event would have made a takeover imperative. A power vacuum had been created, and it had to be filled—quickly. Perhaps, as happened in the East Indies in the aftermath of the 1883 Krakatoa eruption, there were now major rebellions against the central authorities by a populace seeking someone human to blame.

It is also possible that when faced with a Greek invasion, the Minoans living in centers outside of Knossós might have put up much more resistance than the Greeks had anticipated. Cretans have never taken kindly to foreign occupations, and in the centuries since, they have repeatedly resisted such intrusions with a fierceness that, for instance, neither the Turks nor the Nazis will ever forget. Thus, the fact that at this time, most of the Cretan palaces were burned to the ground may have had less to do with earthquakes than Greek anger at the Cretans' intransigency.

All that is known for sure is that sometime in about 1480 B.C., after years of mutual peace and prosperity between the Minoans and the Greeks, the latter suddenly launched an invasion of Crete that resulted in the destruction of every major center of Minoan power except Knossós. From here, as the Minoans' once-proud civilization lay strewn about them in heaps of collapsed and smoking ruins, the ruling Greeks began refashioning the cosmos in their own image. In the process, they would bury that of the Minoans in near-complete oblivion.

The time had come for the birth of Zeus.

PART TWO

THE SON

5

CRADLE TO GRAVE

Come, let us begin with the Muses,
Who gladden the heart of their father Zeus in Olympus,
Telling of things that are and shall be
and that were aforetime.

HESIOD, *Theogony*

Many stories have since entwined themselves, umbilicus-like, around the birth, death, and resurrection of the infant Zeus. Some of them come from the tales heard by the Greeks on their trading forays to the east, when they would be treated to wondrous accounts of the creation of the world and of the gods from the Babylonians and Phoenicians, who had gotten many elements of their stories, in turn, from the Hittites and Hurrians. Most seminal of all, however, were those mystery rites that had been conducted by the Minoans in what was now the Greeks' island.

For thousands of years, the Minoans had held these ceremonies atop the island's tallest mountain (today called Mt. Ida, or Psilorítis, the "High One"), which rises in almost the exact center of Crete, about twenty-five miles (as the eagle flies) southwest of Knossós and the modern capitol of Iráklion. The purpose of these rituals was to celebrate the death and rebirth of a shadowy male divinity, one whose name and existence are only hinted at in the otherwise enormous amount of religious material uncovered at various centers of worship on Crete. Occasionally the visiting Greeks would see images of him on Minoan rings and seals—at times an infant, at others, a young man—always smaller than the Great Goddess, of course, and ever obeisant to her. But for the most part, he remained in the background, as mysterious and hidden in the labyrinthine Cretan ceremonies as the reclusive Minos himself.

The boy—or young man—was apparently a consort of some kind to the goddess, a prince or companion. Some said he may even have been, once upon a time, Minos himself. While Minos was said to have been sacrificed (at least, symbolically) as a bull every seven years, the ritual killing of the boy was an annual event, which occurred, as did that of Minos, within the palace labyrinth on the night of the winter solstice. But every spring, as soon as the snow cleared on the passes up to the high, white mountain, and day and night were of equal length, the boy would undergo a resurrection, thus guaranteeing the rebirth of the world itself and of all its plant and animal offspring.

The Minoans said that the event took place in a huge cave near the top of the mountain. For thousands of years, the cave had been one of the most sacred of sites. Proof of its sanctity came from the hundreds of bees—regenerating epiphanies of the Great Goddess herself—who had built their hives within. In winter, when snow began to blanket the mountain and its meadow below, the colonies would seem to disappear into these hives, which would become their funerary jars of hardened wax and honey. Then, three months later, as the snow melted and the meadow began to fill with grass and flowers, the golden, fiery bees would return, resurrected souls of the dead, to once again sweeten life with honey, which was thought of by the ancients as the elixir of immortality and ambrosia of the goddess.

Once the Greeks had conquered the island, it would not have taken them long to conclude that the Divine Child the Minoans had been worshipping all these years had been none other than Zeus himself.

What required considerably more ingenuity, however, would be a refashioning of earlier myths to show that the sole purpose of creation had been to bring about this blessed event. For this, the Greeks turned to the stories that they had picked up on their travels to the east. Out of these, they would create a particularly Greek blend of horror, humor, and high purpose, the whole spiced with enough blood and sex to satisfy the tastes of even the most battle-hardened of their warriors. At the same time, however, this creation myth would also pay due deference to the power of the Great Goddess, whose volcano was still simmering out there in the Aegean and whose presence remained firmly embedded in the faiths and the landscapes of both Crete and the mainland.

THE BIRTH OF ZEUS

As the story and its entangled begettings wandered their way down through the centuries to Homer and Hesiod, it would develop, in brief, into something like this:

> In the Beginning, there had been the yawning emptiness of Chaos and, as well, the first Beings of the cosmos: Earth, Hell, and Love. Love, whose name was Eros, was the most powerful of them all. Barely pubescent, half-girl, half-boy, he was incomparably beautiful, but as deadly and intoxicating as Egyptian opium. He unhinged the mind and inflamed the body, moving all things, mortal and immortal, to couple with one another, heedlessly. He was desire and longing; he was creation; he held the world together and made it go round. He was also blind.
>
> Eros made Earth, whose name was Gaía, seethe with such fertility that, on her own, she brought forth a male companion to satisfy her desires. He was Ouranós, the immense Sky, who would arch above her body, covering it from end to end and showering

her with fruitful rain. Through the agency of this rain, Gaía began to give birth to all the other beings in the universe, including those giant, godlike creatures called the Titans.

But many of Gaía's children were monsters: among them, huge thunder lizards and giant rats. Others were half-human—some of them with only one eye in the center of their foreheads, and others with a hundred arms and fifty heads. The disgusted Ouranós decided that the moment they were born, he would take and hide them away deep within the earth, in a place so secret that not even she would know where to find them.

But the Earth Mother missed her children, however deformed they might be. As she started to bloat from the pressures within her body, she understood what Ouranós had done. And vowed to wreak revenge upon him. Groaning in the fullness of her misery and her anger, she called upon her other sons, the seven male Titans, for help. She had taken from within her body the hardest of stones, diamond-like gray adamant, and fashioned it into a giant, razor-sharp sickle. She promised all of Ouranós's power to any of her sons who would use the sickle against their father as she wished. Only one of them stepped forward, the largest and craftiest of them all. His name was Krónos.

That night, while Ouranós was spread out upon Gaía satisfying his usual nocturnal desires, Krónos snuck up behind his father and, with a single, quick cut of the sickle, sliced off his genitals. But instead of immediately tossing the grisly trophy over his shoulder as Gaía had instructed, Krónos let out a howl of triumph and raised the severed family jewels above his head, unable to resist the temptation to bask in his triumph. As he did, great drops of blood dripped down upon Gaía's body and immediately began burning their way into her, blindly seeking nurture in her womb.

Some of these drops would become the Giants of the Earth, the Yenénis, disgusting creatures with legs sprouting serpents' tails, who dwelled in the Land of the Burning Volcanoes, their bodies impervious to death even at the hands of the gods. Other drops ended up in Tártarus, where they festered, sluggishly blackening, multiplying, and dividing, until there blossomed forth out of this filth the hideous, serpent-wrapped forms of the foul-breathed Furies, their eyes dripping a yellowish ooze, nostrils flaring, endlessly sniffing out the droppings of sin.*

Thus did Retribution make its appearance in the world, with Krónos doomed to become the first to suffer its lashings. He was told by both his mother and father that although he was now king of the Titans, he would eventually be attacked and overthrown by one of his own children—just as he himself had usurped the throne of Ouranós.

Krónos, in a futile attempt to forestall his fate, began gobbling down his progeny as fast as his sister-wife, the Titaness Rhéa, could produce them. In five years, he devoured a handful of glorious offspring: Héstia, Protectress of the Home; Deméter, Keeper of the Earth's Fertility; Héra, Guardian of Women and Marriage; Hádes, Ruler of the Underworld; and Poseidon, Earth Shaker and God of the Sea. Now, with Rhéa again pregnant and nearing the end of term, Krónos was once more impatiently pacing the halls of his palace on the mainland, ready and waiting to wolf down the next in line: the child that would become, if it survived, the mighty Zeus.

This time, Rhéa went to her parents, to Gaía and Ouranós, for help. For reasons that only certain warring married couples can fully understand, these two were still together, in spite of Ouranós's spiriting away of her children, and Gaía's urging Krónos to castrate him. They counseled Rhéa not to despair. They had been told by Eros, who had set this family romance in motion eons before, that Rhéa's

---

* Hesiod also tells us that when Ouranós's members splashed into the sea there arose from the foam (*aphrós*) the goddess of love, Aphrodite. But Homer had previously stated in the *Iliad* and *Odyssey* that she was a daughter of Zeus.

next child would be saved. Therefore, on the night Rhéa was due to give birth, Gaía did what had to be done and spirited her away to Crete, to the only cave large and sacred enough to hold such a divine and magnificent child. Rhéa went into labor, and as she did, there arose within her womb a terrible burning and tearing sensation, as if this new child were in fact a beast, as monstrous as a fully grown bull, intent on ripping her to pieces as he tore his way into time. The energy released sent such a fiery light radiating out of the cave that it seemed the air itself might even be set ablaze.

[As it happens, I can personally attest to the authenticity of this part of the myth, having, in 1978, witnessed a similarly awesome (and truly terrifying) phenomenon from the rooftop of a house I was renting in Réthymnon, Crete. I had been awakened in the middle of the night by a noise that sounded as if an ammunition depot was suddenly being ripped apart by a sustained series of detonations. When I went up to the roof, I saw that the sky above Psiloritis was exploding with a thunderous crackling of flames that seemed to emanate from the peak itself, leaping back and forth from one roiling mass of clouds to another and growing louder and louder with each passing moment, a wildfire of lightning that was threatening to set the very atmosphere alight. It went on and on, for perhaps twenty minutes or more. Then, as suddenly as it had appeared, it burned itself out. And the heavens, after a few intermittent, sputtering flashes, settled back into the soothing deep-blue darkness of a spring night. As I watched, I kept reassuring myself that it was (probably) only an electrical storm (not the end of the world), but I didn't find the thought very comforting (and probably still wouldn't). Imagine, then, what the ancient Greeks and Minoans must have made of such a sight, one which they must have most certainly witnessed more than once over the many years that they were on the island. Certainly it would have seemed as if such a phenomenon were heralding something of great importance. Perhaps even the birth of the god, of he who would someday be called the Great Thunderer.]

And suddenly there was the divine child, lying between Rhéa's legs, a naked little baby boy, smeared with the glistening, honeylike *ichor* that flowed in the veins of all the gods, totally vulnerable—and, in fact, almost human.

Rhéa quickly roused herself and, leaving the infant Zeus, in the care of Gaía, hurried home to present her husband with what seemed to be his latest child, a brand-new bundle of joy wrapped in a swaddling blanket. Krónos immediately gulped the bundle down without realizing that the weight resting inside the blanket was nothing but an enormous stone.

THE DEATH OF ZEUS

While Hesiod tells us that Krónos lived on in blissful ignorance of this son's existence, in many other tales and traditions, we are told that the Titan not only learned that the infant was still alive, but would send assassins to both murder the babe and eat it.

The identity of these killers is disputed by both the tale tellers and scholars. Some say they were the Koúrites, successors to the Idaían Dactyls, young warriors whom Gaía had stationed to guard the infant. They were supposed to prevent Krónos from discovering Zeus's whereabouts by beating their bronze shields and cymbals together to cover the noise whenever the baby Zeus let out one of his thunderous squalls. Others say it was the Titans themselves who had banded together to kill the boy. To disguise themselves and protect them from whatever powers might be guarding the god, they covered their bodies with a magical white clay taken from the foot of the Holy Volcano. Then they gathered around the mouth of the cave and dangled an array of delightful toys to lure the babe out of the safety of his sacred birthplace.

Like all infants everywhere, the child would have found such glittering enticements irresistible. And so, he eagerly crawled out of the cave and into the arms of his killers, blissfully believing that all the world was his plaything. As soon as he emerged, they went at him with their long knives, not even bothering to see if he was dead before slicing off the most succulent portions of his flesh to eat while it was still quivering with divinity.*

HIS RESURRECTION

All Zeus could ever remember about the incident were flashes and fragments: the killers' white, white faces, eyes bloodshot, the inside of their mouths a glistening, screaming red, the glints of fire on their weapons, flashes of light behind his eyes and within his brain, and then, a sudden, blinding brilliance . . .

. . . and out of the light, as if no time had passed at all, there was the soothing hum of bees, like a mother's song, and the sweet taste of honey bathing his entire being, as if he were suspended within it, as if he were again within Rhéa's womb. Suddenly, he opened his eyes, and it was spring. A nanny goat was licking the honey—or was it *ichor*?—off his face. Her name, he knew, was Amálthia, and he knew that until his mother returned, she would nurture him. He also knew that although he had been given the shape of a man, beneath this semblance he was still what he always had been: the god of thunder and lightning, a bull-like mass of pure primal energy who would as soon kill you as look at you. And that this was what his murderous father, Krónos, would learn, the moment the child had grown into manhood and could marshal enough forces to obliterate the Titan supremacy.

---

* Over the years, stories of Zeus's death on Crete and the presence there of his tomb gained such credibility that the poet Kallímachus was moved, in his *Hymn to Zeus* (c. 340 B.C.), to call all Cretans liars, a condemnation repeated by St. Paul in his Letter to Titus (1:12). See also the endnote on p. 248 keyed to the phrase "quivering with divinity."

* * *

Under the new rule of the Greeks, the lightning-browed Idaían Cave quickly became the epicenter of the cult of Zeus Kritayenís—literally, "the Cretan-born Zeus"—whose death and resurrection would be celebrated at various venues around the island, most importantly at the caves on Mt. Díkte (also thought to be a birthplace of Zeus) and Mt. Ida. Plato would set the dialogue of his *Laws* during a pilgrimage from Knossós to the cave (presumably on Ida), and the cult would continue to attract pilgrims—among them, the mystic-philosopher Pythagoras—from all over the pagan and emerging Christian worlds well into the reign of Emperor Julian, which is to say, some 360 years after the birth of Jesus.

In the 1980s, the Greek archaeologist Iánnis Sakellarákis undertook the first systematic excavation of the cave on Mt. Ida since the nineteenth century and unearthed tens of thousands of votive offerings and cult objects brought there over a period of some two thousand years. One of the first items found by Sakellarákis was a shepherd's knife, which had been left around the turn of the twentieth century. In his book on the digs, he includes, without comment, a photograph taken at the time of a flock of sheep (one appropriately black) lined up to enter the cave. It therefore seems that this site of Zeus's nativity has been fairly continuously used—since, perhaps, those prehistoric times when the Koúrites' predecessors, the Idaían Dactyls, were said to have invented the art of sheepherding—as a manger.

Today, the drive from Iráklion to the cave (some eight thousand feet above sea level) takes roughly two hours over a series of tortuous zigzags across the foothills and then up, down, and around increasingly steep ridges, gulches, valleys, and ravines. In ancient times, over virtually the same route, it would have required at least two days and would have probably taken place in the often brutal heat of the midsummer, when the snow within the cave would be guaranteed to have melted—something that was not the case when Fárzaneh and I arrived in our rented car two days before Easter.

We pulled into a wide parking lot outside the cinder-block lodge and restaurant that marked the end of the journey. Below the restaurant was the enormous Nida Plateau, snowbound in winter but on this day in early April, graced by flocks of tiny sheep milling across its acres of undulating, flower-filled grassland. Above us stretched a grassy slope which led upward toward the granite mass that was the peak. Somewhere along the way, as yet invisible from our vantage point, was Zeus's birthplace.

Since our guidebook said that it was just "a 10-minute walk up a rough track," we decided to forgo lunch until after we had made our pilgrimage. Some thirty-five minutes later, soaked in sweat, jackets off but sandaled feet frozen blue from slogging through the sometimes foot-deep snow that blanketed the final fifty-yard stretch of rocky terrain, we at last reached our destination: the front edge of a gargantuan cavern that had housed the earthly birth of the great Greek Sky God.

The snow outside had just been a mild prelude to the mounds that were piled up within. It blanketed the fifty-foot width of the entrance and extended down an extremely steep slope to what we could only assume was the cave's floor, at least another thirty yards into its shadowy interior. There was no telling how deep the mound was. It seemed entirely possible that you could take one or two steps inside and sink into a drift twice your height. Even a group of hearty Greek mountain climbers who were gathered at the lip peering down into the snowy abyss had made sure to keep a respectful foot or two away from the edge, lest they slip into depths that could only be guessed at, but never—except of course by fools—treaded upon.

CHILDHOOD

As you stand in front of the cave and take in the view below, in particular, the enormous flower-filled, mountain-ringed, stream-crossed meadow of the Nida Plateau which stretches out before you almost from horizon to horizon, it is easy to envision how glorious Zeus's childhood must have been. Tales of his early years, however, are few. Like many other gods and heroes, from Oedipus to Moses, Jesus, King Arthur, and our own Superman and Luke Skywalker, Zeus was an abandoned child growing up under a threat of death. But unlike them, Zeus had neither foster parents nor mentors to guide him—except for, perhaps, the occasional, clandestine counsels of Gaía and Rhéa, whose visits would have been less devoted to mothering him than to keeping lit the fires of vengeance against his father.

We do, however, hear of the infant Zeus being suckled on the teats of his nurse, the goat Amálthia, and drinking from her horns, which were said to flow with ambrosia and nectar, the food and drink, respectively, of immortality. Amálthia (who some say was really a nymph) also protected the child by hanging him in a golden cradle from the branches of a willow that grew in the mouth of the cave, thus suspending him between Heaven and Earth, of and not of mortal flesh, and in neither of the realms where Krónos might seek to murder him a third time. And when these duties were done, and Zeus was sending her off into the heavens as the constellation Capricorn, it is said by others that Amálthia's final gift to her former nursling was, literally, the skin off her back, a woolly pelt which the god would forever wear as his magical *aigís*, symbol of his lordly power.

We can imagine, too, how wonderful it would have been for the formerly amorphous god to now experience the joys of having a body, in particular one which he could use to practice the splendid, godly art of shifting from one shape to another, reincarnating himself in wondrous states of being, notably those for which he would become most notorious—the eagle, ram, snake, dragon, lion, panther, bull, flame, shower of gold, and, last but not least, swan—in preparation for his eventual mastery over the cosmos now ruled by his Titan father.

Then there were the nymphs. Who provided them is uncertain, but inasmuch as the ancient Greeks who imagined the stories considered these lithe and lovely creatures to be especially amorous, we must assume that one of their duties was to educate the rapidly maturing young god in the facts of life—in preparation for the time when he would need to populate the offices of both Heaven and Earth with his own progeny.

So when you drive down from the mountain and through the rolling hills and fields of the glorious Cretan landscape, lush with all manner of flora and fauna, it is delightful to imagine how it must have been for the pubescent Zeus as he, too, was brought closer and closer to human affairs—exuberantly tumbling and frolicking over the undulant hills and dales of ancient Crete, across fields that were then without walls of any sort, playing hide-and-seek with the nymphs in the great forests that covered most of the island, resting in sylvan glades beside bubbling brooks as the hot winds from Africa swept through the trees, making clothing of any kind (except perhaps the revealing gossamer wisps that nymphs like to loosely twine about their limbs) completely beside the point.

On the other hand, the art of lovemaking would never become Zeus's strong suit. His talent would lie in seduction solely for the purposes of dominance and procreation. Thus, if a brief whispering of sweet nothings failed to achieve the desired results, he would blithely turn to force as a natural alternative, as his lordly right. The new world that his followers had ushered him into was a rough one, with little time for courtly flutterings.

6

THE ROAD TO POWER

War, father of all things, is of all things, king.

HERACLITUS, *Fragment 44*

For the Greeks, the subjugation of Crete meant that they now dominated nearly all the central Greek islands and large parts of the mainland, while also taking as their own the Minoans' trade routes to Asia Minor, the Levant, and Egypt. On the mainland, they possessed major strongholds at Pylos, Athens, Orchomenos, and Thebes, with their most powerful citadels—at Tíryns, Mycenae, and Argos—governing both the fertile plains of the Argolid and the main roads between the Peloponnese and northern Greece. In the *Iliad*, Homer referred to these people as the Achaeans and Argives, although scholars doubt that this is what they called themselves. Modern-day archaeologists have since resurrected them as the Mycenaeans.*

From within the ever-thickening walls of their fortresses, the Mycenaean royal families managed an empire whose reach and volume of commerce would expand, over the next two hundred years, as far west as England, north to the Black Sea, east to the coasts of

* The term *Mycenean* was first applied to this culture by a Greek archaeologist, Christos Tsountas (1857–1934), who followed Heinrich Schliemann in excavating the site.

Asia Minor, Lebanon, and Israel, and south to Egypt and Libya, and also come to constitute one of the great naval and land war machines of the Bronze Age era.

As part of this process, they would establish their god of gods as the supreme deity of the territories they dominated, setting shrines to him on various peaks around the country while establishing his main center of power atop the great massif that they now called Ólympus. At 9,570 feet, this was the highest mountain in the land, twice the height of his birthplace on Crete. From here, Zeus and his fellow Olympians could survey the world as their fiefdom, just as the Mycenaeans were doing from their hilltop fortresses on the mainland and Crete. At the same time, these new rulers were building their own myths on top of those already current among the natives and, in the process, dominating most of the tales by placing Zeus and his cohorts at their core, with the indigenous deities as their consorts or offspring. Later, as the various communities began generating their own traditions, the great Mycenaean heroes would come into being, each claimed by a particular city or region, but celebrated, too—especially in the case of Hérakles—as the pride and joy of all Greeks.

Eventually, these tales would most certainly become the greatest of all the treasures that the Mycenaeans accumulated during their reign, much more fabulous than that hoard of beautifully wrought artifacts of gold and precious jewels unearthed in the late nineteenth century by the great amateur archaeologist Heinrich Schliemann (and his much more professional successors) at Troy and Mycenae. In the Mycenaeans' priceless trove of myths, folktales, and legends, we have been handed down our most celebrated pagan deities and superhuman heroes and had our culture enriched by such incomparably tragic human archetypes as Odysseus, Medea, Eléktra, Helen, Oréstes, and Oedipus—all of whom, not coincidentally, would trace their lineage and their individual fates back to the one who might justifiably be called the great founding father of Western civilization: Zeus.

* * *

The young god's sudden eruption into manhood makes it difficult to pin him down to an orderly chronology. So many places would lay claim to his presence during this fertile era that he seems to have been everywhere at once: dashing all over the eastern Mediterranean making love to this goddess and that mortal, battling Titans, giants, and fire-breathing dragons, quelling rebellions against his authority, destroying and then resuscitating mankind, and in general intruding himself into the world with all the tangled pervasiveness of Life Itself.

THE WAR WITH THE TITANS

As Greek mythographers tell the story, it was the aid of Gaía, the Great Mother, that made possible the first phase of the venture: Zeus's return to the mainland and his battle with Krónos and the Titans.* Zeus, she advised, could never triumph over the Titans alone; he would need the help of his five siblings: the sisters Héstia, Héra, and Deméter, and the brothers Hádes and Poseidon. Yes, their father, Krónos, had swallowed them years before, but, being immortal, they were still there, floating around undigested in the Titan's very large large intestine. All Zeus had to do was get them out.

With the help of his mother, Rhéa, and her sister Titaness, the ocean nymph Mítis, Zeus contrived to slip the unsuspecting Krónos a powerful emetic in his evening cup of mead, with the young, unrecognized Zeus himself, assigned by Rhéa to be Krónos's cupbearer, carrying him the honeyed drink that Mítis had prepared. The king of the Titans quickly became violently ill, first disgorging the great stone that Rhéa had substituted for the infant Zeus at the time of his birth, and then vomiting forth his five children, all of them now fully grown. Amid the filth and confusion brought on by this monumental

---

* In Greek literature, the war with the Titans is called the Titanomáchy.

regurgitation, Krónos was able to flee. But the band of siblings were at last reunited and ready to do battle.

Deposing Krónos and his fellow Titans would still not be easy. They were as enormous as their name implies. In addition, their numbers had grown considerably since Gaía had given the original twelve dominion over the six planets. By now they had had many powerful children, including the mighty Atlas and his cunning brothers, Epimétheus and Prométheus.

So Gaía counseled Zeus to get further help by also liberating those formidable children of hers—the Cyclopes and the Ekatonhíres (Hundred-Handers)—whom her husband, Ouranós, had imprisoned deep within the earth all those eons before. These one-eyed Cyclopes were much different from the more famous ones encountered by Odysseus in Homer's *Odyssey*. The latter were savage giants who lived in caves on an island now believed to be Sicily. These, on the other hand, were a trio of very sympathetic and powerful misfits whom Ouranós had unjustly sent to their hellish underground incarceration. The Ekatonhíres were even more deformed and misunderstood. There were three of them, each with a hundred arms and fifty heads. To free them, Zeus made the dangerous journey down into Tártarus, killed their Titaness jailer, and brought them all back to the surface, where he plied them with ambrosia and nectar to rebuild their strength and courage. Afterward, they would become the god's most trusted of servants, to whom Zeus would assign the task of keeping those he had punished safely incarcerated in the Underworld.

The grateful Cyclopes presented Zeus with three important weapons which they had forged prior to their imprisonment. Henceforth, these would become the storm god's signature trademark, the force majeure with which he would wield power over mortals and immortals alike: his awesome lightning bolt, its terrifying flash, and the deafening clap of thunder that followed. The Cyclopes also gave Zeus's brother Poseidon his famous trident, and the other brother, Hádes, a helmet of darkness to make him invisible.

It was with these formidable weapons and allies that Zeus was said to have engaged the Titans in battle on the great, mountain-ringed plain of Thessaly, which lies between the mighty massif of Ólympus in the north and the broad, southern range of Mt. Óthrys, home of the Titans. This was the only arena on the mainland large enough to hold such gigantic combatants. It was also of great strategic importance to the Mycenaeans. Since the Greeks' arrival from the Caucasus, most of central and western Thessaly had remained largely independent of their control. So Zeus's impulse to establish hegemony over the entire area and its fertile plain may have been a reflection of the Mycenaeans' desire to do the same. Last but not least, part of the Titans' mountainous redoubt to the south included Mt. Parnassus, which nestled on its slopes the Great Mother's highly influential oracle at Delphí.

In Hesiod's telling, the war was a decade-long series of clashes that raged back and forth across the plain and plunged deep into Tártarus, the most abominable region of the Underworld, shaking the world's foundations and turning Greece's incomparably blue heavens as dark and roiling with fiery clouds as the very depths of that stygian abyss. In fact, the effects described are strikingly similar to those of a volcanic eruption: The land seethes, the waters boil, and blasts of scalding vapor fill the air, while a stupefying heat grips the Underworld and terrible, roaring winds precede a torrent of earthquakes, dust storms, thunder, and flaming lightning bolts. To think that Hesiod wrote his account nearly one thousand years after the Santoríni event is to be reminded once again how deeply the destruction of the Holy Mountain must have been seared into the Greek collective unconscious. This forgotten but unforgettable trauma, with its weakening effect on the hegemony of goddess-worshipping Crete, had begun a process that would, with the victory of the Olympian gods, forever change the course of history.

* * *

Krónos, devourer of his own children and once the most-favored son of the earth goddess Gaía, was the last to be captured. The aging Titan had not been on the field of battle, having ceded command to his more vigorous nephew Atlas. But Zeus and his brothers, Poseidon and Hádes, had circled behind the lines to get at their father in his mountain redoubt. Hádes, invisible because of the Cyclopes' helmet of darkness, entered Krónos' chambers first and stole his weapons. Poseidon then diverted the Titan's attention by threatening an attack with his trident. This allowed Zeus to strike their father with a massive thunderbolt, stunning him into submission. At long last, the old man was at the mercy of his sons. But before his punishment could be carried out, the Titan cursed Zeus as he himself had been cursed by his castrated father, promising him that one day, he too would be overthrown by an offspring more powerful than himself.

What happened to Krónos then is uncertain. Hesiod implies that he was imprisoned with his fellow Titans in Tártarus, sealed behind a bronze door put there by Poseidon and guarded by the trio of fierce Hundred-Handers. Before the door stood baleful Night's black-clouded abode, and next to this crouched the unfortunate Atlas, receiving special punishment for his role as the Titans' commander in chief by being condemned to forever support the sky on his head and shoulders.

Other stories have Krónos (and perhaps his fellow Titans) exiled to the edges of creation, out beyond the Pillars of Hérakles—which is to say, the Straits of Gibraltar, the pillars being the Gibraltar to the north and the Atlas Mountains in the south—where the great stream of Okeanós girds the earth. There he was confined to quarters on what Plutarch says was one of the islands of Britain, from which he would never again threaten Greece.

Meanwhile, the tale tellers say that Zeus and his Olympian cohorts had allowed the female Titans to remain free. This was ostensibly recognition of the aid given by Rhéa, Gaía, and Mítis, but also an acknowledgment of the continuing power of the Great Goddess among her many devotees on the mainland and Crete. The natives in both places would have still had deep attachments to their old-time religion and the goddesses who embodied it. In addition, as noted, the Mycenaeans seem to have been a people who liked to cover all the sacred bases, just in case. Moreover, their personal favorite, Zeus, would have an enormous number of posts to fill in extending his power throughout the cosmos. Every little rock, tree, and breeze seemed to require its personal deity. Consequently, he would have need of an endless number of the resident female divinities (Titanesses, nymphs, Olympian goddesses)—and the occasional mortal—to carry his seed. So, as is always the case between the sexes, mortal or immortal, accommodations had to be made.

AFFAIRS OF STATE

But few of Zeus's prospective conquests would submit to him as easily as the hot young god had hoped. Most of the goddesses and nymphs were allies or surrogates of the Great Mother and were not about to so readily yield to his authority. Although the first female he chose to be his consort, the Titaness Mítis, had helped slip that emetic to Krónos, she was, when it came to bedding her, a slippery, shape-shifter who took days to tussle into a form he could hang on to. Then, just as he was savoring this conquest, Gaía arrived to warn him that Mítis would eventually bear him a son stronger than himself. Panicked, Zeus turned and swallowed the poor Titaness on the spot, not knowing that she was already carrying within her womb the embryo of a daughter. Consequently, the god himself was now pregnant, albeit unknowingly. Far too busy with his fatherings to notice the fetus's burgeoning presence, Zeus also brushed aside his mother, Rhéa's demands that he cease having sex with his subjects and act like a proper king. In response, he replied that he would continue to do *what*ever he wanted with *whom*ever he wanted *when*ever he wanted, and that if his mother didn't mind her own business, he would start with *her*. Horrified, Rhéa instinctively sought to protect herself by turning into that most inaccessible of creatures, a giant serpent. Changing into a snake himself, Zeus lashed his muscular coils around his mother, twisted their bodies into a nearly indissoluble knot, and proceeded to relieve himself of his rage, leaving his mother to slither off in mute and humbled mortification.

Some of the Great Thunderer's liaisons were, however, all that could have been wished for. Beautiful, fish-tailed Evrynómi, sister of Mítis, bore him the three fair-cheeked Graces of Beauty, Gentleness, and Friendship. Subsequently, in nine glorious nights of ardent lovemaking with Mnimosíni, Goddess of Memory, he fathered the Nine Muses. Then, upon the Titaness Thémis, he begat the Órai, or Seasons.

But his second batch of triplet daughters with Thémis proved much more problematic. These were the Moírai, or Three Fates: Klothó, who spins the thread of life; Lákhesis, who decides upon its end; and Átropos, who cuts it. They would turn out to be the only deities over whom the Great Thunderer had virtually no control. Fate was Fate, and its implacable ways were often mysterious even to the greatest of gods—a fact that was destined to cause Zeus considerable anguish over the centuries, not to mention chagrin: What kind of head of the family was he, anyway, when his own daughters could tell him what to do?

Which brings us—and him—to Héra.

HÉRA

The first time Zeus laid eyes on her, she was a mess, having just emerged from years of sloshing around in her father, Krónos's, large intestine. Nevertheless, it had taken only a single glance for the two of them to know that they were meant for each other. Insatiably so. Lust for Héra wrapped Zeus's loins in its embrace from the very start, and even during the dogged, decade-long conflict with the Titans, he would sneak off into the countryside to grapple with his sister at every opportunity, the divine siblings hidden from curious eyes by curtains of glistening dew and a glorious golden cloud, mutually drugged with desire as they tried, unsuccessfully, to merge their bodies into one. Finally, Zeus understood that they would never be at peace until he, the great god of the Greeks, and she, the supreme surrogate of the goddess, were united by more than just physical hunger—until, in fact, the father of gods and men had this divine female exactly where he mistakenly thought he could put her: under his royal, husbandly thumb.

And so he took the final, fateful step—and with it, guaranteed himself at least a millennium of more misery than he could possibly have imagined. It was—as Zorba would term his own fall into matrimony centuries later—the Full Catastrophe.

The Great Thunderer could be, if he wished, extremely charming. And on this particular occasion, instead of coming to Héra in one of his usual guises (bull, eagle, or any of those other brutes), he manifested himself, much to Héra's delight, as a tiny and utterly enchanting cuckoo bird—feathers an iridescent emerald, bright yellow breast gleaming golden green in the moonlight. And he fluttered to her bosom, perching upon the edge of her gown as if he were giving himself to her in the form of a brilliantly bejeweled brooch.

Then the Sky God used his powers to make a silver rain drift gently down from the cloudless sky, and Héra immediately understood that she must protect this precious bird, this *pouláki*, by sheltering it beneath her skirt.* She also knew that if she did so, she would be giving the gift of herself in return. But by then, it was too late. She was being pulled forward as if in a dream. Leaning back, Héra lifted her

* In modern Greek, *pouláki* means "little bird." It is also affectionate slang for "penis." Who's to say that a folk memory of this myth was not its source? And, perhaps not coincidentally, in Farsi (the language of Iran), the word *pouláki* denotes a tiny sweet, like a sugar cube, that one takes with tea by sucking on it.

gown and allowed the bird to enter, its silken feathers whispering along her thighs, metamorphosing even as it waddled toward its goal, swelling inexorably into the god himself.

Stories of where the royal couple spent their wedding night would claim as many spots in ancient Greece as George Washington's sleep-overs did in colonial America. One authority lists Plataía, Euboea, Athens, Hermione, the Argolid, Arcadia, Samos, Crete, and, in Italy, Falerii—adding that there were probably many more. But a pair of these particularly stand out: Samos and the Argolid.

At both sites, magnificent temples not only honored the goddess (and her marriage to the Great Thunderer) but rivaled those erected elsewhere solely for Zeus, just as Notre Dame de Paris rivals, say, St. Patrick's in New York. They were called Heráeums, literally "Places of Héra."

The imposing sanctuary on the island of Samos was begun in about 525 B.C. and worked on over a number of centuries, but its scale was so monumental that it was never completed. Said by Herodotus to be the grandest of all Greek temples even unfinished, it was enclosed by 134 pillars (the Parthenon had 92) and approached via a Sacred Way whose three-mile length was flanked by two thousand statues.

Samos was widely believed (not least by the Samians) to have been the site of both Héra's birth and her sacred marriage to Zeus. She was said to have been born beside the river Imbrasus beneath a willow tree. This tree, says Pausanias, was still growing within the Heráeum when he visited it as a child, in about A.D. 150. Pausanias also states that the wooden statue of the goddess in the sanctuary may have brought to the island by settlers from Argos and that it might have been carved by Daídalos, the Athenian-born architect who would later become the builder of the Minotaur's labyrinth.

The island held two annual rituals to celebrate Héra's marriage to

Zeus. During one, the goddess's statue was draped in bridal veils in observance of her betrothal, and in the second, it was taken out of the temple and hidden away until the ceremony, just as brides the world over are concealed from their husbands before marriage. Famously, the divine couple's lovemaking after the wedding was said to have lasted three hundred years, a record of some sort, even for a supreme god and his goddess. Near the river where they lay, a wooden relief from what may have been a bed was found and displayed in the Heráeum. Still extant, it shows Zeus with one arm around his bride's shoulders and the other possessively clasping her breast, while between their heads, that of a cuckoo bird peeks out.

However, Héra's power in the arena of the marriage bed was made most manifest at her magnificent hilltop Heráeum in the Argolid peninsula, three miles south of Mycenae. Rebuilt in 423 B.C. after a fire destroyed the old, seventh-century-B.C. temple, it housed a seated, ivory and gold statue of the goddess that stood comparison—in splendor (if not size)—with Zeus's chryselephantine colossus at Olympía. Of her sacred marriage to the god of gods, however, there were only two, small reminders—although both were highly significant. The first was a replica of the famous cuckoo bird, which sat perched, petlike, atop the royal scepter that Héra held in her right hand. The second rested on a table near the altar: a votive image of Héra holding the Great Thunderer completely in her power, his penis enveloped by her lips.

Héra was not much as a mother. While she and Zeus would produce three children, they were nowhere near as distinguished as many of the god's other progeny with lesser goddesses. Their first daughter, Hébe, was little more than a cupbearer for the gods. Their son, Áres, although the God of War and one of the twelve Olympians, was often a figure of fun and had little of the fearsome clout of his Roman successor, Mars. Meanwhile, their second daughter, Eileíthia, became venerated only because her mother gave her the duties of being Goddess of Childbirth, Héra herself apparently wanting to have as little as possible to do with that aspect of womanhood.

Which raises the question: If dominance over the cosmos through his sexual conquests and his progeny was supposed to be Zeus's priority, why had he (and the Greeks) chosen Héra as his consort? Why had they not, instead, picked one of Zeus's other sisters, the housewifely Héstia or fecund Deméter, to be his wife? Héstia was the Goddess of the Hearth, a true homebody, while Deméter, whose name meant "the mother," was the preeminent goddess of earthly fertility. In contrast, the jealous, strong-willed Héra was about as motherly and subservient as a rattlesnake, and even while you had her in bed, you could never really have her, not even for all the golden apples of the Hesperides. Wouldn't either Héstia or Deméter have seemed a much better choice?

The answer is that while the production of progeny was possible anywhere, anytime, with anyone, Héra's prestige among the people—as queen of the Olympians, she was embraced as the successor to the Great Goddess—made her an even more valuable catch for Zeus than, say, Jackie Kennedy was for that other great Greek, Aristotle Onassis. She was also, as Homer has her point out in the *Iliad*, older than Zeus and thus, by implication, his superior. Celebrated throughout the land as the patron saint of marriage, as its guardian and sanctifier, Héra was venerated above all else as the force that held the family and thus the tribe together. In her bed, the making of children was only secondary. What really mattered was a marital balance of power. Héra was the only one of all the goddesses (and gods, for that matter) who was able to persistently stand up to Zeus and demand that he stop running around and tend instead to his full responsibilities as father of gods and men. Whether or not she was successful was, of course, another matter. But she herself would remain, at her core, unpossessed. Like Jackie.

At the beginning of his reign, Zeus's appetite for the opposite sex remained undiminished, even by marriage or those legendary three hundred years of lovemaking with his new bride. In the course of doing what he (and, doubtless, most Mycenaean males) saw as his most pressing duty, the indefatigable Great Thunderer would continue to produce offspring at an astonishing rate: some of them gods and goddess, such as Apóllon, Athína, and Diónysos; others, the founders of Greece's most prominent royal families, including those of Crete, the Argolid, and Troy; and still others, those favorites of the people—the great, legendary heroes like Perseus and Hérakles. But at each and every liaison and birth, there was Héra (and often, Grandmother Gaía), resisting these intrusions into their realms with tooth, nail, the occasional claw, and all the feminine wiles at their disposal.

PART THREE

THE FATHER

7

SPREADING THE FAITH

Longings for love and lusts for power
Make poor bedfellows 'neath the wedding bower.

OVID, *Metamorphosis*

After winning the Great War with the Titans, Zeus's first priority was to establish a pantheon of the gods and goddesses to dwell in regal splendor atop Mt. Ólympus. In the Bronze Age, this lengthy east-west mountain range was thought of as the natural northern border of Greece—with all that was behind it (i.e., present-day Macedonia and Thrace) a shadowy hinterland roamed by savage beasts and their barbarian hunters. Viewed from the south, Ólympus's broad, snow-crested heights (which can often be seen rising above a line of low-hanging clouds) look completely flat, much like the Acropolis at Athens. So it is not surprising that the Greeks should have imagined that upon the latter's heavenly counterpart there should sit a splendid celestial abode, that which Homer describes as

the everlasting home of the gods
[where] no wind beats roughly, and neither rain nor snow can fall;
but it abides in everlasting sunshine and in a great peacefulness of light,
wherein the blessed gods are illumined for ever and ever.

From the perspective of the east and north, however, Ólympus is a forbidding mass of rugged peaks and valleys, with its summit a snow-covered slope known as the "Throne of Zeus." This, presumably, is where the gods would assemble for their debates. (My son, who has been up there, tells me that the area of this "throne" is only about ten yards square. In the middle is a pillar where you can hang on for dear life while you sign a guestbook certifying that you had been insane enough to complete the ascent. "Otherwise," says my son, "you don't dare move. The edge is everywhere." Hardly enough room, it seems, for one god, much less twelve.)

Zeus and his siblings—Poseidon, Hádes, Héra, Héstia, and Deméter—comprised the first six of the Olympians. Next would be the Great Thunderer's son, Áres, born of his contentious relationship with Héra and thus, inevitably perhaps, named as the God of War. With war thus in place, Love, in the form of Aphrodite, was not far behind, although there are differing stories as to how and when she was born. As noted earlier, Hesiod tells us she arose out of the foam generated when Ouranós's severed members hit the sea off of Cyprus. A more conventional begetting, mentioned by Homer in the *Iliad*, came out of Zeus's very early liaison with the nymph Dióni, a shadowy consort who was celebrated at Dodóna, site of the oldest oracle in Greece, as Zeus's primal feminine half, perhaps even as the "Broad One" herself.*

APÓLLON AND ÁRTEMIS

Next to be included in the pantheon were the divine twins, Apóllon and Ártemis. Although Zeus had gotten their mother, the Titaness Litó, pregnant months before his marriage to Héra, the moment the latter

* Thus, Aphrodite may nearly be as old as Eros. Certainly, both kept the world going around and offered cruel indifference along with their ecstasies. It was said, however, that Aphrodite tamed Eros to such an extent that she was able to bring him with her to Ólympus.

heard that Litó was about to give birth, she unleashed the full force of her queenly authority and forbade any land on Earth where the sun shone to provide shelter for the event. She then sent the giant female serpent Python, Gaía's daughter, to relentlessly hound the poor Titaness out of every place she tried to settle. Zeus finally got around his wife's dictate by sending Litó to the Aegean island of Delos, which the myth tells us was then floating unanchored just beneath the surface of the sea and thus, technically, not a land where the sun shone. Here, as their mother clung for support to a palm tree, the twins were finally born. But even though Poseidon afterward raised the island above the waves and anchored it to the bottom with four adamantine pillars, Apóllon and Ártemis soon left, with Apóllon nevertheless swearing to forever hold it dearest in his heart, and his sister, in turn, retaining a lasting affection for watery, marshy habitats, areas off on the edges of civilizations, places where she would never be tamed. Both became highly important deities in the Olympian pantheon: Ártemis, the huntress, and Apóllon, golden god of the arts, of music, and of prophecy, destined to be, next to his father, the most revered god in all of Greece.

ATHÍNA

All this time, Zeus had been suffering from a series of increasingly intense headaches. The agony finally became so intolerable that the Cloud Gatherer seized an ax and swung the sharp edge of its blade in a vicious arc down upon the top of his skull—desperately hoping that this would either kill or cure him.* Much to Zeus's surprise—and subsequent delight—out of the fissure made by the ax, there sprang

* Most mythographers say that it was the Olympian blacksmith Hephéstos who did the deed. However, as we shall very shortly see, Hephéstos wasn't born yet. There is nothing strange about having Zeus swing the ax himself. Many visitors to Greece have had similar impulses when racked by headaches caused by an excess of Greek spirits.

forth the daughter whose fetus he had inadvertently swallowed all those years before in angrily devouring his first wife, the pregnant Mítis. Now their child sprang from his head fully grown and fully armored, too, as if her father's many battles while she was gestating within his body had prepared her to take on all comers the moment she hit the ground.

Her name was Athína, and of all his children, she would be Zeus's greatest pride and joy—though sometimes, his greatest bane as well. Just as he was equally her father and mother, so Athína seemed at times to be equally his daughter and his son. Like her half-sister Ártemis, she was happy being a virgin, unencumbered by masculine demands. But whereas Ártemis actively disdained the company of men, Athína loved to join them in their exploits, most particularly their battles—"foremost, fearsome, tireless, battle-rousing and -devouring queen of clamorous combat," Hesiod calls her. Thus, she was the patron saint of war and of the cities that war protected, which included not only Athens but, among many others, Argos, Sparta, and, surprisingly, Troy.*

HEPHÉSTOS

Héra, of course, couldn't have been less welcoming. In fact, when Zeus pointed out to her that he, technically, had been Athína's mother as well as her father, the furious Héra promptly became pregnant herself—by herself—creating from her unfertilized egg a son. The goddess was mortified to see, however, that in her anger, she had spewed forth a deformed child, lame in one leg, his face permanently

* Homer, however, would later make up for this by having her help the Greeks build the wooden horse that brought down the Asian city that had so honored her as its protectress. Scholars are uncertain whether Athens is named after her or she acquired her name as protectress of that city. The Athenians called her simply *ee theh-ós* (the goddess). (Walter Burkert, *Greek Religion*, pp. 139–40.)

blackened as if charred by the flames of her rage. Immediately, she flung the baby into the sea. There he was rescued and raised by the sea nymphs Thétis and Evrynómi, who would teach him the arts of the forge. This knowledge he would eventually take with him to Ólympus, where he would become a member of the pantheon and blacksmith of the gods—Hephéstos.

HERMES

Zeus found Héra's presumptuous self-impregnation yet another excuse for not honoring his nuptial vows, and so, while she was sleeping, he snuck off for comfort and sympathy with the shy and lovely nymph Maía, daughter of Atlas. Out of their union would be born Zeus's next addition to his royal family, that clever little streak of lightning Hermes, so swift that the Olympians made him their messenger, their "luck-bringing angel." Hermes invented the sacrifice and, said some Greek mythographers, fire to go with it. His role in Zeus's revolutionary regime was to upset the old ways of doing things, and he was constantly at the ready to go anywhere and try anything, regardless of the consequences. As a result, this virile and mercurial god, with his swift golden slippers, rapidly emerged as the gods' Johnny-on-the-spot, proving himself invaluable in getting them out of innumerable difficulties. Equally as important was the fact that the moment he was born, he had also charmed the formerly implacable Héra by depositing himself on her lap before she even knew what was happening, and sucking so sweetly and convincingly at her breast that she instantly took him as her foster child.

With twelve deities in place, Zeus's pantheon appeared complete. But the Great Thunderer had still not fathered that most remarkable and disturbing of all his children—the interloper, Diónysos, god of wine and ecstasy—he who would push Héstia out of her place in the pantheon. However, Zeus would first have to deal with a most unexpected assault on his regime—by none other than Mother Earth herself, the heretofore extremely helpful Gaía.

ZEUS AND THE DRAGON OF CILICIA

Hesiod and his successors tell us that Gaía had become angered with Zeus because he had imprisoned her defeated children, the Titans, in the Underworld rather than sending them off to someplace more suited to their former stature as rulers of the cosmos—to the Blessed Isles, say, with their leader, Krónos. The furious Earth Mother therefore returned to her original home in the East, where she settled in a cave in the mountainous wilds of Cilicia (on the border of present-day Turkey and Syria) to plot her revenge. There, with Aphrodite's help, she mated with her hellish son Tártarus, dweller in the lowest depths of the Underworld, and out of their dark commingling came the last of Gaía's children and the final defender of her faith—one who would, she hoped, destroy the Olympians and rule the universe in her stead—a monstrous child named Tiphón.*

Tiphón was an enormous, chimera-like admixture of a winged anthropoid and serpent. He had the shaggy body of a man or ape down to his thighs and from there on, the coiled, lashing tail of a huge snake. His hundred heads were snake- and dragonlike. His burning eyes and fearsome, flickering tongues flashed fire, the hundred mouths clamoring in a cacophony of bulls' bellowings, human speech, lion roars, snake hisses, the whimpering squeals of dogs, and indescribable noises whose meaning only the gods could possibly comprehend.

The appearance in Greek myths of such a fiendish creature may have been an attempt by the Greek patriarchy to identify Gaía as the

---

* Alternately named Typhoeus (pronounced *Tifo-éfs.*)

mother of a horrific form of evil hitherto seen only in the shamanistic religions of Mesopotamia—a vision of a world without gods, haunted instead by swarms of evil beings whose only purpose was to bring about the innumerable miseries which plagued the people's daily lives. It had been brought into the area by the Sumerians in the fifth millennium B.C. and planted in what had been a peaceable, Neolithic Garden of Eden. As the region became increasingly ravaged by imperial power struggles, these demonic seeds would metastasize into an army of infernal beings—monstrosities with such gnarled monikers as Pazuzu, Ashag, Semihazah, Lilitu, Ullikummis, Anath, Azazel, Mot, Beelzebub, Mastema, and Belial—who would eventually slither forth to also plague the Western world, lurking in its religions, its literature, its popular culture, and its worst political nightmares.

For the early Greeks, however, the world's evils did not have a supernatural source. Rather, they were a fault of human nature and entirely different in substance from the malevolence found in the East. Socrates, for example, thought the greatest of all evils lay in doing injustices to others, and when Oedipus discovers that he has unintentionally murdered his father and committed incest with his mother, he doesn't blame a demon for his actions, but instead, punishes himself for not having known what he was doing. Meanwhile, the evils that Pandóra lets loose upon the world are spoken of as "illnesses," which is to say, human fallibilities. And although the Furies and the goddess Némesis seemed to resemble Mesopotamian demons in the fear and horror they inspired, it was not they, but the humans they were pursuing, who had been responsible for bringing wrongdoing into the world.

On the other hand, the Greeks were not averse to evoking the eastern specter of evil when it suited their purposes. Particularly when it came time to demonize the Great Goddess—she who had, after all, come out of the east in the first place, brought into Greece in the seventh millennium B.C. by Neolithic migrants making their various ways to the mainland and islands. A perfect model for these purposes had already been provided by the great Babylonian epic *Enuma Elish*, written, scholars estimate, sometime between the eighteenth and twelfth centuries B.C. In it, a brash young god, Marduk, dares to challenge the supremacy of a Great Goddess whom the Babylonians had also demonized as a bloated, monster-spawning creature named Tiamat, Goddess of Chaos and the Primordial Ocean, who, says the poem, "spawned monster serpents, sharp of tooth, and merciless of fang, with poison instead of blood . . . set up vipers and dragons, and the monster Lahamu, and hurricanes, and raging hounds, and scorpion-men, and mighty tempests, and fish-men, and rams."

With its powerful, negative propaganda and gory details, the poem made an immense impression on a Mesopotamian region now shifting, c. 1200 B.C., from goddess-oriented societies to patriarchal ones, and it was only natural that when the tale made its way along trade routes to Greece, Zeus worshippers there would borrow liberally from its bloodcurdling incidents.

Although Zeus's confrontation with Tiphón was much shorter-lived than his decade-long battle with the Titans, it proved to be nearly as apocalyptic. Once again the earth shook, the waters boiled, and even the denizens of deep Tártarus were afraid that the end of the world had come. In one variant, the fiend rips the tendons from Zeus's hands and feet, hides them in a bearskin, and carries these and the god's crippled body to the dragon's cave to be disposed of at its own malignant whim.

But ever-resourceful Hermes and his son, Pan, come to the rescue, outwitting the she-dragon whom Tiphón had left to guard his spoils and refitting the tendons on the Cloud Gatherer. Resurrected once again, resilient Zeus takes the battle to the great beast. In a conflict that rages across the entire eastern Mediterranean, the father of the gods and men, armed with his smoking thunderbolts and the very same diamond-hard sickle that his father had used to castrate Ouranós, finally overcomes his horrible adversary, Gaía's hideous child, by stunning Tiphón with a blast of lightning and quickly throwing him down to imprisonment in Tártarus, where (say many) he still lies today, just below Mt. Etna, his hundred dragon and serpent heads continuing, some 3,400 years later, to vomit up murderous fire.

But no sooner had Zeus buried Tiphón beneath Etna than Gaía was back with another attempt to undermine his regime. This time, however, she would employ her feminine wiles in a much subtler manner, acting in the guise of yet another of her surrogates, the Titaness Thémis, already the mother of Zeus's intractable daughters, the Fates. Under the guidance of Thémis, Gaía's new attack would be much more insidious, coming from within the Cloud Gatherer's ranks, from Thémis's own son, a young demigod whom Zeus thought of as one of his most valued allies: the turncoat Titan Prométheus.*

* Prométheus is given so many different mothers in various myths that scholars rightly suspect that all are really aspects of Gaía herself, reinforcing the suspicion that she was also behind his rebellion (see Karl Kerényi, *Prométheus*, p. 34).

8

PROMÉTHEUS, PANDÓRA, AND OTHER MATTERS

Zeus is hard to be entreated,
As new-born power is ever pitiless.

AESCHYLUS, *Prométheus Bound*

In the story of Prométheus, we see the first glimmers of the Greeks' emerging pride in their own considerable accomplishments: the great palaces they had built, their accumulated wealth, the trade routes that they had taken over from the Minoans, and the taming of the natural world, the Great Mother's domain, through organized farming communities that stored grain and oil in the palaces as a protection against drought and other calamities that were thought of, as they are now, as acts of the gods. At the same time, however, the savagery of Zeus's response to Prométheus's defiance of his authority also gives us a vivid picture of the despotic brutality of the Bronze Age, a thousand years before the advent of democracy, when populations were growing, crowns beginning to sit uneasily on the rulers' heads, and any threat against a regime, internal or external, demanded swift and ruthless retaliation.

Nearly everyone is familiar with the broad outlines of the story: how Prométheus stole fire from the gods and gave it to mankind, and how Zeus subsequently chained him to a mountaintop and sent an eagle to feast for eternity upon his liver. Many are also aware that since that time, Prométheus has been viewed as something of a hero—a near Christ-like figure martyred for the sake of mankind after gallantly losing the good fight against Zeus's Implacable Absolute. However, in Hesiod's version—which is to say, the earliest that we have—it is Prométheus, not Zeus, who is the villain. In it, Prométheus is consistently called "cunning" and "devious," and is fully blamed for the sufferings that resulted from his theft. For the most part, Zeus is shown as being as completely justified in his wrath as Yahweh was over the transgressions of Adam and Eve. But even in Hesiod, we see the beginnings of a bias against Zeus that would become near total in subsequent versions of the myth, as the near apotheosis of Prométheus as the people's champion gained increasing currency, put into circulation by Greeks of the emerging democracies of the Archaic and Classical ages, for whom Zeus's long supremacy had become too autocratic and pompous for its own good.

This turning against one's rulers, good as well as bad, is part of a long Greek tradition. In Classical times, it would be the great saviors of democracy, Themistocles and Pericles, who were sent packing; in the twentieth century, it was the masterful Cretan politician Elefthérios Venizélos, hero of his island's successful struggle for independence from Turkey and the greatest of Greek prime ministers, voted out of office and forced into exile at the height of his powers. In Prométheus's rebellion, we see the manifestation of this impulse in the earliest days of Greek society, when the very human beings who had first imagined Zeus in power now began envisioning the possibilities of taking it from him.

THE STORY OF PROMÉTHEUS

During the war with the Titans, Prométheus—whose mother had imparted to him a knowledge of future events that not even All-Seeing

Zeus could divine*—had come over to the side of the Olympians after failing to persuade his fellow Titans to accept what he knew would be Zeus's inevitable triumph. Thereafter, Prométheus's foresight and cunning had contributed mightily to Zeus's victory, and the Great Thunderer seems to have regarded the recruitment of this charismatic Titan as a fine strategic coup. But had Zeus been able to peer into the future as well as Prométheus, he would have sent the young demigod packing off to the Underworld along with the rest of the Titans. Instead, the Great Father stubbornly kept him on, as if helpless to change what had been written.

As recounted by Hesiod, Prométheus's first undermining of Zeus's authority took place during the initial phase of the Cloud Gatherer's rule, in those days when the gods were still living among men and dining with them. In their first meal together, Prométheus took it upon himself to apportion the sacrificial bull. He set the best meat before Zeus but cleverly folded it within an unappetizing wrapping of hide and belly flab. At the same time, he offered the mortals a large, juicy helping that glistened with fat on the outside, but inside, contained a meager bundle of leftover bones and intestines. Wittingly or not (there are differing opinions), Zeus switched the portions. Thus, thanks to Prométheus (who already knew that his future fame would rest with mortals), only the hide and bones of a sacrificial animal are offered to the gods, while the best parts always belong to mankind.

Zeus, furious at being made a fool of, then decided to punish Prométheus's favorites (but, strangely enough, not the demigod himself) by depriving them of fire, which had heretofore been given them by the Great Thunderer's lightning strikes, the embers then being carefully nurtured and preserved by the tribal priests. Once again, however, Prométheus saved the day. As the Greeks well knew, the fire for Zeus's lightning bolts was kept at the top of Mt. Ólympus. But

* His name literally means "foresight."

how to find the way up there so that he could get his hands on the sacred fire? The only solution was to persuade one of the Olympians to lead him. But who? Not one of Zeus's siblings. Nor Hermes, Zeus's lackey. And not his son Áres, the god of war, either. Nor Áres's paramour, Aphrodite. Apóllon, too, was not a possibility, so perfect a son was he and near mirror of the god himself. And certainly not Apóllon's sister, Ártemis, who hated men and was anyway always off by herself in the woods, consorting with the animals. That left the heretofore impenetrable Athína. Although still a virgin, she clearly loved the company of men, reveled in being out there on the battlefield with them, exalting in the blood, the tears, and the sweat. Tough and smart she was. Just like Prométheus. Yes, Athína would be the one.

The mythographers do not tell us what wily combination of mind and body the resourceful Fire Bringer used to seduce this favorite daughter of Zeus, just that he was able to accomplish the miracle and persuade her to lead him up to the top of Mt. Ólympus. There, she showed him where the fire was kept, in the burning wheels of the chariot of the sun. Whereupon he stole a portion of it by thrusting a torch into the wheels, then carried the flame down the mountain hidden within a stalk of fennel.* Whereupon he presented it to mankind—to these mortals who were now so beholden to Prométheus that in later centuries, they would honor him as their creator.

This was a most serious transgression. In those days, as fire was the earthly embodiment of the Great Goddess, so, too, in the Olympian scheme of things, was it the supreme manifestation of Zeus's awesome powers, fire from Heaven shooting down as lightning bolts to make sacred whatever piece of Earth it touched, or mortal it consumed. So to steal fire and parcel out its powers to anybody and

* According to the Roman naturalist Pliny the Elder, there is in Greece a species of fennel that he describes as being about five feet tall and three inches thick, "with a white pith which, being very dry, catches fire just like a wick; the fire keeps alight perfectly in the stalk and consumes the pith only gradually, without damaging the rind; hence people use this plant to carry fire from one place to another."

everybody, to ordinary mortals, was akin to subjecting Zeus to the same kind of humiliation suffered by his grandfather Ouranós, so suddenly castrated at the height of his powers.

As expected, the Great Thunderer's rage was monumental. As was the punishment he meted out—first to mankind and then, at last, to Prométheus himself.

Zeus's vengeance began exquisitely, with the creation of the very first woman, a vision of loveliness whom the father of gods and men would name Pandóra—"All Gifts." She was fashioned on Zeus's specifications by the artisan of the gods, Hephéstos, who made her out of clay. Sweetly, bewitchingly beautiful, the picture of absolute, untrammeled innocence, with the most alluring adornments the god could bestow, Pandóra was created, says Hesiod, as "an evil to mortal men with a nature to do evil," and finished to perfection by the finest hands on Mt. Ólympus. Athína, after breathing life into Hephéstos's clay, enveloped her in a rainbow-tinted gown of sheer gossamer. Aphrodite, the Goddess of Love, then polished her with a sparkling sheen of charm and beauty, which the Three Graces festooned with jewels, and the Seasons with a garland of spring flowers woven through her golden tresses. Hermes, patron god of thieves, then put the final touches on this paragon of femininity by schooling her in perfidy and guile—giving Pandóra (again according to Hesiod), "the shamelessness of a dog and the lies, wheedling words and treachery of a thief."

The Great Thunderer thereupon had Hermes present Pandóra to Prométheus's thick-headed brother, Epimétheus.* The latter was so instantly smitten that he promptly ignored Prométheus's warnings to beware of gifts from Zeus and installed the lovely maiden in his house. Just as the Cloud Gatherer had planned, Pandóra began snooping through Epimétheus's belongings. Soon, she came upon a giant, tightly sealed *pithos*, or jar,† suspiciously hidden away in a back

---

* Whose name means "Afterthought."

† Not a box (see the endnote keyed to the phrase "the sole resource . . . we mortals now have").

storage room. (The box was an invention of that great humanist scholar Erasmus of Rotterdam, 1469–1536, who inexplicably translated Hesiod's *pithos* as *pyxis*, or "box.") Prying it open, Pandóra let loose everything that Prométheus had hoped to keep bottled up inside—all the illnesses and sorrows that now plague mankind. Although Pandóra quickly shut the lid, she was only able to trap Hope inside—often the sole resource, however illusory, that we mortals now have.

Zeus thereupon ordered Prométheus taken out of Greece to the mountains of the Caucasus, those desolate, windswept edges of the world where the Great Thunderer had once ruled as the primal God of the Bright Sky. Here, on the heights of the tallest mountain, Zeus had Hephéstos fasten the Titan to the rock with unbreakable bands of bronze and iron and then, as a brutal finishing touch, drive through his chest a wedge of adamantine—the same diamond-hard material that Gaía had used to fashion the saw-toothed sickle that had castrated Ouranós—piercing Prométheus's breastbone and penetrating deep and inextricably into the rockface. Prométheus's screams of defiance echoed across the mountains, but distant Zeus did not deign to reply. And would not for eons to come.

Meanwhile, however, Zeus's own troubles were far from finished.

THE REVOLT OF THE GODS

No sooner had he returned to Ólympus from the Caucasus and settled down on his royal couch for a nap, letting Hýpnos, the God of Sleep, lull him into a deep, dark slumber, than Gaía struck again, this time through the agency of her mighty granddaughter Héra.

Homer tells us that when Zeus awoke from his nap, he found his body being bound in a snakelike coil of chains, its grip already so tight that he could not find the leverage to break free. Surrounding him and helping in the binding were the eleven other Olympian deities, led by his wife, Héra, brother Poseidon, favorite daughter, Athína, and favorite son, Apóllon.

Homer does not explain the reason for this revolt. Robert Graves, citing a scholiast, says that it was because Zeus's tyrannical behavior had become intolerable. H. J. Rose suggests that it might contain an echo of a recognition that Zeus, unlike the other gods, was a foreigner from the northeast, from the Russian steppes. There was also the above-mentioned Greek penchant for getting rid of rulers who had become—or seemed to have become—too full of themselves.

At no other time would Zeus find himself so close to inhaling the foul breath of defeat—not even in his vicious battles against the Titans and Tiphón. This time, it was his own kind who had him at their mercy, who were jeering at his helplessness and already beginning to argue over who would be anointed his successor. But before Zeus's chains could be fully wound and fixed into place, a gargantuan form rumbled into the room, its hundred hands and fifty heads thrashing and roaring about with rage at what was happening to its benefactor. This terrible being was Briáreos, one of the three Hundred-Handers whom Zeus had brought to aid him in the war against the Titans. Briáreos had been sent for by the principled and good-hearted sea nymph Thétis, who had feared that the new reign of the gods might quickly dissolve into a destructive civil war.

Briáreos marched his writhing bulk in between Zeus and his assailants, hundred hands a blur, and instantly loosed the Great Thunderer's chains. Upon being freed, Zeus went straight for Héra, while her fellow conspirators scattered in fear. Zeus bound was one thing. Zeus unbound and backed by Briáreos was entirely another. What happened next is recounted, in Homer's *Iliad*, by none other than Zeus himself, as he reminds Héra of what he did to her back then, of the time "when I hung you aloft / With anvils strung from your feet / And unbreakable golden bands binding your wrists / Dangling in the ether and the clouds, / Your fellow far-off Olympians helpless to help you."

How long this punishment lasted is not known. Zeus seemed to have spared the others, with the exception of Poseidon and Apóllon, whom he sent to work for one year for Troy's notorious skinflint of a king, Laomídon. The myth tells us that in their servitude they raised the walls of the city to such an impenetrable thickness and height that, years later, a besieging army of Greeks would have to build a wooden horse to breach them. But Laomídon failed to pay the two gods for their work. What followed is too much of a lengthy mess to be recounted here; suffice it to say that when the Greeks finally took Troy from Laomídon's son, Priam, one of the first things they did was despoil and obliterate the lying penny-pincher's tomb.

Zeus would always be beholden to Thétis. As a result, he would later spare her from a fate worse than death at his own hands and instead give her as a bride to Peleús, the king of Aegina, with whom she would give birth to the great Greek hero Achilles. Zeus would also do everything within his Fate-limited powers to guide her son to victory at Troy—even though, as we shall see, he himself had destruction in mind for both the Trojans and the Greeks.

Later that night—the night of the Olympians' failed conspiracy—while giant Briáreos prowled protectively in the ravines around Ólympus and the other gods cowered in their quarters (Héra continuing to dangle by her wrists in the sky, body stretched to the breaking point by the torturous weight of the anvils pulling down on her ankles), Zeus stood alone upon the massif's highest peak, brooding over the day's events.

As the Great Thunder's simmering anger roiled the heavens, dark clouds began to gather around the peak, blotting out the stars above. Below, however, Zeus could still see, in the blackness spreading out before him, the thousands of fires that humans had built with Prométheus's stolen goods, twinkling like stars in the nighttime sky. For a moment, just for a moment, it was as if the cosmos had been turned upside down, and Zeus was hanging in its center, gazing upward—at a firmament of mortals living as gods.

9

DIVINE RIGHTS

We boast that we can trace
High as Zeus our ancient race:
Sojourners were we at birth;
This is home, this parent earth.

AESCHYLUS, *The Suppliant Maidens*

By the beginning of the thirteenth century B.C., the various Mycenaean overlords—their bronze weaponry and body armor now being mass-produced on an unprecedented scale, chariots inventoried in the hundreds, and sleek warships powered by banks of twenty to fifty oarsmen*—soon began to see themselves as deserving of a touch of divinity. To this end, their tale tellers embarked on the elaborate process of going back in time to once again refashion the myths, in this instance to create legends about how the Great Thunderer had planted his immortal seed in the royal bloodlines from near the very beginnings of the cosmos. At the same time, they also had their ancestors come into the country not from the primitive, frozen wastes of

* Capable of rowing at a speed nearly equal to that of the huge ferries that ply the Aegean today.

the north, but out of the same lush and fecund Nile Delta that had produced the mighty Egyptians.

The stories that they now told were doubtless much different from those that have come down to us through the later Greek mythographers. While the former must have foreshadowed much greatness, the latter, written after the holocaust that claimed the Mycenaeans, were deeply shaded by the knowledge of how the best-laid schemes, especially of kings, can go devastatingly awry. So even in the most triumphant of these tales, there are dark and often bloody undertones. As Aeschylus would write as he looked back on the story of the first Mycenaeans to come to the mainland, a group of suppliant maidens fleeing Egypt:

Zeus' desires are hard to fathom.
What is shiningly clear for him
Is shrouded from mortals in obscurity . . .
The path of his purposes
Beyond understanding, tangled in darkness.
From the high towers of their hopes,
Zeus hurls humans down to doom.

THE STORY OF IÓ

In choosing the woman upon whom he would found these lines of kings, Zeus selected a maiden princess from the Argolid, a descendant of the Pelasgians, the first inhabitants of Greece. Her name was Ió, and she was the daughter of Ínachos, the king of Argos. She was sprightly and beautiful, with the raven-black hair, olive-gold skin, and flashing, long-lashed dark eyes that the women of her race had brought with them out of Mesopotamia. But she had already dedicated herself to being a priestess at Héra's principal sanctuary in the region, the Heráeum, and was so devoted to her vocation that, at the age of fourteen, she was granted guardianship of its keys and was dreaming of remaining a virgin for the rest of her life.

To his credit, Zeus approached the young lady as delicately as he could, first coming to her only in her dreams, sending his night thoughts winging out like eagles from the heights of Ólympus, south across the great Thessalian plain, past the mountainside sanctuary of Delphí, over the moonlit waters of the Gulf of Corinth, and down to her father's darkened citadel in the Argolid—dreams in which the god whispered of the delights he would bring her if she would let him be her friend. He spoke of the many splendid vistas that would be opened to her and elaborated the favors he would lavish on her and her family, if only—if only, murmured the god, she would consent to lie with him and let him hold her in his arms.

Night after night he came to the girl, and so insistent and seductive were his words that even when Ió was awake, they continued to wrap her in their hypnotic murmur. Haunted by this incessant voice inside her head, she began to fear that she was going mad and prayed to Héra for relief, but the goddess, still stretched from the sky upon Zeus's rack, seemed unable to even hear her.

Some say that Ió then went to her father for help, but that Ínachos, out of fear of Zeus, expelled her from his house and his land. Because of this, say others, Zeus finally managed to lure the maiden to the nearby meadow of Lerna where the king grazed his cattle. Here, Zeus disguised Ió as a beautiful white heifer and himself as a bull. He then drew a cloud around them for privacy and was about to mount the poor, befuddled princess when suddenly Héra appeared in the meadow, her fury so intense that the cloud instantly evaporated.

Just as quickly, Zeus also dematerialized, changing back into his godly aspect and abandoning poor, plaintively lowing Ió to the not-so-tender mercies of his jealous wife. Héra took revenge by leaving her former priestess trapped in the body of a cow while appointing the fearsome herdsman, Árgus, a monster with a hundred eyes sprouting all over his body, to ensure she stayed that way.

Ió couldn't have been more miserable. Even her father didn't recognize her when she went to him and pressed her velvet snout into his hand. Nor could she understand why the god who had so recently implored her to come to him now seemed so callously indifferent to her fate. But Zeus, who was engaged in founding dynasties and empires, had little time for sentiment. And although he did send Hermes to free Ió by lulling Árgus to sleep with music and then lopping off his head, the god nevertheless kept Ió confined to that bovine prison. In fact, she was destined to remain a cow until the very end of her travails, doomed, as humans so often are, to suffer the consequences of acts that had not been of her own doing.

Héra, meanwhile, dispatched a vicious gadfly, its bite as fiery as a hornet's, to attack her and, for good measure, sent the hideous ghost of the beheaded Árgus to hover around them as the fly's dreadful familiar.

Pursued by these furies, Ió fled the Argolid, galloping away as fast as her awkward little heifer's hooves could manage, her epic odyssey ever after memorialized in the names of two of the places she passed during her flight. One is the Ionian Sea, west of the Peloponnese, site of the islands of Corfu, Ithaca, Kefalonia, and Zakinthos; the other is the Bosporus (literally, in ancient Greek, "cow-" or "ox-" ford)—the strait where the Black Sea joins the Sea of Marmara—across which Ió swam in her increasingly crazed attempt to elude the relentless pursuit of Héra's vengeance.

Halfway through the journey mapped out for her by the Fates, Ió scrambled up the snowbound heights of the Caucasus mountains. Here she came upon Prométheus, still pinioned and chained to the rock where Zeus had sent him as punishment for stealing fire. In his play *Prometheus Bound,* Aeschylus describes their momentous encounter. The ever-defiant Prométheus has just told a sympathetic chorus of ocean nymphs that he will one day be liberated from the rock, and that then, in a manner he is not now free to reveal, it will be Zeus who will be made to suffer. At just this moment, Ió stumbles onto the stage in a state of near madness. It is a stunningly dramatic moment, this meeting of the ancient world's two greatest unfortunates, each the other's peer in unparalleled misery.

Prométheus, gifted with foresight by his mother and strengthened by the fierceness of his resentment against Zeus, offers what little solace there is to be found in both their fates. He tells Ió that one day Zeus will end her sufferings by depositing in her womb a son from whom there will eventually issue—in the thirteenth generation—the greatest of all Greek heroes (i.e. Hérakles), who will also release Prométheus from his tortures. If this does not happen, says Prométheus, then Zeus himself will fall, brought down, as was his father (and father's father), by a son even mightier than himself.

Ió can hear no more. Terrified that Prométheus' brash pronouncements will provoke Zeus to another attack, she rushes off on her anguished odyssey, pitifully trying to flee a destiny that cannot be escaped.

Immediately afterward, Hermes arrives on the mountaintop, dispatched by eavesdropping Zeus to learn the identity of this woman who will bear the god such a mighty son. When Prométheus refuses to reveal her identity, Zeus launches an enormous lightning bolt, splitting the mountaintop and engulfing the still-impaled Prométheus within its impenetrable walls. In Aeschylus's play, the rebellious Titan's final cry is to Gaía—"Earth, reverent mother!"—exhorting her and the heavens to witness "how unjustly I suffer!"

But there is as yet no such thing as justice in the world in which Prométheus and Ió bear their bitter punishments. This is nearly a thousand years before the glory days of Athenian democracy and the magnificent formulations of justice which accompanied it. Zeus is not yet fully secure on his newly won throne, and the giants Vía and Krátos (Violence and Power) still stalk the earth on his behalf, ruthless in his defense.

* * *

Meanwhile, Ió, still pursued by the gadfly and Argus's ghost, gallops frantically around the edges of the known world, passing through all of Asia, India, and then Ethiopia before finally arriving in the land that has not yet been named Egypt, where she collapses in utter despair and exhaustion at the mouth of the Nile. Here, in the delta's torpid heat and humidity, strange beasts slither in the waters' primordial slime: the terrible, sacred crocodile with its lacerating claws and glistening, saw-toothed mouth; and the river horse, half elephant, half ox, tusked like a boar, and bigger than a bull. Here, the sandpiper plucks leeches from within the crocodile's open, slavering jaws, and the phoenix arrives from Arabia every five hundred years to bury its parent, encased in a lump of myrrh, in the temple of the Sun. And here Ió, the human heifer, has reached the nether point of her fate.

We are now back at the beginning of the world as the Mycenaean tale tellers wished to present it—back at the creation of a new order out of which generations of their gods and heroes would spread forth to settle and give names and rulers to many of the great centers of the eastern Mediterranean, from Sidon in Phoenicia to Knossós in Crete, to Mycenae, Tíryns, Argos, and Thebes on the Greek mainland, the legitimacy of all of them grounded in the union which would now take place between Ió and Zeus, father of gods and men.

Egypt was the perfect spot to anchor these beginnings. The Mycenaeans had been familiar with the area since being introduced to it by the Minoans, whose trade routes they had taken over entirely after subduing Knossós in about 1400 B.C. At this time, Egypt was the most powerful nation in the region, its pharaohs controlling territories as far east as Babylon and north to the edges of the Hittite empire. Egypt's capital, Thebes, luxuriated in wealth nearly beyond imagining, and the great pyramids and mysterious Sphinx of Giza rose as awesome reminders of Egypt's past accomplishments, while the just-completed Colossi at Memnon and the enormous temple at Luxor told of its equally impressive present. That the Mycenaeans would have wanted, in one way or another, to be associated with this magnificence is beyond doubt. Some scholars even speculate that their enormous beehive tombs and the massive walls of their citadels at Tíryns and Mycenae were directly inspired by the Egyptians' taste for the monumental.*

The Nile delta was also the spot where life on Earth was believed to have begun. The Sicilian-born Greek historian and mythographer Diodorus Siculus, writing in c. 50 B.C., cites as proof of its fecundity the fact that the soil was continuing to generate prodigious numbers of creatures, some only half formed, "the rest of the body still retaining the character of the earth from which it came," while Herodotus tells us that the names of most of the gods came from that country. Ió's great-granddaughters, the suppliant women in Aeschylus's play of the same name, called the delta "Zeus's sacred garden"—the spot where the god had first planted the seeds of his all-conquering Mycenaean dynasties.

As Ió lay splayed out in the cooling silt of the river, her mud-splattered flanks heaving with exhaustion, hooves jerking as if she were still on the run, Zeus came to hover over her and caress her quivering hide with his presence. It was a gentle, amorphous touch, one which would not only make the young princess an immaculate maiden again, but also leave her heavy with child—with Zeus's child, a son of god. The boy would be called Épaphos, a name whose original meaning is still found today in the modern Greek noun for "touch"—*epafí*.

Subsequently, Épaphos would marry Memphis, a daughter of the river Nile. They would have a daughter, Libya, upon whom Poseidon would then sire two sons, Agínor and Bílos. It is through the separate branches of these sons' families that we can trace the genealogies of the gods, kings, and heroes who established Greek supremacy on

* The pyramids and the Sphinx were all constructed during a sudden flowering of the arts and technical know-how in the period of the Old Kingdom, c. 2700–2160 B.C.

Crete and the mainland. While much of this comprises a tangled bank of begettings too complicated to go into here, there are certain births which stand out, all of them so significant that the tale tellers would reinsert Zeus into the gene pool to emphasize the fact.

The first concerns a daughter of Agínor for whom all the land north of the Peloponnese may have been named: the beautiful maiden princess Evrópi.

10

THE CRETAN SAGA

The virgin did whate'er a virgin cou'd
(Sure Juno must have pardon'd, had she view'd);
With all her might against his force she strove;
But how can mortal maids contend with Jove?

OVID, *Metamorphosis*

In the beginning, long before he took on human form for the first time, All-Seeing Zeus had looked down upon the island of Crete, made note of its abundance, and decided that he wanted a son of his own to be its king (so said the bards of the Greeks, now the new rulers of Crete). With this in mind, the god turned himself into an eagle and flew eastward (where the best civilizations of the time were located) in search of a human female—preferably a princess—worthy of carrying his seed.

Now in the land of the Phoenicians,* there was just such a creature. Her name, in Greek, was Evrópi. She was very beautiful, very headstrong, and completely innocent in the ways of the world, having been brought up to believe that when you were the daughter of a king, particularly one as powerful as Agínor, who was said to be a son

* Today, a part of Syria and Lebanon.

of Poseidon and grandson of Zeus, nothing bad could ever happen to you, no matter what. So on many a spring morning, she would lead her maiden playmates to pick flowers in a broad meadow by the sea, near the city of Sidon, completely ignoring the warnings of her parents and her guardians to stay away from the shore lest she be seized by pirates. Or a wandering god.

Thus it was that eagle-eyed Zeus came to spot her as she frolicked among the flowers, her many-colored gossamer gown fluttering around her as radiant as the wings of a butterfly. And instantly, Zeus knew that she was the one.

For the briefest of moments, hovering on the wind, the god was poised to swoop down in all his brute beauty and take her with his talons just like that, off to Crete. But she was so lovely! So young and so vibrant! Suddenly, his feathers felt funny, his wings weak. They could hardly hold him aloft. He himself didn't know what the matter was. But Hesiod and the other poets—particularly that lascivious Roman Ovid—would tell us, in detail. For the very first time, Zeus was being assailed by human feelings. He was falling—almost literally—in love.

But how would he appear to her? Obviously, not as himself. No human being could look upon his divine incandescence and survive. What he needed instead was an outward shape that was not only seductively beautiful and appropriately masculine, but large enough to be able to whisk the girl off to Crete before she could do anything about it. A bull. Just as with Ió. But not the black, ground-pawing, thundercloud type. Rather, a smallish white one, about the size of a Shetland pony, color pure as untrodden snow, hide soft as that of an unborn calf, and horns so delicately wrought as to seem carved out of ivory and mother-of-pearl by a master jeweler, a Bronze Age Cellini.

And so it was that Zeus materialized in the midst of a herd of cattle grazing in the meadow and was almost upon Evrópi before she even noticed him. But when she did, she was enchanted. At the time, Evrópi was barely in her teens, and the bull seemed to her to be about the same age, standing before her like a bashful, newly pubescent boy. As she gasped in surprised delight at his sudden appearance, he shyly lowered his long-lashed eyes and shook his dewlap as if pretending he was preoccupied with something else, his well-muscled shoulders flowing beneath his pearly hide like water rippling over rocks in a brook. Then Zeus snorted softly, little more than a breath, and, lo!, between his lips there appeared, as if by magic, a golden crocus, the powdery cloud of its saffron drifting upward to settle upon his moist, pink nostrils, turning them gold.*

Delighted, Evrópi clapped her hands together, dark eyes flashing like star sapphires. She was easily the most beautiful creature the god had ever seen, ringlets of her black, curly hair seductively curtaining her face as she bent over him, skin as golden as virgin olive oil, her lips soft and pink as sweet briar roses. She took the crocus and, in return, entwined a chain of flowers between his horns, draping a loop, garlandlike, around his neck. As she did so, the Great Thunderer sank to one knee, seemingly overwhelmed by her presence.

Evrópi, taking this genuflection as a sign that she should sit on his back, hitched up her skirt and did so.

"No!" cried her friends.

But it was too late, and besides, Evrópi was not in the habit anyway of heeding the advice of underlings.

Zeus then heaved himself to his hooves, and as he rocked upward, he seemed to grow much larger than before. Evrópi, clinging to his back, gave a high-pitched giggle; the ground suddenly appeared much farther away than she had expected. Meanwhile, her playmates began backing away in fear, and the herd bolted toward the inland hills and the safety of their palace corral.

"Let me down!" cried Evrópi.

---

* In Persia, where saffron is an ingredient in numerous dishes, both savory and sweet, one is advised to be judicious in the amount used, since it is both a stimulant ("It makes you laugh a lot," Fárzaneh says) and an aphrodisiac ("Probably for both men and women," she continues, and then adds, "but nobody talks about the effect on women—of course!").

But before she could even consider jumping onto the soft grass of the meadow, the bull had bounded from there to the beach and thence into the sea, breasting through the incoming waves with all the ease of a great white whale barreling toward the freedom of the deep. And he headed toward Crete, some 550 miles away.

How long did the journey take? None of the poets tell us that. For Zeus, feeling the pressure of Evrópi's soft body upon his back, the crossing must have seemed interminable. Evrópi, meanwhile, was nearly drowning, swamped not by seawater (Zeus was careful to keep his prize as high and dry as possible) but by riptides of conflicting emotions. Frightened to death of the full fathoms of both the sea and the bull (having never been on either before), she nevertheless had to cling to the latter for dear life. He may have been her abductor, but he was also, she realized, her only savior, too.

Meanwhile, the weather had become eerily, almost supernaturally, calm. A delicate fog had gathered around them, softening the glare of the sun, and the sea had flattened to nearly imperceptible swells; it was as if the bull were an eagle, and they were gliding through clouds, not water.

After a while, lulled by the cadence of the waves and the warmth of the beast beneath her, Evrópi found herself beginning to relax, to appreciate the animal's power and to find a strange and increasing kind of comfort in it. The garlands of flowers she had woven around his horns and neck were still there, calming her with recollections of how gentle and boyish he had seemed when she first caught sight of him.

Dolphins appeared on either side, guarding their flanks, a procession of them, like bridesmaids at a wedding, thought Evrópi, drowsily, smiling to herself. Succumbing to the rhythm of the bull and sea, she leaned forward, entwined her arms and the folds of her butterfly gown through the bull's horns, and fell asleep . . .

So exhausted was she, in fact, that when they came ashore on the southern coast of Crete and the bull-god let her slip from his back beneath a great, inland plane tree, Evrópi slid to the ground with hardly a murmur and instantly fell again into the arms of Hýpnos, the soothing God of Sleep, son of Night and brother of Death. To Zeus, she looked so innocent, lying there in the spangled shade of the tree, sunlight flickering on her limbs, that it seemed a shame to disturb such purity. But the Great Thunderer's energy (particularly as confined within the body of a mere bull) was up. Gazing down at the pastel gossamer of Evrópi's gown, still wet and glistening like a thin film of oil upon her flesh, painting her body with a swirl of colors, the god suddenly let out a bellow of pent-up passion.

Jolted awake, Evrópi sat up, eyes widening in terror. What had been her gentle companion, her savior, was now metamorphosing into a giant eagle, its imperial talons bared, wings slashing the air. Then he was upon her, forcing her backward, smothering her in the reek of his feathers, and although the violation of her body was over in a matter of seconds, the horror she felt at the shuddering of his loins would stay with her forever.

As the eagle pulled back, Evrópi spat at him, bits of feather floating lazily down through the dappled sunlight. Some of these landed between her legs, where a dark stain was seeping into the folds of the gossamer shift that her mother—had it been only the morning before?—had so admired on her figure, now already beginning to swell from the burgeoning of the three divine seeds planted within her womb, one of these destined to become the next king of Crete.

"Oh, yes," said our hostess, "*that* tree. It's still there, you know."

It was Easter Sunday, and Farzaneh and I were now on Crete, celebrating the holidays with a family of old and new friends from the island, thinking that we would take an afternoon's respite from chasing after Zeus. But in Greece, serendipity (as it happens, a word of Persian origins) is more often than not the order of the day, and when it appears, you must heed its call; otherwise marvelous opportunities may be lost.

So as I was telling the guests about our project and mentioned the tree, our hostess told us that it not only still existed, but happened to be just a half-mile down the road. "But you knew that," she said.

No, I didn't. I knew that the place where Zeus had supposedly taken Evrópi ashore—now the archaeological site of Górtyn—was there, but I had never dreamed that the actual tree was thought to still be flourishing. If so, it would be about 3,400 years old—an impossibility. Such trees, commonly called plane trees in Europe and sycamores in the United States, don't survive longer than 500 years. Besides, Górtyn had been a major Cretan settlement since Minoan times, was mentioned by Homer as a major contributor to the war effort against Troy, and during the Roman subjugation had become the most powerful city on the island, covering some 370 acres with a massive complex of buildings, including temples to Apóllon, Athína, and the Egyptian deities Isis and Serapis. Moreover, in the early Byzantine era (fourth to sixth centuries A.D.), the Christian faithful had managed to squeeze six basilicas into a little more than an acre in the heart of the city. So it seemed highly unlikely that in all this activity, the tree hadn't been totally trampled under long before our own era. But, of course, we had to take a look anyway, and so we promptly left the party and hurried down the road to Górtyn, hoping that for the sake of tourists, the site would be open even on Easter Sunday.

So inconspicuous is Górtyn's entrance that we sped right past it and over a small river before realizing that all the signs announcing its entrance were now on the other side of the road and pointing in the direction from which we had come. So we doubled back and pulled into a small graveled area by the main gate. Miraculously, a guard was on duty, seated outside at a wooden table on the gravel parking area. He was a pleasant-looking, pear-shaped gentleman in, perhaps, his sixties, with a full head of white hair, several gold fillings, and a freshly washed Sunday shirt that sorely needed ironing. Beside him on the table was a battered portable radio, out of which floated the faint undulations of an Eastern Orthodox liturgy.

He gave us a bright smile as we stepped out of the car, and said, in English, "Closed." And then, in case we hadn't understood, added, "*Geschlossen*" in German.

Although he was pleased to learn that I could speak Greek, this did not make a dent in his iron refusal to let us into the site. Yes, he acknowledged, there was such a tree inside, and in fact, it was just on the other side of the ruins of that basilica. But no, we couldn't sneak into the site, not even for a peek. Not on his watch, and especially not—he pointed to the radio—on Easter Sunday. So why didn't we return tomorrow, when it would be open? I explained that we had to catch the evening boat for Athens and wouldn't have time. Too bad, he said.

I decided to try what was beginning to look like our trump card: "Yes," I replied, "really too bad, particularly for my wife, who is Persian, you know, and on her first trip to Greece."

In an instant, everything changed. Suddenly, it was he, the guard, who was insisting that Fárzaneh must see this famous tree. No, he still couldn't open the gate, but if we climbed over those rocks to the right and followed the fence around to the side, along the riverbank, we'd soon be able to at least get a look at it. It was just behind the Romans' music center, the *odeíon*. We couldn't miss it. It was a huge tree. The guard grinned. Very big. Like Zeus.

And so we made our way around and along the fence. Just past the crumbled apse of St. Titus's, we saw the *odeíon* and beyond that, the tree. The guard had been right. You couldn't miss it. About thirty feet tall, it towered behind and over what looked to be a large, reconstructed section of the backstage area of the *odeíon*, and nearly engulfed a poor little palm tree that had had the bad luck to grow up next to it. Unfortunately, the *odeíon* completely blocked our view of the lower half of the plane tree. As a result, we could not see what would have been its most impressive aspect: the massive trunk and lower branches, which often spread out as wide as the tree is high and bend so low at their ends that they touch the ground, creating a perfect circle of privacy for anyone beneath it. Once again—as we had been at the snowbound mouth of the Idaían Cave—Fárzaneh and I were denied access to the precinct of the god. And so there we stood, a good seventy-five feet away, our noses all but pressed up against the chain-link fence, gazing longingly at our unattainable goal like homeless street urchins before a department store window at Christmastime.

I consoled myself with the thought that the tree didn't look to be all that spectacular anyway—particularly not to those of us who hailed from the land of the giant redwood and spreading chestnut tree and, moreover, had just experienced the thrills and chills of a climb to Zeus's colossal birth cave on the heights of Crete's highest mountain.

And in truth, it really wasn't all that much to write home about. Nor would it have been to Zeus. What mattered was the act itself: the impregnating stamp that he would put on Minoan civilization in fathering not just a line of Cretan kings but, in the centuries that followed, the glory that would be Classical Greece.

According to Theophrastus, a fourth-century-B.C. botanist and philosopher whom Aristotle designated as his successor at his school in Athens, not only did the tree exist, but it stayed forever green in commemoration of this momentous coupling between Zeus and the Asian princess. And now, when all else was said and done and all the Roman temples and Byzantine basilicas that had been put up to supplant the original myths were little more than piles of nearly forgotten rubble, the tree and its tale were indeed still here—ever green—just as Theophrastus had claimed.

After Zeus had forced himself on Evrópi, his subsequent treatment of her—particularly the way he showered the poor girl with magnificent gifts—shows a surprising amount of remorse at what he had done. Those strange emotions that had so confused him when he had first laid eyes upon the princess had clearly not evaporated after the satisfaction of his sexual needs. Within seconds of assaulting her, he seems to have felt such pangs of conscience at what he had done that he instantly cast off his brutish animal form and set about finding ways to make it up to her. But as far as Evrópi was concerned, he had simply disappeared—and were it not for her strange, new surroundings, the bits of eagle feathers still drifting in the air, and the inescapable stain on her shift, she might have thought that it had all been nothing more than a terrible dream.

She would not, however, be alone for long. Within minutes, a handsome young Cretan happened to wander by this very spot, silently guided there by the Great Thunderer himself. This good-looking youth was none other than the king of Crete, Astérios, out on a hunting expedition. As soon as he saw Evrópi, he became as bedazzled by her beauty as Zeus himself had been. So much so that he hardly questioned why and how she, an Asian princess, had wound up in the woods of Crete. Shortly afterward, he not only took Evrópi as his consort but agreed to act as the father of the three children now taking form in her womb, no questions (apparently) asked.

The gifts that Zeus bestowed upon the happy couple were clearly designed to reward Astérios for stepping so handily into the breach: a hunting dog that would unfailingly bring its prey to ground; a magic spear that never missed its mark; and, last but certainly not least, a giant man made entirely of bronze, whose job it would be to guard the kingdom by circling Crete's shores three times a day and hurling rocks at any hostile approaches. His name was Talos, and some say he was a bronze bull or had the head of a bull. Some third-century-B.C. coins from Crete also show him winged. He was said to be indestructible, but later, in that mythical time a generation before the Trojan War, after Jason had escaped from the Caucasus with the Golden Fleece and the sorceress Medea, the latter would use her wiles to kill Talos by removing a pin from his ankle and draining out the immortal *ichor* in his single vein.

Astérios, whose father was the mythical colonizer of Crete, was not only the island's first king, but he also happened, conveniently, to be childless. As a result, the sons he adopted from Evrópi and Zeus's union—Minos, Radámanthys, and Sarpedón—were directly in line to succeed him. Thus did the Greeks' god of gods, through the abduction and ravishment of an Asian princess, become the father of the Cretan royal line—from virtually its very inception.

But the bull from the sea—or another one suspiciously like it—had not finished with the kings of Crete.

THE MINOTAUR

Upon the death of Astérios, Evrópi's three sons, fell into an angry dispute over the succession. Since all had been conceived by Zeus and then born at the same time, none seems to have been able to claim the right of primogeniture. Minos asserted, however, that the gods favored him. To prove this, he prayed to Poseidon to send him a bull to sacrifice. Immediately, a magnificent white bull arose out of the sea, cresting to shore among the foaming breakers. The Cretans were so impressed that they forthwith proclaimed Minos king of Crete, with his true father, All-Seeing Zeus, being the power behind the throne.*

Minos, however—like kings everywhere—quickly began to mistake the god's power for his own. He decided not to sacrifice the bull from the sea, but rather to hold on to it as a testament to his eminence. So he offered a substitute bull to Poseidon instead, keeping the first one in the palace corral, where he and his beautiful queen, Pasiphái, could enjoy its impressive presence at their leisure.

All-Seeing Zeus knew this would happen, of course, and in turn, he instructed his brother Poseidon to punish Minos by causing

* This, we must remember, is the Greek version of events. In this version, the Minoans' Great Mother is given only scant and primarily decorative importance, with some of her aspects, such as Pasiphái and Ariadne, subsumed into Minos's family.

Pasipháі to develop an irresistible urge to couple with the bull and bear its child. It seems likely that Pasipháі had already heard from her mother-in-law, Evrópi, how Zeus had once appeared to her, Evrópi, in that very same guise and manner—as a white bull from the sea—and carried her off to Crete. So Minos's queen may have already been primed to imagine herself also in thrall to the Great Thunderer. But Pasipháі seems to have also been aware that she was in the grip of some kind of derangement, divinely inspired or not. Euripides tells us as much in that fragment of a lost play, *The Cretans*, when Pasipháі explains that "her passion for the bull was a form of madness inflicted on her by Poseidon."

Try as she might, the Cretan queen could do nothing to rid herself of this obsession. Nor, on the other hand, was she able to arouse a reciprocal madness in the white bull, who, Zeus or not, stood passively staring at her with utter, cud-chewing indifference, no matter what she did to arouse it. Desperate, Pasipháі confided her crazed desire to a distinguished foreigner from the region of Attica on the mainland,* a man of sophistication and experience, someone who could be counted on to both understand her frustrations and remain discreet about them—because he too had recently fallen victim to an irrational passion and was now in exile as a result.

The man's name was Daídalos. Before his exile, he had been an artist of the first rank, celebrated because of the lifelike quality of his paintings and sculptures. But one of his apprentices had had the effrontery to upstage him by inventing not only the saw (out of a snake's jawbone) but a two-legged compass for geometric drawings, and the potter's wheel. In a spasm of jealous rage, Daídalos had pushed the boy off the Acropolis. In broad daylight and in front of scores of witnesses. The authorities had had no choice but to charge him with murder and send him away in exile. King Minos, fully appreciative of

* From, in fact, the town that was gathered at the foot of the Acropolis, which had not yet been named Athens.

Daídalos's talents, had not only welcomed the poor man but decided to keep him permanently on the island—by force if necessary.

Daídalos, perhaps hoping both to gain a modest revenge against Minos for his de facto imprisonment and to find favor with Zeus and Poseidon, not to mention Pasipháí, quickly came up with a way to satisfy the queen's illicit passion. He constructed a hollow wooden sculpture of a cow, covered the structure with cow hide, and sewed Pasipháí inside. He then rolled his creation into the bull's corral, where the great white beast completed Zeus's design by mounting the poor, god-crazed queen and getting her with child.

The result of the bizarre coupling was the Minotaur—a hulking monstrosity with the body of a man and the head of a bull. The embarrassed Minos immediately hid this abomination in a labyrinthine prison beneath the palace, designed by Daídalos so as to be both impenetrable and inescapable.

In the second part of the tale, which takes place at least two decades after the Minotaur's birth, Minos has now sired nine children upon Pasipháí, including his daughters Ariadne and Phaedra, and a favorite son, Andrógeos. The king is also being regularly counseled by Zeus, whom he visits in the Idaían Cave every nine years to receive, in the manner of Moses, new laws to bring down the mountain to his people.* During this favored period, the Minoan Empire reaches its greatest heights, with the Aegean becoming a Cretan sea and all the people within and bordering its shores subject to Minoan dictates.

But such fruitful hegemony was not to last forever.

The death of Minos's son Andrógeos on the mainland was the

---

* Moses and Zeus were, for all intents and purposes, contemporaries. Moses was born in about 1571 B.C. (say some authorities), and he was about eighty years old at the time of the Exodus, just about the time when the cone of the volcano on Santoríni may have collapsed and sent out a second tsunami, this one paving the way, perhaps, for both the birth of Zeus and the parting of the Red (or Reed) Sea.

first sign that things might be changing. Andrógeos had come to the relatively insignificant little kingdom of what would later be called Athens for an athletic competition and, as a king's son should, dominated the events in which he entered. But then, suddenly, he was dead—gored, said the mainlanders, by a bull, a white bull, which had been terrorizing the plain of Marathon outside the city.

The dread that Minos then experienced, compounded by his rage and sorrow over his son's death, was unlike any feeling he had ever had before. That bull—it must have been that bull—was back again. He should have had it killed many years before—should have sacrificed it to Poseidon when it first appeared to him out of the sea—or at least slaughtered it after it had impregnated his wife. But when his men had gone to do just this, the bull had disappeared. How it had done so was a mystery. The gates of the corral were all locked. It was as if it had transformed itself into something else—"An eagle!" was what Pasiphái, in her temporary derangement, had cried—and vanished, seemingly forever.*

But now, here the bull was again. As if it had been waiting all these years to bring this misery to Minos.

When news immediately followed that Aegeus's son, the crown prince Theseus, had captured and killed the bull, Minos did not feel any better. The dread was still there, curled up like a fetus in the pit of his stomach, ready to spread its terrible wings. So Minos went to war against Attica and its neighbors, as if only the victorious bloodbath that was certain to be his could put this fear to rest.

But Attica did not fall. The fortifications of its acropolis could not be breached—a second sign that things were changing. Never before had the mighty Minoan fleet failed to bring an opponent to its knees.

For the first time in a long time, in matters of military significance,

* Later myths would credit Zeus's son Hérakles (after whom the city of Iráklion was named) with ridding Crete of the bull, which had been ravaging the island. After capturing the bull, he set it free on the mainland, where it had found its way to Marathon.

Minos turned to his father, Zeus, for help. The god's response was seemingly all that Minos could have wished for: terrible plagues and pestilence were visited upon the people of Attica, drying up its rivers, blighting the arable land, and decimating its population.* And if that were not enough, the oracle at Delphí told King Aegeus and his emissaries to give Minos everything that he desired.

What Minos wanted was blood for blood: an annual sacrifice of seven maidens and seven youths to be sent to Crete for the Minotaur to feed upon. And he wanted Aegeus's son, Theseus, to be first among the first of these. A prince for a prince. It seemed to make sense. But in choosing Theseus, Minos was unknowingly bringing about the beginning of the end of Cretan dominance. By now, the balance of power between the mainland and Crete had definitely shifted. With it, so, too, had Zeus. Soon the god would completely abandon his former favorites, the Cretans, and their king, his son, leaving them to twist slowly in the prevailing northern wind—the one which had already brought the Greek invasion fleet on its first foray into the Aegean hundreds of years before.

King Aegeus, of course, had no inkling of this. He was horrified at the prospect of sending his son to Crete to be torn apart and eaten by the Minotaur. But the brash young prince was bursting with confidence. He promised his father he would kill the beast, rescue the other hostages, and return to Attica on the same ship. So the king reluctantly let Theseus depart for Crete but made him swear, on the return trip, to change the ship's black sails to white to signal his success, so that his father would be able to know the outcome without having to wait for their landfall.

Theseus vowed to do this. But instantly let the promise slip from his mind, which was filled with many more urgent matters.

---

* About the same time that Yahweh was visiting similar disasters on Egypt. And all of this, of course, could have been (say many authorities) the result of the catastrophic explosion of Santoríni's volcano.

Upon his arrival at Knossós, the handsome young Theseus was spotted by Minos's teenage daughter, Ariadne, who promptly fell in love with him—as teenagers often do with impossible objects. Or, as her mother had done with that apparently unattainable bull from the sea.

And, again like Pasipháí, Ariadne went to Daídalos for help. Daídalos advised giving Theseus a ball of thread to attach to the opening of the labyrinth and unwind as he penetrated its depths. By following this, Theseus would be able to find his way back out once he had dispatched the Minotaur.

Secretly, Ariadne visited Theseus in his cell and promised to help him to escape if he would swear to take her with him and marry her on their arrival in Attica. Theseus agreed. But only, it seems, in principle. Clearly, he had little or no interest in the girl. His taste ran to more dangerous types—as would be evidenced in his later affairs with Hippolyta, the queen of the Amazons, and Ariadne's mad, destructive sister, Phaedra. But these are other stories, for other times, and other books.

Apollodorus says that Theseus killed the Minotaur with his bare hands, but many vase paintings of the event show him with a sword or a club. Whichever, he did away with the monster in short order, freed the other prisoners, and fled with them and Ariadne on that black-sailed ship, which had been waiting for them in the harbor.

On the way to Attica, they stopped off at the island of Naxos for supplies. While they were docked, Ariadne, curious as a kitten and delighting in her newfound freedom, went to look around the island. The impatient Theseus then ordered the ship to sail—without her. Some say that he was in such a hurry to return home that he forgot to see if she was aboard. Others, that he simply abandoned her. In any case, Ariadne was left behind. Sometime later, after falling in with a crazed group of maenads—female followers of the God of Wine, Zeus's son Diónysos—she would be carried off to immortality by that very god. Eventually, Diónysos would marry Ariadne and honor their nuptials by having her wedding garland set into the heavens as the constellation Corona Borealis.

Meanwhile, Theseus, in his haste to get home, forgot to change the ship's sails from black to white. His father, King Aegeus, who had been anxiously on the lookout atop the acropolis, saw the black sails and, thinking his son had been devoured by the Minotaur, leaped to his death.

As king, Theseus redeemed himself by gathering the people of Attica into a great, democratic city-state, which he named Athens. In later years, however, he was forced to flee the city he had founded after he had brought the wrath of Sparta down upon its people by abducting its king's twelve-year-old daughter, Helen, later of Trojan fame (see chapters 17 and 18). Theseus went into exile on the island of Skyros but was murdered by its king, who pushed him off a cliff.

Several centuries later, in 490 B.C., after Theseus's fully armored ghost was seen leading the Athenian charge against the Persians at the Battle of Marathon, the oracle at Delphí ordered his gigantic bones dug up and returned to Athens. In 475 B.C. a great tomb was built to honor him. The tomb, said to be on the spot of Ptolemy's Gymnasium, just to the south of the Athenian agora, has never been found.

Meanwhile, Minos, his world falling apart around him, had turned his fury against Daídalos, the man who had not only helped Pasiphái cuckold him with that white bull but then facilitated both the murder of his fearsome symbol of power, the Minotaur, and the abduction of his eldest daughter. But no sooner did Minos imprison Daídalos and his son, Icarus, in the labyrinth than they escaped (adding insult to injury) by famously flying off the island on wings that the great artificer had fabricated with wax.

Although Icarus perished because the wax melted when he flew too close to the sun, plunging into the sea near the island, Icaria, that now bears his name, Daídalos managed to reach Sicily, where its king gave him refuge.

Minos then became so obsessed with finding Daídalos that he completely abandoned his family and his kingdom to chase after this foul architect of his humiliation, scouring the length and breadth of the Mediterranean for news of his whereabouts.

Eventually, he arrived in Sicily, where the very same king who was harboring Daídalos offered him the hospitality of his citadel. There, as the exhausted Cretan monarch sat naked in a tub awaiting a warm bath, the daughters of the king poured boiling water over him while Daídalos, from a nearby room, listened to his dying screams.

The shade of Minos was then sent to spend eternity in Tártarus, in the very depths of Hádes' kingdom. Here his father, Zeus, took posthumous pity on him by making him, renowned in life as a giver of laws, the supreme judge of the ghosts who wander these dark and fittingly labyrinthine recesses. In fact, Odysseus himself would see Minos there and return to tell the living of "Zeus's glorious son enthroned, golden scepter in hand, passing out judgments upon the dead."

The violence and brutality of these ancient beginnings seem to have permanently soaked into the Cretan soil, leaving a pool of darkness beneath its verdant landscape which even the recent glittering overlay of new highways, upscale boutiques, and shiny beachfront resorts can barely hide.

When you live on the island for a while and learn about Cretan history, you start to catch glimpses of this below the surface, the way the Cretans do—particularly of the still-resonant Ottoman occupation, which lasted from 1669 to 1898. And then, when you sit in Iráklion's main square, as Fárzaneh and I were doing on that bright Easter Monday morning, savoring warm, sugar-dusted *bougátzas** for breakfast and

* A delicious, cream-filled pastry about the size of an omelet that is often prepared piping hot right in front of you. I am mentioning this because Iráklion's are perhaps the best I have had.

watching the water bubbling merrily out of the square's lion-sculpted fountain, it is hard not to be reminded of the times when this water ran red with blood, as it often did during the time of the Turks, and to see, beyond the fountain, the eerie ghost of another plane tree, as green as that at Górtyn, its long, thick, low-hanging branches festooned with bodies.

In those days, in reprisal for some rebellious offense committed in the Cretans' constant lust for freedom, the Turks would abruptly lock Iráklion's gates and wallow in a nightlong slaughter of the locals trapped inside. Nikos Kazantzákis, the Cretan-born author of *Zorba the Greek*, recalls being taken to the tree by his father on the morning following one of these rampages, in about 1891. They walked right up to a branch where the corpses of three Cretan men, dressed only in their nightshirts, were dangling, their feet bare, "deep green tongues hanging out of their mouths."

His father first forced Kazantzákis to touch the cold, crusty skin of the dead men's feet. Then he commanded that his son kiss them. When Kazantzákis, then all of six years old, tried to pull away, his father grabbed him, lifted him up, and forcefully glued his mouth to their cold and rigid surface. "That," said the father, "was to help you get used to it."

The Greeks call this honoring of tribal honor *filótimo*. *Filótimo* is in the blood. And in Greece, the blood is of prime importance. You cannot, for instance, become a citizen, as you can in America, simply by being born here. You must have the blood. Perhaps this idea started with Zeus and his followers. He was an immigrant god—conceived of in the Russian steppes and later smuggled to Minoan Crete inside his mother's womb. So the moment Zeus had taken power from his father, the tale tellers saw to it that he had relations with every suitable female, mortal and immortal, he could get his hands (or paws, claws, talons, and webbed feet) on—all for the purpose of infusing the region and its religion with his own, overwhelming bloodlines.

One glance at the males of Crete, particularly the blond and blue-eyed ones from the mountain villages, will tell you that these are nearly direct descendants of the Bronze Age Greeks who poured into the country from the Caucasian north—their luxuriant mustaches, flashing eyes, and proud staglike stance blood-forged in more than three thousand years of stalwart resistance against intruders from both the West and East. In them you see the blood of the young, Cretan-born Zeus. The one that was raised to the clanging of shields in its wild mountains, his newfound body ministered to by nymphs and fed on honey dew and the milk of paradise, yes, but also slashed to pieces by agents of his father and his infant flesh eaten while still quivering with life.

"For the first time," wrote Kazantzákis about the morning when his father took him to honor the Cretan dead, "my childish mind saw life's true face behind the beautiful mask of sea, verdant fields, fruit-laden vines, wheaten bread, and a mother's smile. Life's true face: the skull."

In the middle of the fifth century B.C., the abductions of Ió and Evrópi would be recast as historical facts when the great Greek historian Herodotus conducted his "inquiries"* into the causes of the recent wars between the Greeks and Persians, in order to preserve for posterity "the great and marvelous deeds of both the Hellenes and the barbarians . . . and the accusations which caused them to make war on one another."

The first of these accusations, and the one with which Herodotus opens his inquiry, was made by the Persians, who blamed the Phoenicians for starting the series of incidents that led to the war, and the Greeks for keeping it going. Many years before, said the Persians, the Phoenicians, who were in Argos on a trading expedition, had abducted a number of Greek women. Among them was the king's daughter, the

* In ancient Greek, *istoríes*—which we have since transliterated into "histories."

princess Ió, who had come to the seaside with friends to see the Phoenicians' wares. While they were bargaining, the sailors seized them and headed quickly out to sea. There, they ravished the lot and when they were finished, discarded their used-up trophies in Egypt—which, says Herodotus, is how Ió really came to that country.

In turn, said the Persians, the Greeks* later sailed to the Phoenician port of Tyre and made off with the Phoenician king's daughter, whose name was Evrópi. When no retaliation to this was forthcoming, a Greek expedition under Jason and his Argonauts further exacerbated matters by abducting another Asian princess from her father's kingdom at Colchis, on the eastern edge of the Black Sea. Her name, they said, bringing yet another mythological figure into history, was Medea.

Therefore, continued the Persians, when the Asian prince Paris fell in love with the beautiful Helen, wife of Menélaos, the king of Sparta, he, Paris, felt perfectly justified in spiriting her back to Troy. It was nothing for anyone to get upset about. In Asia, women were abducted all the time, and, in most cases (as in Helen's), they wanted it that way. Otherwise, they—the women—wouldn't have allowed the abduction in the first place. But, the Persians complained, the Greeks couldn't let matters be. They had to go and raise an army and invade Asia and destroy the Trojan Empire just because of the work of that she-devil from Sparta, Helen. And it was for this reason, said the Persians, that they regarded the Greeks as their everlasting enemy. Asia, they said, belonged to the Persians and to the people who dwelled there, and the Greeks, who were of a distinct and separate race and geographic area, should stay out of it.

Thus the myths of Ió and her great-great-granddaughter Evrópi (not to mention Medea and Helen) metamorphosed into historical facts and became the causa belli not only of the wars between the

---

* Most likely Cretans, according to Herodotus. He also notes that the Phoenicians categorically denied this, saying that the fault was Ió's, that she had fallen in love with their captain and run off with him. (*Histories*, I.5.)

Greeks and Persians, but—one might reasonably argue—of that series of conflicts between East and West that has continued to the present. In fact, the consequences are so catastrophic that one is tempted to search for a much darker original sin than the abduction of Ió. If a pagan Greek were living today, he or she might discern in all this the implacable hand of Zeus (and/or of his daughters, the Fates) still wreaking havoc on mankind for its hubris in committing the true original sin—accepting Prométheus's tainted gift of fire—and thereby presuming to harbor for themselves power and knowledge too dangerous to be wielded by anyone but the gods.

On the other hand, a Greek might also point out that the union of Zeus and Evrópi did, after all, father the magnificent Minoan Empire, and that the glories of that civilization gave birth to the great Classical Age of Greece, which in turn engendered the incandescent renaissance of Europe—an area of land that the Greeks to this day, in a mostly unconscious recognition of those long ago beginnings, still call Evrópi.

11

THEBES: THE ILL-FATED MARRIAGE OF KADMOS AND HARMONÍA

Two great urns sit upon the floor of Zeus's palace,
Filled with gifts of the god, some of sorrow, others joy.
From these Zeus, lightning-lover, allots a mix of good and bad.
But when he gives solely from the jar of sorrow,
That man he makes mad, driving him outcast across the
sacred earth,
Honored by neither gods nor men.

HOMER, *Iliad*

When Evrópi's father, King Agínor of Phoenicia, learned that she had been abducted, he had no idea where the white bull might have taken her after he disappeared over the waves. So the king immediately sent his three sons to search for their sister in different parts of the world, charging them not to return until she had been rescued. As a result, the second line of Zeus and Ió's descendants would come to mainland Greece, carried there in the person of one of Evrópi's brothers, the young prince Kadmos; and although he would never find his sister, the gods would grant him the privilege of founding one of the greatest cities in all of Mycenaean Greece: mighty, seven-gated Thebes, whose renown, for better and for worse, would echo down the ages.

THE STORY OF KADMOS

In a fruitless search for Evrópi, Kadmos and his contingent of Phoenician soldiers scoured northern and central Greece before finally trudging up to the mountainous redoubt of Delphí to ask its oracle for aid. In those early Mycenaean times, before a total religious patriarchy had been imposed on the people's beliefs, the voice that spoke through the oracle was still worshipped as that of Gaía herself, the goddess's enigmatic utterances rising from the gaseous crack in the earth called the *ómphalos*, or navel, of the world, her giant python guarding the sanctuary as it slithered through the hot, fume-wrapped darkness of the nearby cave that housed her sacred spring.

In no uncertain terms, Gaía's oracle informed Kadmos that his quest for his sister was hopeless, that the bull that had abducted her was no ordinary creature, and that its will was not to be thwarted. Nevertheless, Kadmos would be greatly rewarded for his efforts. First, said the oracle, the prince would have to go to the lowlands to the north, where he would come upon a heifer that had the markings of the full moon on her flanks. Kadmos was to follow this heifer wherever she would lead him, and on the spot where she lay down to rest, he would found a city that would become one of the most powerful in all of Greece.

The prince, deeply impressed, proceeded to do exactly as ordered. He and his soldiers went down the mountain and north to the plains of Thessaly. Here, lo and behold, they soon came upon just such a heifer, her auburn hide emblazoned on both sides with a pale-yellow, moonlike circle. When Kadmos and his soldiers approached the heifer, she moved away and began meandering southward, into what is today Viotía. Kadmos and his retinue patiently followed, until the heifer at last slumped exhausted to the ground atop a large plateau in the hills of Viotía. This plateau, more than half a mile long and a quarter mile wide, was perfect for a fortified acropolis. Below it lay a valley of fertile, forested alluvial ground plentifully watered by rivers, streams, and springs.

To thank the gods and goddesses for having shown him the way to this near paradise, Kadmos decided to sacrifice the heifer on the spot and dedicate it to Zeus's daughter Athína. Hearing the gurglings of a nearby spring, Kadmos sent his soldiers to bring water for a proper purifying bath. But as the soldiers approached the spring, they were assaulted by a huge, fire-breathing dragon. The beast managed to kill several of the soldiers before Kadmos could come to their aid. Enraged, the hot-blooded young prince attacked the monster and, after a furious battle, sliced off its head.

As Kadmos was still a relative youth and not yet entirely accustomed to the murky machinations of the gods and goddesses, he had no idea whom the dragon represented or what a dangerous offense killing it might be. Although the dragon was later said to be an offspring of Áres, Zeus's son, and that Kadmos would sow its teeth to produce the first brave citizens of Thebes (the Spárti, or Sown Men), serpents and dragons were also likely to be familiars or even embodiments of the Great Goddess herself, and therefore highly dangerous to fool around with, much less to kill. Thus, even though Kadmos was honored for his heroics, the city he then founded—first called Kadmía and later Thebes—would be thereafter ridden with inexplicable tragedies, with no perceptible cause, except perhaps, his slaying of that dragon. And maybe his subsequent marriage to a goddess.

This goddess was Harmonía, the entrancing daughter of Aphrodite and Áres, and her hand in marriage was said to be a gift from Zeus to Kadmos in payment for the eight years of penance he was said to have undergone for slaying the dragon. The wedding of Kadmos and Harmonía was a landmark in Greek mythology—the first in which a mortal man was granted the privilege of marrying a goddess and also the first to be attended by the entire corpus of Olympian deities, all twelve of whom descended to Earth at Kadmía and bestowed magnificent gifts upon the bride and groom while the Nine Muses sang their golden songs in the surrounding hills. Among the gifts that Harmonía received was a golden necklace famous for having been forged by Hephéstos and first given to Kadmos's aunt Evrópi by Zeus—a token, it was said, of his rough affection for Minos's mother.

But for mortals to become too familiar with the gods was, as everyone knows, a dangerous game. In the old days, before worshippers had begun to picture their deities in human form, a more respectful (and much safer) distance existed between the heavenly and earthly realms. At that time, these amorphous entities could only be approached through prayer and propitiation. Familiarity (even a simple handshake, to say nothing of sex) was out of the question, out of the realm even of fantasy. Since Zeus's "human" birth, however, the barriers had begun to dissolve. As the idea of anthropomorphic deities caught on with his Mycenaean worshippers, the more enticing it became to imagine the possibility of physical intercourse between humans and their gods. And while the Olympians seemed to enjoy what the poets called *mingling* with humans, it was risky for humans to presume that this was a two-way street. The deities, particularly Zeus, were famous for allowing humans only so much intimacy before slapping them down again, often fatally.

For both Kadmos and Harmonía, the punishment would be particularly terrible, mainly because it was so incomprehensible. They had done nothing, they thought, to deserve the seemingly unending string of afflictions that would plague them. The killing of the dragon had been paid for—hadn't it?—by Kadmos's eight years of penance. Maybe not. Maybe the Great Goddess was still not satisfied. In addition, the couple had also disregarded a primal principle in the relationship of a man with a goddess. They had dared to fall in love.

Zeus, of course, had known from the beginning that this would happen. So had Gaía when she sent Kadmos on his journey down from Delphí. The story had already been written. Thebes had to be founded. And, most important for Zeus, Kadmos and Harmonía had to marry so that they would produce the daughter upon whom Zeus could father the last of his Olympic pantheon: the great god Diónysos. This was necessity. The rest—the fate of the humans involved—was of little consequence.

The name of this daughter was Seméli, and of the many horrors that would beset Kadmos and Harmonía and their descendants, it would be Seméli who would endure the worst. Because it would fall upon her to love, and be loved by, Zeus.

THE STORY OF SEMÉLI

So enthralled, in fact, was the god with this last and loveliest daughter of Kadmía's king and queen that when he appeared to her as a handsome young mortal, he couldn't resist making the terrible mistake of not only boasting about who he really was, but promising, moreover, to grant any wish she might ask, as long as she would let him lie with her.

As expected, the innocent young princess was so flattered by such attractive attentions that, as he drew her into his passionate embrace, she forgot all thoughts of making a wish. At the same time, Zeus's disguise was so effective that the affair was in its seventh passionate month before Héra, always the last to know anyway, finally realized what was going on.

The queen of the Olympians, furious that Zeus was back to his old tricks, quickly devised a particularly horrific punishment for poor, god-stricken Seméli. Coming to her in the guise of an old and trusted nurse, Héra suggested that Seméli's new lover might not be the god he claimed, but just another ordinary mortal plying her with lies, as all men do, just to get into her bed. "You should," counseled the old woman, "make him prove that he is what he says. Ask him to grant you the wish he promised. Demand that he show himself to you as he really is, exactly as he appears to his wife—as Zeus in all his glory. If he loves you, he'll do this. If he doesn't, then you'll know he's been lying, and you can break off the relationship."

Seméli had no doubts that her lover was the god. And that he adored her. But it was exciting to imagine herself being made love to by the god in his purest form—and to think of herself, as well, as having the same privileged status as Héra. So the next time Zeus came to Seméli in human form and took her in his arms, the young princess sweetly reminded him of the wish he had promised to grant her. "Anything," murmured Zeus, nuzzling his princely nose into the curve of her neck. "Well," she replied, "I want to see you as you really are, as a god. As you show yourself to your wife."

Zeus did everything he could to make Seméli change her mind. But when the girl persisted and persisted and finally refused to sleep with him unless he did what she asked, the father of gods and men, furious at this lack of trust, abruptly burst forth in his full, thunder-and-lightning glory—and incinerated the horrified teenager on the spot.

Then, as the flames flickered their way through the inner layers of Seméli's charred body, Zeus was shocked to suddenly spot, within the seething amniotic fluids of her womb, the curled form of a male fetus, at least six months old. Swifter than Zeus's thought, Hermes appeared on the scene to snatch the fetus to safety. Immediately, he and Zeus sliced open the god's thigh, embedded his unborn son within, and quickly sewed the wound together—thus making the Great Thunderer for all intents and purposes pregnant for the second time in his brief paternal reign. (And once again ensuring, since he was the mother, that this child, not being born of woman, would not be a threat to its father, would not be a party to that still-disturbing prophecy that the great god would sire a son who would overthrow him.) The name of this child would be Diónysos—an appellation whose meaning and origin are as rich with mystery as his birth from Zeus's thigh.

DIÓNYSOS

While Athína, born from Zeus's head, was the exemplar of well-reasoned judgment, resolutely pure in character and in body, Diónysos was dissolutely the opposite. Emerging from Zeus's overheated loins, he would turn out to be what Kadmos's grandson and successor, Pentheus, would characterize as "a charlatan and sorcerer . . . flush with wine, who mingles with our maidens day and night by stretching forth his Bacchic rule . . . and infecting them with his disease"—a new kind of god who delighted in transgressing the Greeks' cherished and delicately balanced Apollonian limits and granted them instead the transporting ecstasies of both the vine and the theater.

But this would be years—centuries—in the future. At the moment, Diónysos was only a defenseless babe just removed from Zeus's thigh. The Cloud Gatherer, by now knowing that Héra was behind Seméli's tragic cremation—and knowing, too, that if given the chance, her murderous rage would also quickly engulf his newborn son—immediately sent the child away with Hermes, who carried him to Seméli's sister, Inó, for safekeeping. Inó and her husband, Athámas, hoping to hide the boy from the prying claws of Héra's jealousy, disguised him as a girl. When Héra discovered this, she drove the couple insane, causing them to murder their own children, but not before Zeus had saved Diónysos by transforming him into a baby goat and having Hermes spirit him off to the mountains. Here nymphs would shelter the infant, as their sisters had the young Zeus on Crete, until he was able to venture down from the heights on his own. Both of the disguises foisted upon the young Diónysos—those of a girl and a goat—seem to account for his later emergence as a dissolute and nearly hermaphroditic figure who was both a god of fertility and the patron saint of the theater—the Greek word for "tragedy" (*tragoúdia*) meaning "goat-song."

The implacable Héra would nevertheless discover where the boy was and, finally getting him in her clutches, drive him as insane as she had Inó and her husband. As a result, Diónysos would spend years madly wandering the world outside of Greece, cavorting with a band of drunken, lecherous satyrs and his equally addled female followers, the maenads. He finally was cured by a surrogate of the Great Mother known in Asia as Cybele, but in Greece called Rhéa, she who was Zeus's mother. While with her, Diónysos saw a snake (doubtless put there by the goddess) drinking juice from grapes, and all at once, he knew, from words Cybele had spoken to him before, that by stomping on these grapes, he could produce wine, the drink of immortality. Afterward, the young god would travel as far as Egypt and India, spreading the knowledge of wine making throughout the area before reentering Greece to return to Thebes to honor his mother, Seméli, and fulfill the destiny planned for him by his father.

THE FATE OF KADMOS AND HARMONÍA

Meanwhile, the suffering of Kadmos and Harmonía did not end with Seméli's terrible death. One of their grandsons, the hunter Actaeon, happened to see Ártemis naked, bathing in a mountain river; as punishment, the goddess turned him into a stag and had him eaten alive by his own dogs. Another grandson, Pentheus, to whom Kadmos had passed the kingship of Thebes, would refuse to recognize the power of Diónysos, just returned from Asia. For this, Diónysos had him ripped to pieces by a pack of his female followers, one of whom was Pentheus's own mother (for more on this, see chapter 24). And then, of course, there was Oedipus—the great-great-grandson of Kadmos and Harmonía—who would blind himself for having unknowingly killed his father and married his mother, and wander the world a sightless pariah until Zeus took pity on him and summoned him to Heaven.

But the deliverance that the Cloud Gatherer offered the similarly guiltless Kadmos and Harmonía was strangely coldhearted. Having been, for all intents and purposes, the best man at their wedding, he (or some say, Áres) ended their unhappy existence on Earth by transforming them into large, nonpoisonous serpents, which were said to bring good luck to the living. However, the god then sent them to endure immortality in the very same spot where he was said to have exiled Krónos—the Blessed Isles, or Elysian Fields, of the distant Atlantic—a lot more pleasant, certainly, than the Underworld, but not, perhaps, if you were a snake. Such are the portions of fate that the Great Father doles out from the two great urns of joys and sorrows in his palace on Mt. Ólympus. Often, they make no sense at all.

12

THE HEROES OF THE ARGOLID—I: PERSEUS

And Zeus the Father made . . . a fourth generation
of mortal men . . . righteous and noble,
human heroes god-born.

HESIOD, *Works and Days*

At the same time, say the tale tellers, the descendants of the other branch of Kadmos's family—the one sired by his uncle Bílos—were experiencing an equally bloody history. But theirs would be redeemed by Zeus—or more accurately, his sons Perseus and Hérakles, the first of the great Greek heroes.

That the Mycenaeans could imagine such beings marked a highly significant turning point in their relationship with the gods. Before the coming of Perseus, the immortal and mortal worlds had been thought of as being on either side of a nearly uncrossable divide. Although there were points of contact between the two, moving from one realm to the other had always been a rare and highly perilous endeavor. Only Zeus was able to get away with it with relative impunity. The other immortals could not—as we can see from the fates of the goddess Harmonía, not to mention Prométheus, the latter still (at this point in the story) pinioned within that mountain in the Caucasus. But the Greek hero was something new: a unique kind of being able to straddle both realms at once, existing somewhere on that shimmering borderline between the divine and the mundane, mortal in body but able to partake of the powers of the gods. Homer called them "a half-god race of men," while Hesiod, taking an old Mycenaean word, termed them *iróon*: "heroes." The very first of these was Perseus.

The line of his descent went as follows: Kadmos's uncle, Bílos, had two sons, Aýgyptos and Danaós, each of whom, apparently aided by the fertile environment of the Nile, sired fifty children: sons for Aýgyptos, daughters for Danaós. When the brothers inevitably came to quarrel over land allotted to them by their father (Aýgyptos's portion of which he had named Egypt, after himself), Danaós, fearing his brother's growing power, took his fifty daughters out of Egypt and led them to the Greek mainland, where they settled in the area that he knew to be their great-grandmother Ió's homeland: the Argolid. But Aýgyptos immediately dispatched his fifty sons in hot pursuit. Danaós, outmanned (as it were), pretended to accede to their demands and allow a mass marriage between his children and those of his brother. On the wedding night, however, forty-nine of Danaós's daughters, all of whom had been given knives by their father, beheaded their new husbands. The fiftieth, Hypermnéstra, spared hers because he had respected her virginity, and together they began the royal line that would produce, four generations later (with Zeus's divine intervention), the redoubtable Perseus.

The shape-shifting that Zeus had to undergo to father Perseus has become one of the most legendary of his many metamorphoses. It seems that the king of Argos had been warned that his virgin daughter, the princess Danái, would one day give birth to a son who would kill him. To prevent this, the king had his daughter permanently locked away in an impenetrable bronze chamber, which he buried underground with only a small opening for ventilation in its ceiling.

The ever-resourceful Zeus, however, hot on the trail of destiny, turned himself into a golden stream which poured through the opening down upon Danái's loins and into her womb, making her pregnant with Perseus.

The king, refusing to believe this story, put Danái and her baby into a tiny wooden chest and pushed them out to an almost certain death in the treacherous Aegean. But the Fates washed them ashore on the island of Seriphos, where they were saved by a fisherman.*

Perseus's subsequent trials and triumphs, like those of his great-grandson Hérakles, are too epic in scope, covering most of the known world, Hell included, and too teeming with exploits to go into in any detail here. Most significant, however, was the way in which the deeds of both heroes were reflections of their father's battles against Gaía—which is to say, of the Greeks' ongoing struggle to subsume the Pelasgians' old, earthbound, chthonic cults into the brave new world of patriarchal Olympian dominance. Thus, Perseus's most renowned exploit would be his beheading of that superbly demonized version of the Great Mother, Medusa, the terrible, snake-haired Gorgon who dwelled with her equally hideous sisters in a seaside cave near the opening to the Underworld.

In Hesiod's *Theogony*, Medusa is one of a brood of monsters spawned near the beginning of creation. Among her siblings and their offspring are the Sphinx, the Chimera, Kérberos (the serpent-tailed, fifty-headed watchdog of the Underworld), the snake-headed Hydra of Lerna, the Lion of Nemea, the three-headed monster Giryón, and the dragon who guards the golden apples of the Hesperides. Like Tiphón, these disgusting and mostly reptilian creatures were intended to be seen as aspects and/or aides of the Great Goddess, that is, as evil to the core. They are also pictured as being either slain or subjugated not by the gods but by the popular heroes of

* Whose name, Dictys, is modern Greek for "fishing net."

Greek folktales, which is to say, by the people themselves.* Nevertheless, Perseus often had to rely on the Olympians for help. In his encounters with the Gorgons and other monsters, he was guided by Athína and Hermes and given the following supernatural means to aid him: Athína's bronze shield, the winged sandals of Hermes, Hádes' cap of invisibility, an adamantine sickle similar to the one that Gaía gave Krónos to castrate Ouranós, and a special gold and silver sack to hold Medusa's severed head.

On the other hand, even though Medusa is often described in the most nightmarish of terms—as a hideous creature with a writhing mass of snakes for hair and a gaze that turns onlookers into stone, there are sudden moments within these tales that give us glimpses of another Medusa altogether: a "fair-cheeked" woman of such striking beauty that Poseidon couldn't keep from ravishing her even though both were within the sacred precincts of Athína's temple. This so infuriated Athína—already jealous of Medusa because of her allure—that (say some) it was she who changed the poor woman's hair into snakes and threatened anyone who looked at her with petrifaction. But there nevertheless lingers about Medusa echoes of her former radiance—and of the goddess's lost predominance—and this may also explain why her name means "ruler" or "queen."

Medusa lived with her two sisters, Sthenó (strength) and Evriáli (wide-ranging), in their den on the shores of the Ocean, a faraway place on the edge of the world. Apollodorus describes them as hideous, with heads wrapped in dragon's scales, tusks like those of wild boars jutting out of their mouths, and horrible bronze hands. They also had golden wings which enabled them to fly with great swiftness. And they could turn anyone who looked upon them into stone. But Medusa was the only one who was mortal.

---

* Ironically, Medusa has continued to thrive down through the ages—from the works of Homer and Hesiod to Ovid, Dante, Cellini, Marx and Freud, and Sylvia Plath—as one of Greek mythology's most fascinating and emblematic figures. So in the end, one could say that it was she—surrogate of the Great Goddess—who stole the show.

Fortunately for Perseus, when he arrived at their dwelling place, all three sisters were asleep. He crept into the lair backward, guided by Athína's counsel and the reflections in the polished surface of her bronze shield. Hefting the adamantine sickle, he severed Medusa's head from her body, stuffed it into the gold and silver sack which he had secured around his body, and prepared to take flight on Hermes' winged sandals. But unbeknownst to Perseus, Medusa was pregnant from her encounter with Poseidon. So, as her body lay twitching on the floor of the lair, out of her neck sprang a monstrous son, Chrysáor, and the winged colt, Pegasus. The pair caused such a clatter that Medusa's horrible sisters instantly awoke. As they came after Perseus on their golden wings, bronze talons bared, the hero donned Hádes' cap of invisibility and disappeared into the bright sky, the bloody head of Medusa dangling from his waist.

Although the mortal Medusa was now dead, her head, as is the way with serpents, retained its terrible powers. On Perseus's flight back home, he was able to escape capture by Atlas by using its gaze to turn the Titan into the stone of what are now the Atlas Mountains. On the other hand, when he flew over Libya, drops of the Gorgon's blood fell on the desert, producing the abnormal number of poisonous snakes that inhabit its arid wastes. Medusa's stare would also help Perseus save the lovely princess of Joppa, Androméda, from a sea monster, and to free his mother from repeated attempts of the king of the Greek island of Seriphos to ravish her.

When all his great deeds were accomplished, Perseus returned the magical aids to the gods and gratefully presented Athína with the gold and silver sack containing Medusa's head. Apollodorus tells us that the goddess inserted the Gorgon's visage in the center of her shield, but the greater authority of Homer has her placing it as the centerpiece of her *aigís*, the serpent-tasseled breastplate that she wore as her emblem of authority. Homer describes it like this: "Over her shoulders she slung the tasseled, terrifying aigís, panic-crowned and wrought with Hatred, Strife, and blood-freezing Assault, and in its heart, the head of the dreaded, monstrous Gorgon, spewing fear and horror, a sign of aigís-bearing Zeus." As one of his signs or portents, Medusa now belonged to the Great Thunderer through his militant daughter. She was their trophy.

With Androméda as his wife, Perseus then traveled to the Argolid, where he vanquished his rivals to become king of Tíryns. In the process, he not only famously founded the citadel of Mycenae but fathered the first great Mycenaean dynasty, the Perseids. Moreover, among his sons was one Pérsis, who would give his name and royal lineage to a land to be called Persia in his honor—thus further deepening the strange embrace of these two cultures by extending it back to their very beginnings.*

Like all Greek heroes, Perseus would eventually overstep his bounds and, for this reason, suffer a mortal's death. Some say that it was because he dared to confront one of the gods—in this case, his highly dangerous half-brother, Diónysos, by resisting the coming of his cult into the Argolid—but the true cause of his end has remained an unsolved mystery, as if the death of such magnificence could never be fully explained or accepted.

That said, there would be no such ambiguity about the fate of Perseus's great-grandson, the indomitable Hérakles, destined to outshine his ancestor in both life and death.

---

* Much later, at the beginning of the fifth century B.C., the great Persian king Xerxes would use this family connection to successfully persuade the citizens of Argos to remain neutral during his invasion of Greece (Herodotus, *Histories*, VII.150).

13

THE HEROES OF THE ARGOLID—II: HÉRAKLES

So let that noble wife of Zeus break forth in dancing,
beating with buskined foot on heaven's bright floor;
for now hath she worked her heart's desire
in utterly confounding the chiefest of Hellas' sons.
Who would pray to such a goddess?

EURIPIDES, *Heracles Mad*

Two generations after the death of Perseus, Zeus once again replanted his seed in the royal line to father Hérakles, the second of his greatest heroes. Accomplishing this was much easier (and more pleasurable) than impregnating Perseus's imprisoned mother. All the Great Thunderer had to do was assume the likeness of Amphitríon, the king of Tíryns, and slip into the bed of the man's unsuspecting wife, Alkmíni. He then extended the night of their lovemaking to three times its normal length, so that his son might receive as much of the Divine Father's powers as possible. Shortly after Zeus's departure, the cuckolded king arrived in the exhausted Alkmíni's chamber and, unaware of what had happened, impregnated her again. Thus were Hérakles and his weaker, wholly human brother, Iphikles, sent on their nine-month journey into the world, with no one the wiser. In this way, the Great Thunderer hoped to have his son accepted as an ordinary human being who happened to have extraordinary powers—as, in other words, a man of the people, but one whose superhuman abilities would make him an ideal model for his father's cause.

However, as the Greeks well knew, the best-laid plans, even those of the Great Thunderer, often go awry. For it is not the gods who bring all things to fruition, but Zeus's unmanageable daughters, the Fates, often aided by their fearsome elder sister, Áte. Particularly Áte. It is she, Goddess of Ruin, born of Éris, Goddess of Strife, who befuddles the minds of both men and gods with grand illusions and then visits horrible punishments upon them for their follies. Little known these days, Áte was acknowledged by both the Greeks and Romans as one of the most powerful forces in the cosmos, and she is introduced here because her first mention in Greek literature comes at its very beginnings, in the *Iliad*, when Homer tells our present story of how Áte was able to blind even all-knowing Zeus to the stupidity of boasting about his plans for Hérakles to an assembly of the gods, right in front of Héra. "On this day," said Zeus, "there shall be born a child of man, of the line of men born of my blood [i.e., the line of Perseus] who shall be lord of all who dwell in the land around him."

Héra, as expected, did not take this news kindly. Since the victory over the Titans, she had been revered as the Argolid's supreme deity, its very own, native-born goddess, and she was not about to relinquish her primacy, not to Zeus and certainly not to a mortal. But she was nothing if not crafty. Rising from her Olympian throne, she sweetly suggested that her husband was, once again, making exaggerated promises, and that if difficulties arose, he would quickly abandon this declaration, as he had so many others. She challenged him, therefore, to swear in front of his fellow deities that this time he would keep his promise, that a man-child of his blood born on this day would indeed become lord of all the land. No matter what.

Pride-blinded Zeus, suspecting nothing, agreed.

And Héra flew into action.

First, she sent her daughter Eilíthia, the Goddess of Childbirth, to stop Alkmíni's labor in its tracks. Then she herself sped to Tíryns, where, unbeknownst to Zeus, the widow of one Sthénelos, another son of Perseus, was now seven months' pregnant with what Héra knew to be a boy—and induced the woman to give birth prematurely. Thus did Sthénelos's son, Evristhéfs, receive the kingly power that Zeus, in his prideful folly, had sworn to give to the first descendant of Perseus to be born on that day.

When Héra brought the happy news back to Mt. Ólympus, Zeus was beside himself with rage. But he could not strike out at Héra for what she had done. The Greeks and their gods understood that the consequences of Áte could not be laid upon others, that its burden belonged solely to the afflicted. However, being the all-powerful king of the gods, the Great Thunderer could release his flashing anger by grabbing Áte by her greasy locks and flinging the Goddess of Ruin off Ólympus forever. But Áte was far from finished. She landed on Earth, where to this day she infects mortals with her sicknesses and self-infatuations.

Meanwhile, back at Thebes, Alkmíni's twins were finally able to be born, thanks to the cleverness of her maid, who had tricked the Goddess of Childbirth into unblocking the birth canal by pretending that the twins had managed to slip through anyway. When they were born, proud Amphitríon gratefully named the first one in honor of Héra—the appellation Hérakles meaning "Héra's Glory."

The irony of this name must have become, for Héra, a constant, caustic reminder of Zeus's treachery. It may therefore account for some of the viciousness with which she tormented Hérakles for the rest of his earthly existence. But the goddess's main purpose was to demean and if possible destroy this threat to her long-standing preeminence among the people. As a result her subsequent onslaughts upon Hérakles' life and reputation would literally become the stuff of legends.

In the earliest of these attacks, while Hérakles was still an infant, Héra placed two poisonous snakes in his crib. But even as a baby,

Hérakles was more than up to the task of defending himself. Grabbing a reptile in each hand, he simultaneously throttled both to death. It was also said that his mother, fearing Héra's reprisals, tried to expose the baby in the countryside. Zeus, in a brilliant move, countered by having Athína take Héra for a stroll in the same area, pick up the apparently unknown child, and persuade Héra to give the poor thing milk from her breast. By so doing, she made Hérakles immortal. But Hérakles pulled so painfully at her breast that Héra pushed him away, causing her milk to spew across the sky as the Milky Way.

Héra, realizing that any further attempts on his life would be fruitless, turned her attention toward making him as miserable and pitiful as possible. She waited until he was at the height of his powers—renowned for his expertise as a wrestler and a musician, his prowess with the sword, spear, bow, and chariot, and the strength that, in one famous instance, enabled him to use only a club to kill the terrible lion whose skin he now proudly wore. He was also at his happiest—enjoying a fruitful marriage to the daughter of Creon, the king of Thebes, appointed protector of the city, and now the father of several strapping sons. It was then that the jealous Héra chose to strike, sending the Goddess of Madness to drive Hérakles into a homicidal rage, during which he would blindly murder his wife and children.

Tortured by remorse, Hérakles journeyed to the oracle of Delphí to seek a way of expiating his sins. He was told to go to Tíryns and perform the twelve labors demanded of him by its king, Evristhéfs, who had been Héra's personal choice to rule the Argolid. Although the oracle promised Hérakles that if he completed these incredibly difficult tasks, he would be taken up to heaven, the seer neglected to reveal how agonizing such an apotheosis would be.

In this way, Hérakles bound himself in servitude to the man who occupied the throne that should rightly have belonged to him. Even though his prodigious strength, cleverness, and courage were already legendary, it was not until he had to deal with the terrible labors unfairly imposed upon him by Evristhéfs that he became the first true superhero of the people. In the process, his faults also became both legendary and beloved. He had a murderous temper, especially when dealing with wrongdoers, engaged in rampant womanizing (he was said to have slept with all fifty daughters of King Thespíos in one night), and displayed often loutish drunkenness. But these very human weaknesses only further endeared him to the populace. And because of this, the afflictions visited on him by Héra would appear increasingly unjustified, if not downright evil.

A detailed account of Hérakles' subsequent difficulties and heroics would swamp a book such as this—just as, in the heart of the people, they nearly overwhelmed the reverence that the common folk held for the majesty of Zeus. Hérakles' final deeds elevated him to an almost godlike stature, which is how the sixth-century-B.C. poet Pindar speaks of him—as *heros theos*, "hero-god." In the twelfth and last of his famous labors for Evristhéfs, he enters a realm from which no mortal (and few immortals) had ever returned—the Underworld kingdom of Hádes—and returns with the hell-hound Kérberos, guardian of the Underworld's gates, as his prize. It is an achievement whose significance cannot be overstated. Hérakles conquers Death and harrows Hell, proving that Man could even triumph over the chthonian realm of the Great Goddess and break her hitherto unbreakable hold over the cycle of life and death.

As the father of gods and men, Zeus still claims supremacy. On the other hand, it is Hérakles' superhuman feats that attract most people's admiration. Moreover, there are two late tales in which this mortal son actually saves the skin of his immortal father. And this in turn reveals a chink in the Great Thunderer's armor, a suspicious weakness in his supposed Olympian omnipotence, a failing that has been imagined (we must always remind ourselves) by tale tellers sensitive to the needs of an audience that was now beginning to flex its own muscles—to want, for a change, some of the credit to go to mortals, too.

The first of Hérakles' exploits was the liberation of Prométheus and the revelation of the identity of the woman who would give birth to Zeus's usurper. The second centered on a sudden insurgency by Gaía's sons, the Giants, sent by Mother Earth in one final assault against Zeus's regime.

When we last saw Prométheus, he had been entombed within a mountain in the Caucasus by one of Zeus's thunderbolts, still in shackles and still pinioned by the spike that Hephéstos had driven through his breastbone. Some time after this, Zeus brought the Titan back to the surface—perhaps to try again to torture out of him the name of the woman who would give birth to the son who would usurp his throne. To this end, the Cloud Gatherer had sent his ferocious, bloodred eagle to peck and gnaw at Prométheus's ever-regenerating liver day in and day out.

In spite of this torment, the Titan had remained steadfast in his refusal to reveal the woman's identity, irritatingly confident that one day Zeus would ultimately suffer the humiliating downfall that Prométheus had foreseen. And this was an event that would surely have come to pass, had it not been for the sudden intervention of the only person who could possibly have saved the god: Hérakles.

There are contradictory accounts of how this happened. The earliest is by Hesiod, who claims that Hérakles' intervention was entirely Zeus's idea, that the Cloud Gatherer had arranged everything solely with the intention of adding to Hérakles' glory. Hesiod, however, was a strict fundamentalist for whom it was inconceivable that anything or anyone could "deceive or go beyond the will of Zeus."

Aeschylus's trilogy about Prométheus, written some two hundred years after Hesiod by a city man who had soldiered in Athens's great victory over the Persians, takes an entirely different approach. Aeschylus, living at a time when heady dictums such as Protagoras's "man is the measure of all things" were challenging absolute belief in the gods, presents Hérakles and Prométheus as heroes who save the world for both mankind and Zeus.

Although only *Prométheus Bound*, the second play of the trilogy, would survive the book-burning rampages of the early Christians, scholars have located enough fragments of the other two to posit a basic plot. In the first, Prométheus brings fire to mankind. In the second, he is shackled and entombed within the mountain. In the final play, Hérakles arrives on the scene as Prométheus is awaiting the return of Zeus's eagle to feast again upon his liver. Extant lines suggest that Prométheus gives Hérakles advice on his upcoming eleventh labor for Evristhéfs: stealing Héra's wedding gift to Zeus, the Golden Apples kept in her well-guarded Grove of Immortality. In gratitude, Hérakles kills the returning eagle with an arrow dipped in the dreadful gall of the many-headed, serpentine monstrosity, the Hydra, slain in the course of his second labor. But Hérakles then learns that he cannot free Prométheus until a god offers to take his place in the horrid depths of Tártarus. It seems an impossible condition to fulfill.

Unless, of course, you are Hérakles.

Several years before, Hérakles had accidentally wounded the immortal healer Híron (Chiron) with one of his poisoned arrows. This had left Híron in such terrible pain that he longed for the black bliss of death. But being an immortal—a half-man, half-horse centaur sired by Krónos himself—such an oblivion was not an option. The ever-resourceful Hérakles, however, now suggested an exchange: that Híron take Prométheus's place and be allowed to die and descend into Tártarus. Whether or not this was done with Zeus's approval is unknown. But we are told that Híron willingly expired in Prométheus's stead and that the grateful Titan, humbled by Híron's sacrifice, finally revealed his secret: that the woman whose son would overthrow his father was none other than the woman whom Zeus happened to be courting at that very moment: his trusted ally, the sea nymph Thétis.

Thus did the incomparable Hérakles liberate not only Prométheus from bondage but Híron from his suffering. In addition Thétis was spared a looming ravishment by the Great Thunderer and Zeus himself a most humiliating dethronement.

THE GIGANTOMÁCHY

Zeus's hairbreadth escape from this well-baited pitfall so enraged Gaía that she decided then and there to launch her final, massive attack on the god's regime—a violent encounter which the Greeks would later call the Gigantomáchy, or War of the Giants.

While the battle with the Titans (the Titanomáchy) had been literally earthshaking and the set-to with Tiphón an unparalleled fiery cataclysm, they were as nothing next to the scare put into the gods by these monstrous underground assailants. The Giants had been born out of the drops of blood spilled upon Gaía's body when Krónos castrated his father. Thus, they were brothers to the Furies. To Homer, the Giants were an ancient and arrogant race, not quite human and certainly not divine, brought to ruin in the distant past by their equally overweening king, Evrymedon. Hesiod, in contrast, pictures the Giants as very large but also very human warriors whose gleaming armor gave them a noble, almost knightly appearance. Both imaginings were doubtless aided by the unearthing of enormous, fossilized bones throughout the region—those of mastodons, mammoths, and other prehistoric "monsters" whose similarity to human bones led the locals to conclude that in times gone by, a race of giants (and giant heroes such as Hérakles) had stalked the land—and been killed and buried there. In one famous rendering of Hérakles slaying the monster at Troy, the latter is shown firing arrows at what paleontologists have tentatively identified as the fossilized skull of a giant giraffe, a species dating from the Miocene period, which would have made the skull, even then, at least two million years old.

For ages, these monsters had been angrily brooding beneath the surface of the earth, their pent-up force building toward a conflict with Krónos's children, the Olympians, and revenge over the circumstances of their birth. Now, Gaía released them from their bondage, hoping to reverse the order of things and send Zeus and his pantheon to spend eternity in the earth's stygian vaults. How Héra was involved is not mentioned, but in her jealousy over Zeus's fathering of Hérakles, she would no doubt have been tickled pink at the prospect.

In their assault on the gods, the Giants began by piling one mountain atop another so they could hurl immense rocks and burning tree trunks over at Ólympus. Although the Giants were not immortal, they were so "matchless in size and invincible in strength" that even Zeus and his Olympians could not hope to defeat them. However, an oracle said that they could be slain by a mortal—which, of course, could only mean Hérakles.

Hearing this, Gaía attempted to gather a rare magic herb that could make the Giants invulnerable to this threat. But, says Apollodorus, Zeus quickly ordered the Moon to stop shining and the Sun and Dawn not to rise, and in the ensuing darkness, he made off with all there was of the herb. That accomplished, the Cloud Gatherer sent Athína to call Hérakles to the rescue.

In the ensuing battle, Zeus's mighty son was everywhere, even saving the feared Héra from certain rape by one of the behemoths. At the battle's climax, Hérakles dispatched the Giants' leader, Ephiáltis,* with a poisoned arrow in the eye and, as his father hurled thunderbolts at the remaining Giants, finished them off with the same deadly shafts. In the centuries that followed, Greeks living in the region where these battles occurred, farming the fields and exploring ravines gouged out of the land by rainstorms and earthquakes, would find enormous bones testifying to the size of the monsters from whose clutches the gods had been rescued by Zeus's legendary son.

This was Gaía's final great offensive; from now on, she and her

* Whose name is the modern Greek word for "nightmare."

surrogates would wage their never-ending campaign to get back on top by resorting more to feminine wiles and allurements than mannish brawn, with only the occasional eruption or earthquake to remind everyone where the real power still resided: on and in Mother Earth.

HÉRAKLES' DEATH AND APOTHEOSIS

The time would inevitably come—in that mythological era four generations before the Trojan War—for the mortal Hérakles to pass from the scene. Perhaps his popularity had become too much of a threat to the authority of the gods, and so the hero's fans had to be reminded of his fallibilities. Or perhaps, in the interests of peace and reconciliation on Ólympus, it was politic for Zeus to allow Héra's anger to finally have its way. Whatever the reasons, and in spite of the love that Zeus professed for his gallant son, the Great Thunderer now permitted Héra to exact a particularly horrific revenge upon this already badly battered champion.

In a truly appalling sequence of events, rivaled in Greek legend only by Medea's vengeance upon Jason and their children, Héra caused Hérakles' latest wife, Diánira, to send him a tunic dipped in what the latter thought was a love potion. But the potion had been tainted with the same Hydrean venom that had been so effective in slaying Zeus's eagle and the Giants. As soon as the heat of Hérakles' body warmed the tunic, the poison began to sear into his flesh. In his agony, Hérakles tore off the garment, ripping away his burning skin as he did so. With the help of his eldest son, Íllos, the dying, pain-wracked hero managed to make his way to a mountaintop in Thessaly.

Here, the boy built a pyre whose flames would consume Hérakles' mortal flesh and thus the pain that went with it. But Íllos could not bring himself to light the fire. Instead, the badly suffering Hérakles was able to persuade a passing shepherd to do the deed by offering, in exchange, his mighty bow and Hydra-poisoned arrows. (The shepherd, named Philoktítis, would later use these weapons to kill Helen's lover, Paris.)

As the flames licked at Hérakles' bleeding, melting body, a cloud drifted over the spot, and out of it, Zeus sent a great flash of lightning, extinguishing the fire. The Great Thunderer then swooped Hérakles up into Heaven. There, Zeus reconciled Héra with his heroic son, married him to their daughter Hébe, and made him into a god and a constellation. In this way, Hérakles became the only human ever to be granted such an apotheosis. He would remain unique in this regard for about another 1,300 years, until Jesus was taken up in a similar fashion from the Mount of Olives. Or so the Christians claimed.

THE SONS OF HÉRAKLES

After hearing news of Hérakles' death, Evristhéfs set about trying to rid the earth of the hero's enormous number of children, who were called the Heraclíds. Eventually he pursued them to Athens, attacking the city. But in the ensuing battle, all of Evristhéfs's sons were killed instead and he was captured and beheaded. The ancient mythographer Apollodorus tells us that when his head was brought back to Hérakles' mother, Alkmíni, she took up weaving pins and gouged out its eyes.

Afterward, the Heraclíds swooped down to take power in Tíryns and all the other citadels in the Peloponnese. But their triumph was only momentary. A year after their arrival, a terrible plague was visited upon the Peloponnese. An oracle said that the Heraclíds had overstepped their bounds, that Zeus still had unfinished business with the Mycenaeans, those fire-thieving upstarts who had so incensed him over the years. So the Heraclíds retreated to an area east of Athens to wait out the time—three full generations—that Zeus had designated for their return.

The Cloud Gatherer then placed upon the throne of Tíryns the father of the dynasty destined to endure the Mycenaeans' tortured downfall. The name of this monarch, and of his royal house, was Átreus.

14

THE HOUSE OF ÁTREUS—I: THE BEGINNINGS

This house exhales slaughter . . .
Odors from the open mouth of a grave.

AESCHYLUS, *Agamemnon*

The myths and legends that subsequently coagulated about the House of Átreus would arise during the chaos of Greece's Dark Age, that 250-year period between c. 1000 and 750 B.C. when nearly all of the Mycenaean centers of power had been destroyed and their displaced inhabitants were wandering the eastern Aegean sustaining themselves on stories of their heroic past while searching for reasons to explain why they had been brought so low. Because the tale of the Atreids* was so well known, both the *Iliad* and *Odyssey* needed to refer to it only in passing in order to use it as an ominous background for their own sagas. By the middle of the fifth century B.C., when the poets, playwrights, and historians at the dawn of Athens's Golden Age began to write about these happenings, it had become impossible to separate the original stories from the tangle of inventions that had afterward been woven into them. At times, there seem to have been as many variants as there were writers.

* Members of the House of Átreus.

It is also impossible to know how much of the story was based on actual events, although the persistence of the stories and their attachment to the Argolid seem to indicate that bits and pieces of truth are lurking somewhere in the piles of fragments. All we can tell for sure is that when we read about the characters involved or watch them onstage or visit sites such as Mycenae, we have the eerie sense, in spite of the unbelievable horrors, that we are somehow spying on ourselves—adrift in a world made treacherous by the arrogance and flaws of our leaders, where innocents are slaughtered generation after generation and the gods operate in a manner murkier than ever before.

Untangling the convoluted story of the House of Átreus, from its butcher-block beginnings to its Fury-haunted end, is like trying to read the entrails of a badly disemboweled sacrificial beast. Significantly, the Atreids were not Mycenaeans at all, not in the sense of their ancestors having come out of the Caucasus. Rather, their progenitor was from Asia Minor, an area which, as the Greeks are still aware, is the breeding ground of most of the evil in the world. His name was Tántalos, and he was the extremely wealthy and powerful king of Lydia—so powerful, in fact, that people believed him to be a son of Zeus. But this was later denied by many tale tellers, perhaps out of horror at the abomination connected with his name—a deed which not only echoed Krónos's original sin of swallowing his newly born children, but began a tradition of similarly gory get-togethers around the Atreid family dinner table that finally would leave this once-mighty clan literally wallowing in its own innards.

The best-known version of Tántalos's tale begins innocently enough, with the king deciding to throw a banquet for his purported Ólympian relatives. This was back in the days when humans and their deities were still consorting with one another on a fairly regular basis, with the gods often appearing to mortals in human form and sharing not only meals with them but deeper intimacies as well. So Tántalos's plans were not at all out of the ordinary. But, as the Greeks well knew, it doesn't take much to set the heavy wheels of Fate thundering ponderously forward—particularly not when Zeus has already primed them to do so.

Initially, the fault lay with Tántalos's wife, who hadn't adequately prepared for a group as voracious as the Olympians. But it was Tántalos's response to this crisis that tipped the scales. He could have slaughtered another bull or goat or two or even several chickens. Instead, he grabbed his youngest son—the tender, barely pubescent Pélops—hacked the screaming boy into serviceable chunks, and tossed the body parts into the simmering stew, sweetening the pot but betting against the odds that Zeus and the others wouldn't notice what he had done.

They did, of course, having only to sniff the air to know exactly what was on the menu. Horrified at being fed a human sacrifice (and especially that of their host's son) at this late date, when relations with mortals had even passed well beyond mere physical intimacy—and doubtless recalling, too, what it had been like sloshing around in the stomach of their own father, Krónos, for those many years—all the gods and goddesses but one instantly recoiled from the table. Only the goddess Deméter, preoccupied by the enforced marriage of her daughter, Persephóni, to Hádes, failed to notice what was up and distractedly took several bites off the bone of Pélops's left shoulder before anyone could stop her.

An enraged Zeus immediately ordered Hermes to rescue the rest of the boy's remains and have them put back together again. He then dispatched Tántalos to an eternity in Tártarus, where the former king would be continually ravaged by hunger and thirst, submerged up to his chin in water that would recede every time he tried to take a sip, while heavily perfumed fruit-laden boughs hung tantalizingly (as we now say) just above his mouth, forever out of reach.

To help reconstitute Pélops, Deméter brought a special ivory shoulder blade to replace the one she had gnawed into, while Klothó, the Fate who was the best at sewing, stitched the joints together again. Rhéa, Zeus's mother, then breathed life into the unfortunate boy, whereupon he blossomed into a youth so radiant in appearance that Poseidon—not known for this sort of thing—instantly fell in love with him and carried him off to Ólympus until Tántalos was safely out of the way. Eventually he gave the boy a magic chariot drawn by winged horses to transport him back to Earth, to the kingship of Lydia. Once there, however, Pélops's tainted past apparently proved too much for the neighboring rulers to bear, and he was compelled (some say by Ilus, the king of Troy) to take his retinue and leave. Thus, this outcast, stitched-together son of Tántalos was sent off—like a Bronze Age Frankenstein's monster—out onto the drifting floes of a fate that would take him and his damaged seed across the wine-dark sea to their destiny in Greece.

When Pélops arrived in his new homeland, he settled in Elis, a large area to the west of the Argolid that included the sacred grove of the oracle of Olympía. Its ruler was Inómaos, the most powerful king in the region. Now, Inómaos was both blessed and cursed with an entrancingly beautiful daughter named Ippodámia. Blessed because she was all his, and cursed because the oracle had warned him that the man who would one day marry Ippodámia would also be the murderer of her father, the king. Therefore, to protect himself (and, it was said, to keep his lovely daughter for his own incestuous pleasures), Inómaos declared that anyone who wished to sue for Ippodámia's hand would first have to defeat him in a chariot race to be run over a rough, ninety-mile course from Olympía to Corinth—with the penalty for defeat being death. Inómaos had no doubt that he would win; both his horses and his armor had been given to him by Áres, the god of war, which seemingly made him unbeatable. As a result, by the time Pélops appeared upon the scene, twelve suitors had already lost their heads to Ippodámia's charms, with what was left of their shriveled, bird-pecked skulls now festooned above the citadel gates as a warning to any other hot young male foolish enough to hitch his chariot to such an impossible dream.

Pélops, having already survived being eaten by the gods, was not so easily intimidated. In fact, he was the prototype of the many Greeks throughout the ages, from Odysseus to Onassis, who have arrived in strange lands to conquer worse obstacles than mere threats of death. So he quickly devised what has since become a standard strategy for dealing with the powers-that-be in a foreign land: He bribed someone of significant influence on the inside. In this case, his target was the king's charioteer, Myrtílos, a son of Hermes, a god already well known as the patron deity of thieves. The bribe that Pélops offered him was impossible for any red-blooded male to turn down: control of half Inómaos's kingdom plus a night—the *first* night—with the princess bride herself. In addition, Pélops promised him a ride in Poseidon's magic chariot, in which he would be transported high above the Aegean by the god's team of winged horses, with Ippodámia at his side. The price? Simply to replace the metal linchpins of the king's chariot wheels with ones made of wax. Who could have refused such an offer? Not Myrtílos. After all, trickstering, Hermes-style, was in his bones.

And so, on the day of the race, when the linchpins failed and the wheels went shooting off Inómaos's heretofore unbeatable chariot, sending it tumbling and crashing to the ground, Myrtílos jumped free. Inómaos, caught in the reins, was dragged to a beaten pulp before Pélops could catch up and finally administer the coup de grace with a spear to the back. But the dying king was nevertheless able to use his last breath to curse Myrtílos for his treachery, predicting that he too would suffer a similar fate at the hands of the invidious Pélops. Before Myrtílos could even begin to digest this possibility, however, there he suddenly was, soaring over the shining Aegean in Poseidon's chariot, half the kingdom his and a night with the luscious Ippodámia, jostling warm and fragrant between him and Pélops, beckoning from just beyond the bloodred horizon. Which was when Pélops reached over and, with a helpful nudge from Ippodámia, pushed him out.

As Myrtílos plummeted toward the sea, he called upon his father, Hermes, to bring disaster to Pélops and his descendants in perpetuity. Since Zeus was deeply indebted to Hermes for helping him out of numerous difficulties, many mythographers have said that Myrtílos's curse was the one that would eventually seal the doom of the House of Átreus. But, as Zeus had long before made up his mind about finishing off the Mycenaeans, the dying charioteer's call for revenge seems to have been just another strand in the noose.

On the other hand, Pélops himself was allowed to lead a long and miraculously charmed life, virtually unscathed by the offenses he had committed. Eventually, by hook, crook, and an occasional murder, he would place nearly all the territories in southwestern Greece under his rule. In recognition of this, his realm—the large mass of land that hangs off the rest of the country like a huge island or, better yet, a badly mangled, out-of-place heart—would become known as the Pélop-ó-nisos, or "Pélops's island"—to us, the Peloponnese. After his death, he would acquire the aura of a demigod, a near-mythical hero whom the Greeks would venerate above all for his craftiness—an asset which their modern descendants still value far above such impractical virtues as, for example, honesty. Pélops's victory over Inómaos was eventually memorialized by Hérakles, who was said to have founded the Olympic Games partly in its honor. And Pausanias, visiting Olympía in the second century A.D., tells us that a cenotaph, or memorial tomb, to Pélops occupied an important position within Zeus's Sacred Precinct, and that the king was worshipped there "as highly honored among the heroes as Zeus is among the gods."*

* Even in death, Pélops continued to take a vital part in the fortunes of the Greeks. In fact, it was said that in the tenth year of the war with Troy, the Greeks hurried to bring his giant ivory shoulder blade to Troy on the advice of a Trojan seer, who had revealed that they could never hope to win without it. Significantly, Pélops's shoulder bone was lost when the ship sank during the voyage back, found by a fisherman, and then lost again—a portent, perhaps, of how things would go for some of Pélops's descendants when they, too, finally made the long voyage home from the war. Scholars now believe that the bone actually did exist, that it may have been, in fact, the well-polished scapula of one of the mammoths that had roamed the Peloponnese in prehistoric times. Also believed to have existed was Pélops himself, who was said by the Classical Greek historian Thucydides to have been modeled on an actual person, a Bronze Age leader of the forces that unified the Peloponnese.

Of Pélops's many children, his favorite was the bastard, Chrysíppus, whom he had begotten upon a local nymph, and who was so beautiful that Laius, the future king of Thebes (and father of Oedipus), was said to have temporarily abducted him. In turn, Pélops's affection for the boy was so obvious that Ippodámia, fearful that Pélops might make him his heir, persuaded two of her sons, Átreus and his twin brother, Thyéstes, to murder the young beauty. Whether or not they actually did this was hotly disputed in ancient times, but given the twins' subsequent behavior, it is likely that they followed their mother's wishes, killed the boy and, some say, then tried to cover up the murder by tossing him down a well. When Pélops learned the truth about what had happened, he drove the twins and their mother out of his kingdom, adding his curses to those previous ones already weighing down the family line. Meanwhile, Ippodámia took Átreus and Thyéstes to mighty-walled Tíryns in the Argolid, the sole territory in the Peloponnese as yet unconquered by Pélops's forces. In this way, the mysterious workings of Zeus's will brought Tántalos's murderous seed ever closer to its final nesting place, just half a day's journey south of Mycenae.

At that time, the king of Tíryns was Sthénelos, the father of Evristhéfs, he who had, with Héra's connivance, become the heir to the throne that Zeus had intended for Hérakles (see chapter 13). Sthénelos installed the boys and their mother at Midea, a citadel east of Tíryns, effectively giving them their own fiefdom to rule, and here they would remain during the years of Evristhéfs's assumption of power, his enslavement of Hérakles, and his subsequent losing battle with the hero's mighty army of sons, the Heraclíds.

When Zeus subsequently forced the Heraclíds to retreat to Attica by unleashing a terrible plague upon them, the Cloud Gatherer then had his oracle at Delphí declare that the people of the Argolid would have to choose either Átreus or Thyéstes to fill the power vacuum created by the Heraclíds' beheading of Evristhéfs. Beckoned by this opportunity to rule the Argolid, the twins quickly turned their inherited duplicity on each other, engaging in a cutthroat competition to prove which of them deserved Evristhéfs's throne. The details are much too tortuous to go into here. Suffice it to say that Zeus himself ensured Átreus's victory by making it seem that the latter was able to cause the sun and stars to move backward in their course—a kingly attribute if ever there was one.

When Átreus assumed power, Thyéstes prudently took his wife and three boys and slipped away into exile. Shortly afterward, however, Átreus learned that all these years his brother not only had been cuckolding him but had conspired with his, Átreus's, wife to cheat him of the throne. True to his heritage, the new king quickly cooked up a reprisal that would outdo even Tántalos's banquet in its gruesomeness. Keeping his knowledge of his brother's treachery to himself, Átreus invited Thyéstes to dine with him at Tíryns, pretending to effect a reconciliation. When Thyéstes sat back from the table, fully sated by a sumptuous meal, Átreus called upon the servants to bring yet another course. Whereupon they appeared with a huge, bronze cauldron, brought it before Thyéstes, and dumped upon the table in front of him the extremities of his young sons, their tiny hands, feet, and heads all that were left of the little, loving bodies whose tender flesh their father had, moments before, so happily sunk his teeth into.

Thyéstes reeled backward, vomiting forth as many of the half-digested bits and pieces as he could, and stumbled blindly out into the harsh Argolid countryside screaming anathemas down upon his brother and his family as he made his way north into exile, mind seething with images of revenge.

Shortly afterward, Átreus moved his court and his young sons, Agamemnon and Menélaos, to Mycenae. But even within the citadel's massive walls and luxurious surroundings, he was unable to find peace of mind. Nightmares plagued him, as did a great famine which had fallen on the Argolid after he had fed Thyéstes his own children for dinner. An oracle said that he could end the famine solely by bringing

Thyéstes back from exile. And so, Átreus went out in search of his brother, leaving the security of Mycenae behind.

Meanwhile, the Fury-driven Thyéstes had also gone to an oracle, that of Delphi, and had been told that he could only take revenge on Átreus through a son, one whom he must father on his own daughter, the young virgin Pelopía, priestess at a local temple to Athína. So rabid was Thyéstes' thirst for vengeance that he immediately did what he had been told. Wearing a mask to conceal his identity, Thyéstes grabbed and raped his own daughter as she was in the garden of Athína's sanctuary, her robe removed, washing herself of sacrificial blood. During the rape, Pelopía came into possession of Thyéstes' sword, which, as soon as Thyéstes fled the sanctuary, she hid under the base of Athina's statue.

Shortly afterward, Átreus came to the area in search of Thyéstes and, as Zeus and the Fates would have it, fell instantly in love with the now pregnant Pelopía. Neither of them had known of the other's existence, nor did Pelopía realize that the father of her unborn child was both Átreus's brother and her father. When Átreus took Pelopía with him to Mycenae, she brought the captured sword with her, hiding it among her belongings. Just in case.

As soon as her baby was born, Pelopía tried to get rid of it by exposing it on a mountainside. Goat herders saved the baby, a boy, and Átreus had him brought to Mycenae, where he raised the child as his own, naming him, because he had survived on goat's milk, Aýgisthos, or "goat strength."

But, as Thyéstes had still not been found, the famine continued to plague the Argolid. After enduring several more seasons of this, Átreus sent the now grown Agamemnon and Menélaos out to capture their uncle and bring him back. After they had accomplished this, Átreus, ignoring Pelopía's pleas for him to be merciful to the man she thought of only as her father, threw Thyéstes into a dungeon. Some of the tale tellers say that Átreus then sent Aýgisthos to kill him. But at the time, the boy couldn't have been more than seven or so. Perhaps he had come across the sword his mother had hidden, had taken it to play soldier in the dungeons and, while there, went to take a peek at the famous prisoner, his grandfather.

Thyéstes, recognizing the sword and understanding who Aýgisthos must be, told the boy to bring Pelopía to him. When she arrived, and Thyéstes revealed what he had done to her and why, Pelopía, unable to live with such a horrible truth, took the sword and thrust it into her heart. As her lifeless body lay bleeding on the floor, Thyéstes called Aýgisthos to the bars of his cage and whispered to him of the wrongs that had been done: how Átreus had stolen the kingdom from him and then fed him his own sons for dinner; how none other than the great oracle at Delphi had told him to father a son upon his own daughter; and how he, that anointed son, was now fated to revenge the family for all that had been done to it by the monster Átreus, king of Mycenae.

Aýgisthos, borne upon the raging tides of his own destiny, brought the bloody sword to Átreus and told him that Thyéstes was dead. As Átreus knelt in gratitude to the gods, arms high, head thrown back, his seven-year-old nephew viciously slashed the sword across his uncle's upraised throat.

Upon hearing the news of their father's death, young Agamemnon and Menélaos immediately fled the Argolid. Thyéstes then proclaimed himself Mycenae's legitimate king. Shortly afterward, the drought ended, and, as all seemed to be right with the cosmos, the people gave joyful thanks to Zeus, blindly unaware that this was only the beginning of their kingdom's hell on earth.

15

THE HOUSE OF ÁTREUS—II: MYCENAE

At Mycenae the gods once walked the earth, of that there can be no question. And at Mycenae the progeny of these same gods produced a type of man who was artistic to the core and at the same time monstrous in his passions . . . It wears an impenetrable air: it is grim, lovely, seductive,and repellent. What happened here is beyond all conjecture.

HENRY MILLER, *The Colossus of Maroussi*

When Fárzaneh and I arrived in the Argolid on the Wednesday following Easter, we had been in Greece for nine days, traveling several centuries through Santoríni and Crete tracing the advent and birth of Zeus. Now, we had at last come to the place where the great creation and succession myths of the Greeks—those of Gaía and Ouranós, of Krónos and the Titanomáchy, and of Zeus and his many seductions—had had their first shapings, fashioned around Mycenaean hearth fires from the fears and rituals carried from the Caucasus by their ancestors. And here, too, was where the mythmaking would be brought down to Earth, the great imaginings of gods and goddesses, terrifying monsters, and superhuman heroes replaced by the painfully human atrocities at the mighty citadel of Mycenae.

Whether or not there ever was an actual House of Átreus,* it is certain that during the period when Átreus might have existed, Mycenae became even more powerful in its fortifications and holdings than famously strong-walled Tíryns. Its citadel occupied a formidable site on the northern edge of the Argive plain, commanding the mountain passes north to the Corinthian plain and overlooking all of the alluvial farmland down to Tíryns and the sea, nine miles south, its hilltop site bordered on all sides by steep ravines, which made an assault extremely difficult. Moreover, its acropolis was nestled between the massive, protective breasts of two nearly perfect conical peaks that guarded its approaches on either side, giving the impression that the Great Mother herself had created the spot for some powerful, sacred reason—perhaps even for the great royal family of the Atreids, monarchs of all they surveyed and, in those days, equal in eminence to the Hittite Empire to their east and that of the Egyptians to the south.

Mycenae's ruins sit in what is now nearly the middle of nowhere, about two miles off the main highway from Argos to Corinth and well into the scrubby, rock-strewn ravines and foothills of the mountain range that marks the northern edge of the Argive plain. The nearest settlement is the tiny village of Mikine, which itself might now also be abandoned if Heinrich Schliemann hadn't come along in the summer of 1876, his head filled with impossible childhood dreams of finding the grave of Átreus's murdered heir, Agamemnon, and—literally—struck gold.

The village is a stolid collection of decidedly non-picturesque one- and two-story buildings, mostly of cinderblock. The main road, which heads directly through town to the ancient citadel, is lined with rooming houses, tourist shops, and eateries whose names are often

---

* The scholarly jury is still out, although each new archaeological discovery brings its existence ever closer to being what might be called a prehistorical fact.

comic evocations of what the locals have learned are their most profitable legends: the Elektra Bar; the Restaurant Bar Orestes; King Menelaos Restaurant; and, most gruesomely apt of all, the Klitemnistra Rooms with Bath. Finally, there is the now-legendary hotel where Schliemann, already the discoverer of Troy, had set up his excavation headquarters. It was and still is called La Belle Helene (The Beautiful Helen), and if you're lucky (which Fárzaneh and I were not), you can even rent the very room where he and his Greek wife, Sophia, stayed during the excavations.

I had visited Mycenae once before. This was in late June of 1992, in the midst of a scorching summer heat wave. The once verdant early summer landscape had been turned into a rocky, sun-baked kiln. Cicadas buzzed in the desiccated underbrush, and the smell of burned oregano and thyme seared your nostrils. The only signs of animal life were a hawk wheeling high up in the merciless white sky and the anguished bray of a far-off donkey occasionally ripping through the silence. The site felt haunted by death. Making things worse was the fact that there was no place to hide from the heat except the tombs—huge, burrowing, beehive structures that sentineled the approach to its acropolis—*fórni*, the locals called them, because of their resemblance to ovens. As I trudged toward the massive stone Lion's Gate that is the entrance to the acropolis, the forbidding mound of rock and rough stone walls that had been Mycenae proper seemed to thrust itself higher and higher out of the barren ground—as though it were some giant prehistoric beast, the undulating lines of stones like scales on its petrified, armored skin. "This is the great shining bulge of horror," Henry Miller wrote in *The Colossus of Maroussi*, of his visit there in 1939, when Greece was about to be swallowed up by the Nazis' conquest of Europe. "The high slope whence man, having attained his zenith, slipped back and fell into the bottomless pit."

I can't remember how long I stayed on the heights. It could have been only a few minutes. It was impossible to make any sense of the skeletal vestiges of the palace. All I wanted, as soon as I had made it to the top, was to get down off of there as quickly as possible, before my soul boiled over.

Now, with Fárzaneh along and April in the air, things seemed considerably easier. The countryside was lush and green, with the soil between the plantings a rich, moist black. Waist-high carpets of winter wheat alternated with low sproutings of lettuce, dill, onions, potatoes, squash, peppers, and tomatoes. The dark, heavily pruned stumps in the vineyards were festooned with the pale unfurlings of new leaves, and in the long grasses between the fields and the undulating rows of olive and cypress trees, wildflowers had begun to play. Even the thistles on the hillsides were green, their thorns still as soft as kitten fur.

Seeing this abundance made it a lot easier to understand why the Mycenaeans had chosen to place their citadel in a spot so apparently remote and far from the sea. Not only did it command the mountain passes to and from the north, but it dominated the enormously abundant food supply of the plain below. Everything that had been planted there would have gone into the citadel for safekeeping and would have then been distributed by the king only to those who remained in his good graces, loyal to their protector and even willing to die for him. The gold and other rich accoutrements of power would come later; what mattered first of all was food. Which perhaps explains why Átreus (or some ancient king like him) would have gone to such great lengths to stop a drought, even bringing his most dangerous rival back into the citadel if an oracle told him it might help.

But in spite of the April freshness, I soon began to feel suffocated by the same visceral oppression I had experienced on my first visit. As we wandered among the dry, rock-strewn salvages of what had been a magnificent two- and three-story edifice, the crowning glory of the Mycenaeans' proud warrior culture, we were treading atop something we knew to be hallowed and cursed at the same time: the blood-soaked ground zero of a civilization that had delved into the darkest recesses of power and passion, had pushed the gods beyond their limits, and had paid for it by being reduced to these handfuls of dust and rocks. What happened here is almost, as Henry Miller wrote, "beyond all conjecture." It didn't help to dispel my unease to know that this post-Easter period also happened to be the time of year when the Greeks believe the dead are raised to walk the earth.*

The treasures that Schliemann raised from the royal graves were dazzling, in particular the enormous quantities of gold. All totaled, some thirty-three pounds of the stuff eventually poured out of tombs he located. It came in a dizzying variety of shapes and sizes—necklaces, pins, dinner plates, diadems, belts, breastplates, rings, goblets, and—most striking of all—exquisitely modeled death masks, each so individually lifelike that the ecstatic Schliemann, throwing all proper archaeological propriety aside, impulsively raised the most impressive mask of all—that of a bearded, tautly featured adult male—and kissed it on the lips. He then dispatched a telegram to the Greek minister of education declaring that it "resembled the features of Agamemnon as it had previously *appeared* to him."† These discoveries also put a very large nail in the coffin of experts who had contended that the

* Greek Orthodox and folk traditions say that this resurrection lasts for either forty or fifty days, from the Thursday of Holy Week until either Christ's Ascension or the descent of the Holy Spirit on Pentecost Sunday. During their return to the land of the living, the dead crouch in trees and float up against the ceilings of churches, sometimes sitting on the backs of spiders in their webs, to watch and long for the loved ones they have lost.

† The italics are those of a Schliemann biographer, Leo Deuel, who used them to emphasize Schliemann's contention that he had had a visitation from Agamemnon's spirit before actually seeing the mask. The story that Schliemann's telegram said that he had "gazed upon the face of Agamemnon" appears, however, to be apocryphal.

stories of Troy and Mycenae were little more than fairy tales. "I have not the slightest objection," Schliemann later wrote, "to admit that the tradition which assigns the tombs in the [Mycenaean] acropolis to Agamemnon and his companions, who on their return from Ilium [Troy] were treacherously murdered by Clytemnéstra or her paramour Aegisthus [Aýgisthos], may be perfectly correct and faithful."*

During this period the worship of Héra as the patron goddess of the Argolid continued unabated, the supposed preeminence of Zeus and the Atreid patriarchy notwithstanding. A well-traveled path led down from the Mycenaean acropolis two miles south to a shrine of Héra that would become, during the fifth-century-B.C. ascendancy of Argos, her greatest sanctuary, the Heráeum. In addition, recent excavations have shown that on the western slope there was what seems to have been an in-house "chapel" or cult complex for worship of the goddess, and it is now thought the famous Lion's Gate entrance to the citadel, on which two giant, unmaned female lions flank a pillar, may have been topped by a sculpture of the Great Goddess herself—standing there just as the Cretans were picturing the Great Mother atop her Holy Mountain, regnant.

Which once again reminds us that back in the days of the House of Átreus, Zeus and his Olympian brethren were still relative newcomers, despite all their posturings of predominance. The old-time Pelasgian worship of the goddess continued to hold its own, espe-

---

* As it turned out, the graves that Schliemann found were centuries older than the Cyclopean citadel itself, dating to a period about 300–400 years before Agamemnon (if he had indeed existed) would have walked the earth. The great cache of gold and jewels and royal bones that lay in the graves had been buried there sometime between 1600 and 1500 B.C., during the early stages of the Greeks' presence in the Argolid, when they were still maintaining their old ties with the Black Sea and trading with gold miners from the mountains of Transylvania.

cially in the Argolid, where Héra was queen, and nowhere was this more dramatically apparent than in the way her priestesses, most of them earthly queens, were the guiding lights.*

Which, in turn, brings us to Helen, and to Zeus's introduction of her and her sister, Clytemnéstra, into the family fold as the queens respectively of Sparta and Mycenae—all a part of the working out of his implacable will.

* It has been estimated, in fact, that only 5 percent of the images of deities created up to the time of the Trojan War were male.

16

A TERRIBLE BEAUTY

A shudder in the loins engenders there
The broken wall, the burning roof and tower
And Agamemnon dead.

W. B. YEATS, "Leda and the Swan"

She would have been conceived at just about the same time that Átreus's brother, Thyéstes, was impregnating his daughter with the murderous Aýgisthos. Both of these conceptions were the result of rapes, both begot violence, and both were destined to converge upon Mycenae. Aýgisthos was an ugly, drunken monster, with apparently no redeeming qualities whatsoever. Helen, on the other hand, was not only surpassingly beautiful but the very embodiment of Eros—the most dangerous kind of love, that of sexual desire. It is this "terrible beauty" that makes her and her legend so endlessly fascinating.

Whether or not there was an actual flesh-and-blood Helen hardly seems to matter. Much more important was that shimmering, almost ghostly being whom the Greeks called the *eídolon* of Helen—a word meaning both "image" and "phantom"—the mesmerizing construct, the idol and strumpet, which the ancients and then the ages have made of her, a vision which could be said to have blinded Homer himself.

Her world is a bewildering hall of mirrors; in it, everything is doubled or tripled. There are two stories of her conception, two of her birth, two about where she actually was during the Trojan War, and at least two or three about her death. She has twin mothers, twin brothers, and a twin sister, the latter albeit fraternal. She is both mortal and immortal, a princess and a sorceress, a faithful wife and an adulteress, tragic and reprehensible. It is impossible to separate the images from the reality. Each time you reach out to grab her, Helen disappears, leaving behind only the perfumed wisp of a presence that may or may not be a figment of one's own, fired-up imagination.

There are several stories that explain why Zeus brought Helen into the world. Some of the tale tellers, perhaps to shift the onus of such an act away from the god, put the blame instead on Gaía's complaint to the Great Thunderer that the earth—her body, after all—was overrun with too many people, and that she needed a great war to relieve her of the burden. However, most of the bards agree that Zeus, having once ordered the creation of the original woman, Pandóra, to bring illness and misery to mankind, now set about giving the Mycenaeans his only begotten mortal daughter so that they might plunge themselves into near extinction.

As noted above, there are two versions of Helen's conception. Neither of them is immaculate. In one, Zeus chooses to father her upon the terrible goddess Némesis, who punishes evildoers and heartless lovers. Like her mother, the Goddess of Night, Némesis was not partial to the attentions of the male gods, not even to the imperious importunings of Zeus. So as soon as she became aware of the god's intentions, Némesis fled to the ends of the earth, furiously shape-shifting as she went. She had just metamorphosed into a goose when Zeus trapped her at Rhamnous, a hilltop near the plain of Marathon, and, turning himself into a swan, completed their coupling. However, even though a sixth-century-B.C. sanctuary was built on the spot to honor Némesis, this version of Helen's conception never quite caught on. Perhaps because her mother lacked that human touch.

Léda, however, was altogether a different story.

LÉDA AND THE SWAN

She was, first of all, the queen of Sparta, that mysterious citadel in the distant south of the Peloponnese,* and the fact that Zeus was said to have penetrated this heart of darkness to father a child upon her has about it the quality of an invasion, as if he had gone there not simply to rape its queen but to take control of what might just have been the last bastion of pure Pelasgian goddess-worship in the country.

The god's intrusion took place along the banks of the river Evrótas, a wide, slow-moving waterway that meanders down Sparta's lush alluvial plain, just below a rise that once held the Mycenaean citadel. A particular bend in the river, a secluded pool of water surrounded by a towering thicket of bulrushes, seems to have been Léda's favorite spot for an afternoon swim. Here, the queen would sneak off while everyone else in the palace, including her husband, Tyndáreos, was napping, and come unaccompanied to the river.

Zeus was there in advance, hiding among the bulrushes decked out in his newest metamorphosis: that of a swan. He had never assumed this shape before. But it seemed fitting that as the God of the Sky, he should penetrate Léda as a creature of the air, just as he had ravished Evrópi as an eagle all those years before, at the very beginning of his intercourse with humans. For Léda, however, an eagle would have too brutal, too savage. A swan—that most deceptively elegant and beautiful of birds—would be much more appropriate. She was, after all, a queen.

Léda arrived and, as she did every afternoon, dropped her robe at the water's edge to exalt in the flow of air across her body, raising her arms, poised to plunge into the pool and sail through its sky-brightened waters as free as a bird, naked as in the innocence of her maidenhood.

---

* In the Bronze Age, this settlement was not called Sparta. Instead, the citadel and its environs were known as Lakedaímon and its people as Lakedaimónians, both too much of a mouthful. Hence the better-known (and more properly laconic) name Sparta.

All the warning she had was the sudden whoosh of wings coming at her out of the bulrushes. Then she found herself smothered by the heated stink of feathers, webbed feet clawing at her thighs, the nape of her neck seized as if by a giant hand, the flow of blood to her brain cut off, body growing limp, loosened, thrust upon. And, with a shudder, indifferently dropped.

Helen was born inside an egg—as are birds and snakes, symbols of the goddess, and as was the universe itself, hatched from the Universal Egg laid by fish-tailed Evrynómi, the wide-wandering Great Mother. For this and many other reasons, Helen's entry into the world trailed such clouds of glory that she often seems more like a goddess than a mere mortal. The Spartans carefully guarded the egg's broken shell for centuries, tying it together again with ribbons and reverently hanging this relic from the roof of a temple, where Pausanias testified that he saw it in about A.D. 160. Meanwhile, a plane tree associated with her was worshipped as the Tree of Life itself.

Her birth, however, was a crowded one. Léda's husband, Tyndáreos, had also made love to her the same afternoon as Zeus, and so Helen was accompanied out of the womb by a pair of twin boys, Castor and Pollux, and a fraternal twin sister, Clytemnéstra. So close were the conceptions, in fact, that the fatherhood of the boys would become a matter of considerable dispute. Some of the tale tellers said both were Tyndáreos's; others that only Castor was his; others that both were sons of Zeus. In any event, they were known as the Diós Koúri,* meaning "God's Boys," and were celebrated for their boxing and chariot skills, their patronage of sailors, and bravery in righting every wrong they came across.

Clytemnéstra was clearly Tyndáreos's daughter, with his same dark red hair and amber eyes. Helen, however, had locks as golden as the yolk of an egg, luminous pale white skin, and eyes black as a swan's, as polished onyx or obsidian. She was, from nearly the moment she

* Commonly conflated as Dioscuri.

emerged from her shell, utterly enchanting. Although Clytemnéstra was equally beautiful, there was something about her fiery eyes and piercing glance that made you want to look away, quickly, before they could draw you into their depths, where unspeakable urges seemed to be lurking.

Which is one of the reasons that men were always after Helen first. And they weren't content to honor and admire her from a distance. Beauty such as hers must be possessed. Thus, when Helen was barely twelve, she was abducted and raped by the king of Athens, Theseus (that very same hero who had killed the Minotaur), and hidden away in Attica. Tyndáreos's armies, led by Helen's twin brothers, invaded to get her back, plunging Athens into chaos. Eventually, Theseus was sent into exile on the island of Skyros, whose king, jealous of his glory, pushed him off a cliff to his death. In this way, the world was first made aware of the power of Helen's beauty. But as yet, no one could conceive of the dark and tangled web being woven around it by the Great Thunderer.

THE AUCTIONING OF HELEN

Theseus's fate did not deter the rest of Greece's top chieftains when Tyndáreos subsequently put Helen on the marriage block.* Hesiod tells us that "at the prompting of Zeus," shiploads and caravans of these mighty leaders and their gift-bearing retinues descended on Sparta to compete for Helen's hand, despite the fact that she was now no longer a virgin. Among the suitors were Idomeneus, the king of Crete, and Odysseus, the ruler of Ithaca. The advantage, however, was held by the Mycenaean Menélaos. Not only had he and his brother, Agamemnon,

* This would have been at the onset of her puberty, which scientific studies had determined occurred at either eleven or twelve years in Bronze Age girls. (See Bettany Hughes, *Helen of Troy*, p. 62.) To present-day Americans, this seems shocking. In modern Greece, however, it is a recognized fact of life. The same is true in Iran, where some girls are married off at an even younger age.

recently regained power in Mycenae, with Helen's father, Tyndáreos as an ally, but Agamemnon had just married Helen's sister, Clytemnéstra.

Nevertheless, the competition, in which the suitors would engage in contests of athletic prowess as well as gift giving, was apparently aboveboard. Moreover, Tyndáreos would accept no gift until all the suitors had sworn that no matter who won, all would be forever committed to coming to his aid should he ever require it—particularly if anyone should take Helen by force. Still, it seems a foregone conclusion that Menélaos, son of the cursed Átreus, had to win. First of all, as was the custom, Agamemnon, already Helen's brother-in-law, was the proxy who did the wooing for him. Second, as Hesiod tells us, being the wealthiest of all the suitors, he "gave the greatest gifts." Last but not least, Zeus had willed it so.

Menélaos now became king of Sparta, and with Agamemnon on the throne at Mycenae, the House of Átreus had the entire Peloponnese under its sovereignty. In addition, because of the suitors' promise to Tyndáreos, the brothers were also owed the allegiance of all the other great kings on the Greek mainland and islands. With such security at their disposal, there seemed nothing more for the brothers to do except settle down in their respective citadels, get their respective wives with children, and blindly await the consequences of having dared to try to domesticate such dangerous beauties.

17

REMEMBERED PAIN

Zeus rightly leads mortals to the wisdom
Which comes through suffering.
In sleepless nights, remembered pain
Drips unwanted into the heart,
Bringing clarity.
Hard is the grace which the gods force upon us
From the decks of their power.

AESCHYLUS, *Agamemnon*

For centuries afterward, these two fated marriages would produce an uncountable number of plays, poems, epics, and other works of art, from the first anonymous laments sung in the ruins of Troy to the last choruses of the last Athenian play produced by Euripides, in 408 B.C., all devoted to explicating the ways of the Great Thunderer, to understanding exactly why the god had brought this great disaster upon the House of Átreus and thus upon the Greeks themselves. It was, as Aeschylus would write some eight hundred years after the fact, "remembered pain."

To the Greeks of Homer's and Aeschylus's times, the Trojan War and its attendant tragedies were historical events as real to them as Cleopatra and the decline and fall of the Roman Empire are to us.* They also knew that the tales of these happenings held great importance for them—first, as examples of the often heroic heights scaled by their Mycenaean forebears, and second as cautionary tales of the catastrophic downfall that these intemperate roughnecks had brought upon themselves, one which the later Greeks did not want to be condemned to repeat. Thus, their renderings of these dark times are also demonstrations of how much Greek society had improved since then, particularly in terms of reasoned discourse and social justice—testaments of how wisdom and grace had come to them though the mysterious ways of Zeus, now called Soter, their Savior.

THE WEDDING OF PELEÚS AND THÉTIS

The stories of the Trojan War began with the marriage of King Peleús to the goddess Thétis. This union was arranged by Zeus with three purposes in mind. First, to rid himself, he hoped, of a continual urge to bed Thétis, recently revealed by Prométheus to be the woman with whom the Great Thunderer might sire a son greater than himself. Second, to have this union give birth to Achilles, who would not only play a crucial role in the Trojan War but, long after his tragic death, provide Zeus's daughter Helen with the best of all possible husbands. And third, to furnish the occasion for a final banquet between the gods and human beings, before the carnage of the coming war would bring such conviviality, already badly damaged by Tántalos's excesses, forever to an end.

At the wedding feast, Zeus arranged for Éris, the uninvited Goddess

* While the actual historicity of these tales remains in much dispute, a lot of ground has been covered (and uncovered) since Schliemann arrived on the scene in 1870. The recent (and ongoing) discovery and translation of Hittite texts (of whose empire Troy was a part) have tended to confirm that Troy and the Mycenaeans did indeed have a relationship and may have gone to war over, among other things, women.

of Strife, to disrupt the festivities by tossing a golden apple into the revelers' midst. Inscribed on the apple were the words TO THE FAIREST. This started a furious argument between Héra, Athína, and Aphrodite, each of whom claimed the prize for herself. This, in turn, allowed Zeus to intervene and announce that the awarding of the apple would have to be decided by someone impartial: a mortal, preferably a non-Greek, male and happily married. In fact, the Great Thunderer happened to have the perfect person in mind: a prince, the eldest son of Priam, king of Troy, and a trusted trading partner of the Mycenaeans. His name was Aléxandros, or, as some of his subjects called him, Paris.

Zeus had Hermes transport the golden apple and its three claimants to Mt. Ida, Troy's sacred peak,* where Paris was often to be found, wandering the hills with the royal flock. At this time, Troy was a respected ally and protectorate of the powerful Hittite Empire, which controlled most of what is now present-day Turkey, east to the borders of present-day Iraq. Thus there was little need for Paris's father, King Priam, to worry about threats from any quarter. And so, while Paris's younger brother Héktor was busying himself with learning the manly but apparently superfluous arts of combat, Paris often passed his days out on the slopes of Ida, communing with nature among the lowing royal herd—a notably humdrum existence which had most probably left him ripe for Fate's pickings.

When Hermes told Paris that he alone of all the mortals in the world had been chosen by Zeus to judge a beauty contest between the three loveliest goddesses of the Greek pantheon, the handsome prince literally leaped at the chance. The goddesses, each of surpassing radiance, then came to him one by one to make her case. Héra offered Paris worldwide power and wealth if he chose her; Athína, victories in every war and competition he entered; and Aphrodite, possession of

* The fact that it has the same name as the mountain where Zeus was born seems to be just a coincidence.

the world's most desirable woman: Helen, queen of Sparta, famed for her heart-stopping beauty.

It made no difference that Helen was solidly bound to the most powerful royal house of the Mycenaeans. Nor did Paris care that in bestowing the golden apple on Aphrodite, he would earn for Troy the enduring enmity of Héra and Athína. At that moment, the bedazzled prince was so entranced by fantasies of bedding this wondrous queen that he could think of nothing else. In his imagination he was already winging his way across the sea to Helen's sweet embrace, to be made immortal with a kiss.

"Her lips," wrote the British playwright Christopher Marlowe some three thousand years later, "suck forth my soul—see where it flies!"

THE SEDUCTION OF HELEN

Sometime afterward, Paris finally arrived in Sparta, ostensibly on a friendly diplomatic mission, his ship laden with gifts for the king, his mind beclouded by Aphrodite. But Zeus had made certain that Menélaos would be unable to stay and fulfill his obligations as host. The Spartan king had just received news of his father's death in Crete and had to immediately set off for the island. But he told Paris to think of the palace as his own. Meanwhile, the queen would see to his every need.

The moment Helen laid eyes on Paris must have been the moment when she at last understood what little choice she had in her destiny. Even if she had hesitated in taking the offering that the guileless Paris was making of himself, Aphrodite, the Goddess of Love, would have been there to push her forward, driven her to put out her bejeweled and perfumed hand to poor, pretty Paris and welcome this little lamb to the slaughter.

The ancient Greeks always feared Aphrodite, never forgot that she had been born out of rage, out of the foam generated by Ouranós's severed genitals as they hit the sea off the island of Cyprus. Thus, their image of her was much different from ours—that of the blond and modestly beguiling Goddess of Love given to us on the half shell by Botticelli in the fifteenth century A.D. In the *Iliad* and *Odyssey*, Aphrodite is adulterously linked to Áres, the God of War, and there are, as well, strong and repeated connections with dangerous Eros (sometimes pictured as her son) as well as with disruptive Éris, the Goddess of Strife. Meanwhile, love's disastrous effect on mortals was thought of throughout antiquity as "Aphrodite's Disease."

As a result, when Paris had accepted Aphrodite's blandishments and awarded her the apple, he was blissfully taking on much more than he had bargained for. In fact, he and Helen would be inextricably bound to the goddess until both had died, as she perched upon their lives like a carrion bird.

As soon as Menélaos discovered the sudden absconding of not only his wife and dignity, but a good deal of her fabulous dowry as well, he went to Agamemnon for help in raising an army to get it all back. Clytemnéstra did her best to stop them. By this time, Iphigénia, the eldest of her and Agamemnon's three daughters, had just entered puberty. She and her younger sisters, Chrysóthemis and Eléktra, and infant brother, Oréstes, needed their father. But Agamemnon's blood was up. He wanted war, as much for his brother's sake as his own. The Mycenaeans had been probing the western shores of Asia Minor for generations, alternately trading with its various communities and plundering them for goods and women. Troy was the most formidable of all these coastal cities, commanding the entrance to the Hellespont and the wealth of the Black Sea. There were great riches to be had in conquering it. And eternal glory, too.

Agamemnon and Menélaos journeyed throughout Greece marshaling forces by calling on the promises sworn to at the competition for Helen's hand in marriage. Of course, not all the provincial chieftains thought it would be as quick and easy a victory as Agamemnon was picturing. At Ithaca, wily Odysseus feigned madness in order not to have to serve, but he was forced to join when they seized his infant son, Telémachos, and threatened to murder the child on the spot. Even the fifteen-year-old Achilles was tracked down and forced, against his mother's wishes, to join the expedition.

This coalition of the willing and not-so-willing, with its twenty-nine contingents and over one thousand ships, then assembled at the port of Aulis, in the strait between the island of Évia and the mainland, with Agamemnon as its leader. Here, the poets tell us that Zeus sent an omen warning them of the difficulties that lay ahead,* but, as the Great Thunderer doubtless expected, the alliance, sniffing Trojan blood and booty, put aside these portents and set sail. After getting lost on their first attempt to make the two-day crossing to Troy (and sacking instead the wrong city), the fleet found itself back at Aulis bottled up by terrible winds. The fleet's resident seer announced that this was the fault of Agamemnon, who had offended the goddess Ártemis by killing one of her deer, and that in order to repair the damage, he would have to sacrifice his daughter, Iphigénia, to the goddess. Agamemnon bowed to Fate, summoned his wife and their daughter to Aulis, and then cold-bloodedly butchered Iphigénia on an altar overlooking the straits. The Greek armada then set out on its fateful voyage, leaving Iphigénia's mother, Clytemnéstra, behind to nourish her increasingly vengeful grief. In her eyes, the sacrifice had not been that at all. What it had been, pure and simple, was murder.

But this was only the first of many deaths. Over the next ten years, as Homer would write some five centuries later,

---

* The god petrified a snake that the Greeks had just seen eating eight baby sparrows and their mother—the sum of these numbers (including the snake) indicating that Troy would not fall for ten years.

Many a stalwart warrior's soul,
Would be sent too soon to Hades,
Leaving their bodies carrion for dogs and vultures,
All to fulfill the will of Zeus.

One of the most curious aspects of the telling of this war is how Homer pictures Zeus as being clearly on the side of the Trojans. While Troy's royal line had been sired by the Great Thunderer and was therefore under his protection, he was nevertheless, first and foremost, the supreme god of the Greeks. Second, he was supposed to be, at the very least, ostensibly neutral. Instead, he seems to continually give the advantage to the Trojans, which not only results in the death of many Greek stalwarts but badly demoralizes the survivors. Meanwhile, the Olympians themselves are often shown in violent disagreement over which side should win, and while heroic human warriors are dying in droves on the killing fields below, the gods are up in the heavens squabbling over petty jealousies, old feuds, and simmerings of resentment at Zeus's arrogant attempts to bully them into submission. No matter how magnificently Homer tells the tale, it is not—when you look at it closely—a pretty picture.

Meanwhile, back in Greece, the people were also floundering in a sea of confusion, faith in the wisdom of both their rulers and their gods slowly being leeched out of them by the war's increasingly voracious (and seemingly pointless) appetites, and by the self-interested machinations of those left behind, already maneuvering themselves into power. Among the latter were Clytemnéstra and Aýgisthos, Thyéstes' son, now old enough for Aphrodite to suck them into each other's embrace just as inexorably as she had Paris and Helen. "Oh, the two of us!" Homer has Helen crying out to Paris in words that might have equally applied to her sister, Clytemnéstra: "Zeus has planted a killing doom within us both!"

18

THE KILLING DOOM

That it is Zeus who has done this,
and brought all these things to pass,
you do not like to say; for where fear is,
there is also shame.

PLATO, *Euthyphro*

Most of us know at least parts of the rest of the story: that Achilles, in storming the gates of Troy, was slain by an arrow in his heel; that later, the Greeks were able to slip into Troy by hiding in the bowels of a wooden horse; that after sacking the city, it would take Odysseus ten years to return home; and that Agamemnon was assassinated in his bathtub at Mycenae by Clytemnéstra and Aýgisthos, who were, in turn, murdered by her son, Oréstes. Some even know that it was Paris who killed Achilles; that he, too, was slain by an arrow, one which Hérakles had poisoned with the blood of the Hydra; and that in the Trojans' argument over whether or not to bring the wooden horse into the city, two huge serpents came roaring out of the sea to crush a priest named Laocoön for warning the Trojans against Greeks bearing gifts.

Few people, however, are familiar with the ugly orgy of rape and slaughter that went on after the Greeks crept out of the wooden horse at night, opened the gates of the citadel to their compatriots, and overran the city: the old Trojan king, Priam, his throat slit as he sought protection at the altar of Zeus; his queen, Hecuba, her daughter Cassandra and daughter-in-law Andromáche, widow of Héktor, carried off to a Greek camp in Thrace to be parceled out as slaves; Cassandra raped so violently in the sanctuary of Athína that the goddess's statue was toppled to the floor; Polyxéni, her youngest sister, sacrificed and immolated on the tomb of Achilles; and Astýanax, Héktor's infant son, hurled to his death off the walls of Troy. All in all, some six thousand men and women were caught in the assault, the men fated to die, the women to be raped and afterward either killed or sent into slavery.

But this was not the end of the carnage. Once the city was pillaged and the spoils divided, the goddess Athína, furious over the toppling of her statue, persuaded her father to send a terrible storm down upon the departing Greeks. Hundreds of warriors were drowned, and hundreds more blown off course. Still others—most notably, Agamemnon, Menélaos, and Odysseus—would suffer separate catastrophes and delays and have to spend months and even years making their way back to Greece, to those strange and often hostile places that had once been their kingdoms.

Meanwhile, Zeus had seen to it that Helen, the original carrier of this killing doom, escaped the carnage unscathed. Even after twenty years, she still had the power to bewitch Menélaos. When he raged forth from the wooden horse and, sword drawn, came upon her in her quarters, all Helen needed was to proffer a single bared breast to make the Spartan king cast aside his sword and sink defeated into her embrace.

HOME AGAIN

Once back in Sparta, not only did Helen resume her former place as queen but she began, as well, to take on aspects of divinity. Telémachos, Odysseus's son, could testify to this. When the young prince visited Sparta in search of his long-lost father and saw her for the first time, she seemed to him to be very much like a goddess—emerging from her perfumed chambers, as Homer tells us, like golden-spindled Ártemis, trails of nymphlike handmaidens flowing around her. And when the talk of the men turned to the many tragic losses caused by war—in particular Odysseus's almost certain death and the horrible murder of Agamemnon—Helen showed a goddess's power in soothing this remembered pain by ministering to them the Great Mother's sacred mixture of wine and nepenthe (from the Greek *népenthé*, which means "against sorrow"). This was a potion so powerful that no one who drank it, even though he might witness the death of a father or mother or the dismemberment of a brother or son, would be able to raise even a single tear in grief. Thus, when the gathering began to remember events at Troy that would normally have cast a most unfavorable light on Helen, no one raised a hint of recrimination during their telling, but let the past drift by them like an insubstantial mist.

Helen could also read portents. The following morning, as she and the king were outside the palace bidding Telémachos good-bye, an eagle suddenly swooped down in front of them to snatch a goose from the yard and carry it off. Menélaos was at a loss to interpret its meaning. But Helen knew immediately. The eagle was Odysseus returning from his journeys, she said, and the goose, the fatted suitors of Penelope at last getting their comeuppance. Telémachos was so impressed by the queen's reading of this sign that he promised, should her reading prove true and such indeed was the will of Zeus, he would from that time forward worship Helen as the goddess she deserved to be.

CLYTEMNÉSTRA

Clytemnéstra would never inspire such devotion, even though she was Helen's twin and, like her, in the grip of the god. But because she was only human—born from the seed of Tyndáreos, not Zeus—she would have to suffer greatly and be much maligned for having been so chosen. The agony and rage she had felt over her own impotence at Agamemnon's sacrificing of their daughter Iphigénia at Aulis had festered for ten long years, turning every attempt at sleep into a nightmare. She lacked the divine detachment that had protected Helen. She had not been able, as her sister had, to retire to a quiet corner and weave away the horrors of her life into a grander tapestry. Nor did she have the feminine wiles of Odysseus's wife, Penelope, who had undone her weaving every night as an excuse to fend off suitors and remain faithful to her warrior husband. Clytemnéstra did not love Agamemnon. She detested him.

On the other hand, when Áygisthos, the murderer of Agamemnon's father, had come sniffing around several years after Agamemnon's departure from Troy, she hadn't jumped right into bed with him, either. Instead, she had seen the consequences and risen in defiance against them. She was not going to be the pawn of yet another man. So, in the beginning, she had all but spit in the face of Áygisthos's advances, his cajolings and soft mutterings of sympathy.

But then Zeus had suddenly taken her over, pinioning her in his divine will, so that thereafter—as Homer tells us—she finally allowed herself to be enfolded in Áygisthos's deadly embrace and drawn onward to the terrible things she had to do.

AGAMEMNON

Everyone but Agamemnon had seen the inevitable, had known exactly what was going to happen once he returned from Troy. Agamemnon, however, had always treated the world as though it were his by Divine Fiat and that, because of this, things would always turn out for the best no matter what he chose to do. Sometimes, his efforts appeared to be inspired, as in his selecting Clytemnéstra over

Helen. Marrying the second-rate sister but keeping mighty Mycenae as his power base was much cleverer than taking firstborn Helen and having second-rate Sparta to rule over. At other times, however, his decisions seemed destructively thickheaded. As at Troy, when he had arrogantly taken Achilles' war prize, the girl Briseis, as his own, publicly humiliating the great warrior and causing him to withdraw his troops. Putting the whole enterprise at risk just to show who was boss—and then blaming Zeus, Fate, and the Furies for the deaths this folly had caused.

But in Agamemnon's mind, it was important not to admit having made a mistake. After all, people had to trust their leaders. Who else was there? So when Agamemnon returned to the Argolid, he came like a conquering hero, bouncing ashore with that purposeful stride of his and brushing aside the past to such an extent that he even dared to proudly have in tow his new concubine, Cassandra, Priam's daughter, and the two infant children he had sired upon her during the long voyage back.

According to Homer, Clytemnéstra wasn't there to greet the ship. The only welcome Agamemnon received was from a delegation led by a young lord whose face Agamemnon could not place, who must have been just a boy when his king had gone off to war. But the young man knew how to pay proper respect to his betters, and when he humbly begged the honor of being the first to serve Agamemnon and his men a feast at his castle to celebrate their return, Agamemnon grandly accepted. There would be time enough, on the morrow, to head inland to Mycenae.

In Aeschylus's play *Agamemnon*, Clytemnéstra murders her husband in his bathtub, but in Homer's *Odyssey*, the shade of Agamemnon himself testifies that it was Aýgisthos who led the king of kings to the table of yet another of those infamous Atreid family feasts, fed him to the full, and then slaughtered him "like an ox at its trough."

Later, down in the Kingdom of the Dead, Agamemnon's wandering shade would recall the moment most vividly, remember looking up from the widening pool of his own wet blood to see Clytemnéstra standing over him, one hand gripping Cassandra's hair, the other holding the short bronze sword that slit her throat. "She turned her back on me as I lay writhing on Aýgisthos' sword," moaned Agamemnon, "dying, and did not even have the pity to prepare me for my journey here by closing my eyes and shutting the scream of horror on my mouth. Just walked away. The whore."*

Oréstes, barely pubescent, wasn't at the court. His nurse, seeing, as Agamemnon had not, what would happen, had spirited the boy away to a friendly king in northern Thessaly. But Oréstes' older sisters, Chrysóthemis and Eléktra, were left behind to watch triumphant Aýgisthos wallow in the wealth and power of Mycenae, rutting the compliant Clytemnéstra at his will, and grinding the people into poverty.

Eight long years later, Oréstes returned to Mycenae, murdered both Aýgisthos and nightmare-haunted Clytemnéstra, and then mounted a great public feast to celebrate his revenge and their burial. As it happened, this took place on the very day when Menélaos and Helen finally made their tortuous way home from Troy, landing at Náfplion, the port of Mycenae. It would even be asserted (by no less an authority than Euripides)† that less than a week later, the blood-maddened Oréstes would go after Helen. But that is (and was) a story for other times, long after all the personages in this great Mycenaean drama had succumbed to Zeus's punishments and only their shades haunted the shattered landscape of the Argolid.

It would also be claimed that Oréstes' killing of his mother was a foul and unforgivable act, a matricide that demanded vengeance by the

---

* Those who know Aeschylus's version in his *Oresteia* may balk at these details. But this is the way Homer knew it, and his version takes precedence over Aeschylus's by some three hundred years.

† In his play *Oréstes.*

Furies. But in Homer's time, there seemed to be no such taboo. On the contrary, tradition has it that Oréstes was honored as a hero for his deeds and acclaimed king of Mycenae by the other nobles. It would also be said that after Menélaos and Helen had passed peacefully away to the Elysian Fields, Oréstes married their beautiful daughter, Hermione, and thus added the throne of Sparta to his dominion. He would live to a ripe old age, and it is a sign of the great esteem in which he was held by Zeus that only after his death would the Great Thunderer release the impatient forces of the Heraclíds to roar down from the north and finish off the Mycenaeans forever. In the course of the fighting, Oréstes' son and successor, Tisamenós, was killed, and with him the tragic lines of Pélops and Átreus were, at long last, laid to rest.

PART FOUR

THE HOLY GHOST

19

THE VOICES OF GOD

Over the centuries, the race slowly softened,
became civilized. God softened also . . .

NIKOS KAZANTZÁKIS, *Report to Greco*

Historians and archaeologists tell us that in about 1200 B.C., wave after wave of invaders poured down upon Greece and the Near East in a deluge of destruction so inexplicably vast that some experts can find no other explanation for it than various "acts of God" such as drought and earthquakes. The devastation was so complete that the identity and origin of the invaders remains uncertain; the Egyptians called them the "Sea Peoples," and this is the name they are still known by today. Their onslaught not only swept aside the Heraclíds but, in quick succession, laid waste nearly all the mighty empires of the Bronze Age, the Hittites included, leaving only a badly battered force of Egyptians to finally blunt the raiders' advance. On the Greek mainland, tribal migrants known as the Dorians either accompanied the raiders and/or settled in central Greece or the Peloponnese after nearly all the previous inhabitants, except those atop the still-unconquered heights of the Athenian acropolis, had fled eastward.

While Hesiod had written that Zeus was "hastening to make an utter end of the race of mortal man," it seems that with the destruction of the Mycenaeans and the advent of the Dorians, Zeus's thirst to punish mankind for its impieties was satisfied mercifully short of finishing off the entire human race forever. Herodotus tells us that the Dorians had been wandering the north of Greece for centuries, having been pushed out of the area around Thebes when Kadmos had settled there. Not only did they speak a dialect of Greek, but they were followers as well of Zeus. So it seems quite possible that they had arrived in Greece either with or just after the original incursions from the Caucasus and had later developed their own versions of both the language and the god. Certainly they were much more uncompromising Zeus worshippers than their Mycenaean counterparts, who had prudently divided their loyalties between the old goddesses and their new Olympians. The Dorians, on the other hand, were what we might call strict fundamentalists: It was Zeus first and foremost, and all the others—particularly the ladies—a distant second.

As a result, the old Mycenaean tales would be reworked to fit the Dorians' vision of things, as they themselves were legitimized as the Heraclíds, sons of Zeus's son Hérakles, returning to take their rightful possession of the land. It is not within the scope of this book to try and pinpoint which part of every myth and legend was originally Mycenaean and which Dorian. Suffice it to say that the ever-shifting balance of power in favor of Zeus is but one result of the changes that were being wrought. Meanwhile, the Great Thunderer would increasingly be seen as presiding over human affairs from a much more lordly distance than in his lusty Mycenean days. Although not disembodied, he would no longer mingle with mortals in a physical way; he was less a father than a patriarch; and he tended to hover over his earthly children in the manner, one might say, of a Holy Ghost.

The destruction visited upon the Greek mainland had been so total that descendants of the Greeks who survived retained no real record of how it had happened or what had followed during the darkness of the next four centuries. Only that some sort of devastation had occurred, that this had been the will of Zeus, and that its chosen instruments were the invading Heraclíds.

Whatever the actual causes, it is clear that most of the major power centers in Mycenaean Greece and the Near East experienced a violent, fiery destruction and sudden and often permanent abandonment, their past glories little more than dim and painful memories, surviving mainly as cautionary tales to be passed down in song through succeeding generations. While the citadels at Mycenae and Tíryns managed to hang on for another century or so, by the beginning of the Dark Age (c. 1200 B.C.), Mycenae had become little more than a walled graveyard. All knowledge of writing was lost, as was the technique of building in stone. At the same time, with the radical decline in population, those who remained or were migrating in from the north survived through individual subsistence farming, living hard-scrabble off the land like their Neolithic predecessors, and eventually gathering for protection into small isolated communities scattered around the country.

Meanwhile, religious observances seem to have suffered a similar decline. Gone were those clay statuettes of the Neolithic goddess which had previously been as ubiquitous in Greece as Orthodox icons are today, remnants of the old matriarchal religion which had persisted in an uneasy balance with the worship of the Olympians. At the mainland's various sanctuaries and other cult sites, almost all activity seems to have ceased. While some forms of worship certainly existed, it was probably practiced by the faithful on their own or in small groups.

Little by little, however, as the traumas of the Mycenaean collapse continued to recede from memory and the surviving families coalesced into larger groups, pooling their resources and building fortified settlements on nearby hilltops, forays were made back to the dimly remembered sites of the old deities, places that had been clearly marked by signs of their sanctity since the beginnings of creation. Sometimes these were hilltops, clearly special because of their proximity to the heavens. But of equal importance were their near opposite: wide-open plains that were so ringed with mountains as to seem bowl-shaped, the sky above forming, by extension, a domelike covering—a natural, outdoor temple that seemed to have been created by the gods specifically as a place of worship. And last, but definitely not least, were those hallowed locations where the deity was said to commune with the world through the voice of a priest or priestess reading the signs coming from a tree, rock, or gaseous cleft in the ground.

Before the arrival of the first Greeks, all such places had belonged to the Earth Mother, variously known as Gē or Gaía, and had continued, throughout Mycenaean rule, to be her special domain. Now, however, the Dorians were moving in to reconsecrate these sites as sacred to Zeus. Of particular importance were those sanctuaries that had been famed, since time immemorial, for their oracles: Dodóna in the northwest, Delphí in central Greece, and Olympía in the Peloponnese. Here, goddess worshippers had come for more than a thousand years to ask the resident seer (usually a priestess) for guidance in their personal and communal affairs. When the answers were murky (as they often were), the fault was thought to lie with the oracle and her interpreters, not the deity. What was important, particularly to the Dark Age Greeks, was that these were now words said to be from Zeus himself—still out there, somewhere, to help guide them across the darkling plain of their times.

DODÓNA

While all three sites were way off the beaten track, Dodóna, the most ancient, was the farthest, situated in a narrow, remote, mountain-ringed valley in northwestern Greece. Today it is just a few miles south of the enchanting lakeside city of Ioánnina, but in order to reach it, one must cross a high ridge of hills over yet another of those narrow, serpentine roads—always difficult and potentially dangerous—that seem to be the required approach to deities everywhere. When the road to Dodóna finally drops down into the valley, however, you find yourself gliding to a stop in a wide expanse of soothingly level, alluvial farmland. Around you are chains of hills and mountains—one of them a breathtaking, twin-peaked massif dominating the western horizon with the heavens above doming into infinity. This combination of big sky and towering crags has the effect of making the visitor feel like the tiniest of mites in God's eye, a dot in the immeasurable magnificence of his being. Rather than spectacularly awe-inspiring, like Delphí, or as spiritual as Olympía, Dodóna is purely and simply overwhelming.

At the time of the Dorians' arrival, c. 1100 B.C., the sanctuary had already been devoted to the Great Goddess for some 1,400 years. Herodotus tells us that when the names of the new gods came into the country from Egypt (presumably along with the descendants of Zeus and Ió), it was the oracle of Dodóna that approved their use. Shortly afterward, two black doves flew out from Egypt. One of them went to Dodóna and settled on a branch of the Great Mother's sacred oak. Speaking in a human voice, the dove informed the priestesses that this would henceforth be the site of an oracle of Zeus, with the god himself residing within the tree. From that time forward, the priestesses began reading the god's oracles through the sounds made by the rustling of the oak's leaves.*

Some of the most prominent figures in Greek legend were said to have relied on the oracle's powers. In the *Iliad*, Achilles prays to the Dodonean Zeus to aid his friend Pátroklos in beating back Héktor's assault and then to return him safely to the Greek camp. While the god allowed the first request, he ignored the second to stoke Achilles' anger for use in the battle against the Trojans. In the *Odyssey*, Odysseus travels to Dodóna to ask whether he should arrive home openly or in secret. The oracle counsels the latter, thus saving Odysseus from certain

* The other dove flew to Libya, where it announced the establishment of the oracle of Zeus-Ammon at a desert oasis. See chapter 23.

death at the hands of his wife's suitors. And in the *Argonautika*, Athína fits a branch from the sacred oak in the bow of Jason's ship so as to guide and keep him safe in his dangerous voyage to find the Golden Fleece.

But such connections had happened far back in time, before and during the period of the Trojan War, and although Dodóna would continue to flourish as a revered institution well into Christian times, it was too removed from the centers of power farther south—Thebes, Athens, Corinth, and Sparta—to ever gain the prestige or influence of its sister oracles at Delphí and Olympía.

DELPHÍ

This extraordinary site clings to an eagle-haunted aerie in the crags of Mt. Parnassus, just north of the Gulf of Corinth, crouching on a steep slope beneath two massive limestone cliffs whose looming, fissured surfaces look ready to tumble down and push everything in their path into the thickly forested valley below. On the opposite side of this valley rise more of Parnassós's spurs, their rocky ridges and deep ravines extending in every direction as far as the eye can see—a seemingly endless, all-devouring wilderness. To the southwest, waves of olive trees undulate down to the distant, slate-blue inlets of the Gulf of Corinth, site of the ancient port of Kirra (just east of today's Itéa), where supplicants would begin their serpentine five-mile ascent to receive the pronouncements of the oracle at some 1,800 feet above sea level.

The Great Mother's deep connection to the oracle was always acknowledged by the Dorians and their successors. In Aeschylus's trilogy about Oréstes (written in the fifth century B.C.), the opening scene of the final play, *The Eumenides*, is set at Delphí, where the oracle praises the primacy of Mother Earth. Later, the first-century-B.C. historian Diodorus Siculus, whose forty-three-volume history of the ancient world has preserved many traditions that would otherwise have been lost, would write a fascinating and detailed description of how the sacredness of the spot was first discovered and the oracle established:

It seems that long before the coming of the Greeks, back during the time of those Neolithic farmers called the Pelasgians, a goatherd, grazing his flock within the grassy, well-watered mountain hollow that is now Delphí, noticed the odd behavior of the animals whenever they would peer into a fissure on its slope. Abruptly, the goats would begin to leap about and make strange noises much different from their usual bleatings. When the herder peered down into the opening, the smell of something pleasantly sweet reached his nostrils. He breathed it in—and immediately found himself filled with a strange exaltation. It was as if he were being embraced by the goddess herself. Her voice sounded within his head as clearly as the bells hung around the necks of his flock, a tintinabulation of wondrous words, incomprehensible yet more luminous with meaning than anything he had ever heard before. When his friends found him later, he was seated cross-legged at the edge of the crevice, eyes wide and wild, mind teetering on the edge of a rapturous madness.

After several members of his tribe stumbled, similarly intoxicated, into the fissure, rules were established. Only one among them would be allowed to receive this gift of the goddess, and that would be a woman, because women had always been the best intermediaries between the Great Mother and her children. Moreover, the chosen one would be a virgin, since such innocence allowed the purest communion with the goddess.

Thus, the first Delphic oracle took her place upon a stone slab placed across the crevice. Although the visions she had while inhaling the goddess's sacred fumes went unrecorded, there is no doubt that they were momentous enough for her fame to quickly spread down the mountain and far across the mainland.

In fact, so great was the oracle's renown that, around 1600 B.C., the Mycenaeans saw fit to establish a settlement on the slope just downhill from the sacred fissure. As they had with Héra in the Argolid, the

Mycenaeans treated the oracle and her goddess with the greatest respect. But when new waves of warriors and settlers arrived during the Dark Ages, shifting the balance of power decidedly in favor of Zeus and his Olympians, the story of Delphí's beginnings underwent a complete revision.

Now, it was said that the spot had been established by Zeus himself, to determine the exact center of the world so that all the communities scattered by the catastrophe would have a focal point around which they could gather. This he had done by setting loose two eagles from opposite ends of the earth (one atop the Caucasus in the East, the other on the Atlas Mountains in present-day Morocco) and letting them fly at equal speed toward each other. The place where they met (which happened to be exactly above the area where the oracle of the Pelasgians had been working her wonders for all those years), Zeus declared to be the center of the earth. Here he deposited the great conical stone that had saved him from being eaten alive by his father, naming it the *ómphalos* (navel) of the world, while the sacred precinct itself would be known as Delphí (womb). Finally, he appointed the most glorious of his many begotten sons, Apóllon, as its resident god. Thereafter, Apóllon would communicate to visiting supplicants the often enigmatic will of his Great Father, transmitting it through the gnomic utterances of the oracle now known as the Pythia.*

OLYMPÍA

In about 900 B.C., as the descendants of Dorians began establishing a presence south of the Gulf of Corinth, they would make similar doctrinal changes at a sanctuary of the goddess in the northwestern

---

* The name comes from the ancient Greek for "rot" and was used to commemorate Apóllon's slaying of the Great Mother's she-dragon, whose carcass he left to rot out in the open as evidence of his mastery over the site. Thus, the god himself often has the epithet "Pythian."

Peloponnese, one nearly as far from human traffic as those in Dodóna and Delphí.

Here, the Earth Mother's sacred precinct was set at the base of a breast-shaped hill that arose between two of the area's most sacred rivers, the Kládeos and Alphiós, both named after Greek river gods fathered by the Titan Okeanós (Ocean), a son of Gaía. As at Delphí, the goddess's presence was made known through a cleft in the earth through which she communed with her supplicants, sending them dreams as they slept nearby, visions that were then interpreted by the resident priestess. The cleft, since closed by an earthquake, was called the *stómium*, or "mouth," of the goddess. The sanctuary came to be called Olympía, just as the great mountain to the north was called Ólympus, both names meaning, in the language of the natives, "hill" or "mountain."*

When the Dorians arrived to claim the sanctuary for themselves, they also claimed that Zeus had long before come into possession of Olympía by defeating his father, Krónos, in a wrestling match on these very grounds, afterward hurling a lightning bolt down from the top of Mt. Ólympus—some 310 miles to the north—to mark the spot as particularly sacred.

Later, Hérakles would commemorate his father's victory (and the subsequent one of Pélops over Inómaos) by founding the Olympic Games on the premises. He would also bring many trees to beautify the grounds and provide both shade for the faithful and plenteous wood for the sacrifices they would make to his father. In the process, Hérakles named the hill that housed the oracle of the goddess, the Hill of Krónos, and at its foot, in the area struck by the thunderbolt, he established and walled off Zeus's sacred grove, the Altis.

Pausanias is said to have written that Olympía is "where the aura of divinity is most tangible on earth." This is just as true today. The

---

* According to one scholar, there were some fourteen elevations in the region with the same name.

instant you enter the gates of the sanctuary, you are embraced by an extraordinary feeling of tranquillity, as if you had at last come upon (or perhaps, returned to) that other magical place between two rivers, the Garden of Eden. Its spirit seems to reside, as Zeus and Hérakles had intended, in its trees. When Fárzaneh and I made our April visit, Easter had just passed, and the world was in blossom. A profusion of fully grown plane trees, oaks, pines, poplars, and olive trees, descendants of Hérakles' first plantings, forested the Hill of Krónos, spilling across the landscape, while thick growths of grass and wildflowers tufted the grounds between the scattered stones, and a dozen or more Judas trees rose within and around the ruins, bright with cascades of pinkish magenta blossoms.

But I suspect that even during the dreary days of winter, the sanctuary is no less magical. There is something in the atmosphere of Olympía that is more than seasonal, an enchantment that its physical charms can only begin to explain. Like our image of Eden, Olympía radiates an eternal, before-the-Fall tranquillity. The difference is that Olympía's beneficent spirit has managed to remain intact in spite of the centuries of violence that have raged through and around it, retaining a sense of peace so profound that it truly passes all understanding.

Whether or not this extraordinary aura of divinity emanates from Zeus or Mother Earth (one suspects the latter), once you are embraced by it, you understand exactly why Olympía and no other spot—not Athens, Sparta, nor any of a myriad other possible sites—had to be chosen as Zeus's primary sanctuary, the sacred precinct out of which there would develop, from observances to his divinity, the equally sacred Olympic Games.

20

HOLDING THE CENTER

Zeus is ether, Zeus is earth, Zeus is sky;
Zeus is everything and all that is higher than this!

AESCHYLUS, *Fragment*

At the time the Games came into being, c. 800 B.C., civil conflicts were common throughout Greece. The various territories, having outgrown their original settlements, were torn by internal and external rivalries. Coming to the fore internally were councils of *áristi* (best men), usually from those families that had managed, over the previous centuries, to accumulate the largest landholdings. Eventually, these "magistrates" (masters) began consolidating neighboring communities into what came to be called the *polis*, or city-state. This greater organization fostered a dramatic increase in commerce and population. As the old Mycenaean trade routes to the East were revived, new goods and ideas were brought into the country. Along with these came the highly important adaptation of the Phoenician alphabet to the Greek language, the latter having lacked a system of writing for some four hundred years, since the destruction of the Mycenaean power centers. The ability to read and write seems to have rapidly spread across the Greek world, and, aside from the obvious benefits that would accrue for literature and philosophy, this recovered literacy would also be crucial to the eventual emergence of democracy: It was now possible (and even demanded) that the laws of the city-states be written down for all the citizens to see—and so they were, often incised on blocks of stone set up in walls for public viewing.*

Meanwhile, as the city-states grew in size, so did territorial disputes with neighboring communities, often metastasizing into full-fledged wars. Inevitably, the governing bodies of the city-states assumed a military as well as political cast, with religion also becoming a part of military policy, binding the populace under a patron deity. At this time, c. 800 B.C., the first temples also came into being, structures built to both possess the deity and proclaim the local god or goddess—one of Zeus's siblings or his children—as the polis's resident protector.

But Zeus remained above the fray, considered too powerful to be confined within a temple or claimed by any single polis. Thus he held the center for all the people in all the city-states—the omnipresent, omnipotent, and omniscient father of gods and men, everywhere manifest but truly accessible only at his three great oracular sanctuaries, where he would appear to his worshippers as a disembodied voice, mysterious and irrefutable. Here at Dodóna, Delphí, and Olympía, the Greeks from various city-states would encounter others with a similar faith and language, some adversaries in an ongoing war, others strangers from as far as two weeks' journey away.† As a result of these meetings, there arose among the people an awareness that they belonged to a much greater entity than just their villages back

* Some of the earliest of these, enacted in Górtyn in about the sixth century B.C., were inscribed on walls that rose only a few feet away from the spot where Zeus ravished Evrópi in impregnating her with Minos. Perhaps not so coincidentally, one of the items the laws made a point of dealing with was rape. The act was not deemed a criminal offense (out of deference, perhaps, to Zeus?). Instead, the violator had to pay a fine. The amount was determined by a male judge, who was required to base his decision on the social status of both the victim and the rapist, which meant that Evrópi, princess or not, probably wouldn't have had a leg to stand on.

† The time it took to trek from Athens, say, to Olympía.

home—to a clan of kindred souls for which they as yet had no name.

In time, of course, their tale tellers would find an agreed-upon way of explaining these common roots. It would be said that they were all descendants of the man whose parents had been the sole survivors of a great flood sent by Zeus ages before to destroy the human race. The man's name, they said, was Hellen (in Greek, Éllin). So impressive was this story of their origins that the Greeks of today still call themselves Hellenes (Élliness), their language Elliniká, and their country Elláda—all because of what they came to believe some three thousand years ago, in these Dark Age gatherings.*

Thus, the visitors to these sanctuaries began to participate in communal ceremonies to honor the Great Father of them all, Zeus. And out of these, sometime at the beginning of the eighth century B.C., there came the first Olympic games.

THE GAMES

The tale tellers would later say that Zeus originated the idea, basing it on practices that his son Hérakles had instituted at Olympía long before the Trojan War. To honor Zeus's famous victory over Krónos in a wrestling match, Hérakles had included an athletic contest, a footrace, in the observances. He had also proclaimed a regional truce that would allow the various parties to travel to the event without fear of being attacked by rival tribes. Over the years, however, the practice had died out. Now, troubled by the civil wars that were plaguing his worshippers, Zeus had his oracle at Delphí suggest that these ceremonies be revived—that the territory of Elis, where Olympía was located, make

* Hellen's parents were Deucalion and Pyrrha. Deucalion himself was believed to have been fathered by either Prométheus or Zeus, depending, it seems, on whose side you were on: man or the gods.

immediate arrangements to restore the truce and get on with bringing the Greeks into a semblance of unity, all under the auspices of the Great Father.

The proposal was met with considerable interest. It would give the warring factions not only a respite from their incessant hostilities but, in and around Olympía's tranquil glades, an opportunity to practice a bit of quiet diplomacy, all the while, of course, displaying their reverence for the Great Thunderer.

In the beginning, it was solely a Peloponnesian affair involving Elis, Pisa, and Sparta. Eventually, it would expand to include not only the mainland city-states but their colonies from around the far shores of the Mediterranean and Black Sea. At first, the festival itself took only a single day—the time of the full moon in the eighth month of the year, around August, when the need to work in the fields was minimal. The emphasis was entirely on religion, with the athletic contest—still a single footrace—being only a small part of a series of rites in honor of Zeus. The main event was the sacrifice itself: the slaughter of hundred oxen (the amount called a *hecatomb*) on the god's altar and the communal partaking of this sacred meat at a banquet following the race. As the years passed, however, and the festival attracted more and more participants, other athletic events were gradually added, with the armistice eventually being extended to three months to allow for the longer journeys.

What this meant was a quarter of a year of guaranteed peace every four years. To many Greeks and their families, the Great Father's Olympiad must have seemed heaven-sent.

But once the festival was over, the fighting quickly broke out again. This brought increasing unrest to the city-states, resulting in a call for stronger rule and better armies. In some cities, tyrants took over; in others, groups of wealthy oligarchs. Sparta was an exception; it was already governed by a military class made up of all its male citizens and had developed Greece's most formidable fighting force. At first, the new governments provided what they had promised: greater security and a better standard of living for the majority of their citizens. Larger fleets were sent out, trade increased, colonies were founded abroad, and more and more wealth and power flowed into the cities. In order to trumpet these accomplishments, the city-states built bigger and better public works—in particular, ever more massive temples for their resident gods. Meanwhile, finding that the four-year interval between Olympiads was too long to wait to show off their wares, the various powers agreed on three new festivals: at Delphí, Isthmia, and Neméa.

Although a staggered schedule made peace a yearly event, less and less attention was being paid to the god in whose honor it had been declared. Of course, the victorious athletes routinely said that they couldn't have done it without his help, but everyone knew that the skills they displayed at the Games were the result of their own year-long training and inborn physical attributes. While no one doubted that the gods were ever-present, the fact that mortals were increasingly in control could not be denied either. All you had to do was look at those magnificent bodies. And buildings. And the new sculptures and earthenware. Man was rapidly becoming the measure of all things.

21

THEIR FINEST HOUR

Man is the measure of all things;
of what is, that it is;
of what is not, that it is not.

PROTAGORAS (C. 440 B.C.)

It was no coincidence that just as the Olympics were growing into an increasingly secular extravaganza, Homer's *Iliad*, the first epic to be widely disseminated in writing, was being read or listened to all over Greece, spreading its image of the gods as quarreling, self-centered, vindictive, and often capricious meddlers in human affairs.* Nor was it coincidental, in spite of the way the poem glorifies human battle heroics, that in its vivid renderings of the war's grisly minutiae—

The spear struck him where the head joins the spine,
Severing both the tendons,
Head, mouth, and nostrils hitting the ground
Long before his legs and knees

* C. 750–700 B.C. In fact, the Games' rhapsodic contests may have led to the first fixed texts of the *Iliad* and *Odyssey*.

—the poet was reflecting the deep concern of his contemporaries about the worth of blind faith in one's leaders and one's gods. In the poem, neither Zeus nor Agamemnon seems to have much control over the forces he unleashes, while the majority of the humans involved are ground down into little more than things, into slaves or corpses.

Nor was it entirely by chance that a century after Homer, the war's tragic waste of human lives was again emphasized in a famous incident involving the greatly admired Sicilian-Greek poet Stesíchorus. It seems that after making a particularly offensive remark about Helen of Troy's adulterous behavior, he was suddenly struck blind. Exactly what he said has been lost to posterity, but Pausanias tells us that it was apparently bad enough to make Helen reach out from the grave and take away his sight. When the terrified poet realized who had done this to him and why, he immediately penned a public apology. This was in the form of a poem called a *palinode*, or "recantation." In the palinode, he now revealed what he claimed was the real truth about Helen. Its opening lines went as follows:

Not true these words,
Never did you step into that many-oared ship,
Nor come to the walls of Troy.

Upon completion of the recantation, Stesíchorus instantly regained his sight. While the rest of his apology has been lost, scholars have been able to approximate the tale he spun. It seems that when Paris was forcibly taking the poor, unwilling Helen to Troy, a storm blew their ship off course to Egypt. There the Egyptian king, Proteus, learning of Paris's crime, had a duplicate of Helen created, switched this with the real woman, and sent the unsuspecting Paris off to Troy with what was merely Helen's image, or *eidolon*. The copy was so real that even Menélaos was fooled. He would not discover the truth until after the war, when he and the *eidolon* traveled to Egypt. Here, he was greeted by the real thing, the faithful wife who had been waiting for Fate to bring him to her all these years. It had been Zeus, said Stesíchorus, who had arranged this elaborate deception all in order that the war would be fought and his will to destroy the Mycenaeans might be fulfilled—all the while keeping his daughter's virtue intact.

As the great twentieth-century Greek poet Giorgos Seferis would write,

And we butchered ourselves for Helen for ten years . . .
for a linen undulation a cloud,
a butterfly's flicker a fluff of swan's down
for an empty shift, for a Helen.

Thus, even at a time when philosophers were questioning the gods' powers over the world and trying to identify a single, natural substance—fire, water, earth, or air—as the primary material of the cosmos, it seemed the Olympians might still be somewhere up there laughing at these puny efforts to make sense of it all. As a result, with civil conflicts continuing to plague the country, ordinary Greeks more than ever came to look up to Zeus as the sole deity who might bring order and justice to his war-weary flock. In contrast to his sportive early days of mingling with humans down on Earth, he was now seen as a sort of Great Administrator on high, his distant, nearly disembodied presence saddled with duties as protector of the state, the marketplace, the family, personal and political relationships, beggars, strangers, supplicants, justice, and righteousness—with numerous temples, sanctuaries, and statues around Greece, from Sparta to Attica, dedicated to him as Zeus Soter, the Savior.*

As things turned out, this was an epithet that he gloriously lived up to in his finest hour as the god of all the Greeks, when he almost

---

* Pausanias saw many on his travels through Greece. In Egypt, a statue of Zeus Soter had been placed atop the great Lighthouse of Alexandria, one of the Seven Wonders of the World, dedicated to the god and built by Alexander the Great's successor and founder of Egypt's first Greek dynasty, Ptolemy I (also, not coincidentally, named Ptolemy I Soter).

single-handedly saved his followers from complete enslavement by yet another evil beast slouching at them out of the East—this time in the form of what seemed to be several million soldiers of the Persian Empire, the greatest menace to Greece's existence since the Dorian destruction of the Mycenaeans some seven hundred years before.

THE ONSLAUGHT

It had been looming for decades. In 547 B.C., a Persian army under its king, Cyrus, had unexpectedly defeated Croesus of Lydia and taken control of virtually all of present-day Turkey, including the Greek cities along the Ionian coast. In 512, Cyrus's successor, Darius, crossed the Hellespont (today's Dardanelles) to invade northern Greece, absorbing Thrace into his burgeoning empire and making a vassal state of Macedonia, whose southern border was defined by the massif of Mt. Ólympus. The next step would be the entire rest of the country.

In 492, Darius launched a land and sea invasion south from the Hellespont. But it was immediately stopped in its tracks by a huge, heaven-sent gale which crashed down upon the fleet as it rounded the peninsula of Mt. Athos, sinking some three hundred ships and drowning twenty thousand men, many of them, Herodotus tells us, devoured by lurking sea monsters. While Herodotus does not specifically say that the blow was delivered by Zeus, there can be little doubt that the faithful saw it that way. Two years later, in 490 B.C., when Darius's forces reinvaded, this time from the south, the Athenians, buoyed by the Persians' first catastrophe, slaughtered an estimated seven thousand of Darius's foot soldiers on the plain of Marathon, with a loss of only 192 of their own men.* Because of their valor and because the Spartans

---

* Serving in the Athenian army were the playwright Aeschylus and a soldier named Phidipides. The latter ran the twenty-six miles back to Athens to bring the news, his run spawning countless "marathons" ever since.

had been unable to get to Marathon in time to join the battle, the Athenians were now looked upon (along, of course, with Zeus) as the saviors of Greece.

But Athens and Zeus were not finished with their heroics. Nor were the Persians done with their invasions. In 485 B.C., Darius's son, Xerxes, began assembling a force of some two million men to again attempt an invasion of the Greek mainland, this time by land and by sea. In response, the Greek city-states were prompted to form their first all-country-wide alliance, called the Hellenic League. They knew that if the Persians won, it would mean the end of the independence that each state and each individual had so vigorously fought to achieve and preserve during the previous five centuries, particularly in Athens, where the first democratic constitution had recently been adopted. On the other hand, few Greeks thought they would have much of a chance. For many, it simply looked to be a matter of liberty or death.*

Of course, Greeks being Greek, there were a number of hotly contested opinions about the best way of countering the Persian advance. To settle the discussion, a number of emissaries, including one from the people of Delphí, were sent to the Pythia to consult the will of Zeus and see what the future might hold.

First, the god advised the people of Delphí to pray to the winds, as these would prove to be Greece's greatest ally. In a separate consultation, the Spartans were informed that one of two dire events would come to pass: Either Sparta would be sacked or one of their two kings killed. Worst of all, however, was the prediction given the representatives from Athens. For them, the oracle prophesied utter doom, telling

---

* In 539 B.C., when Greece was a muddle of battling city-states ruled by tyrants, Cyrus the Great had been the first to introduce the notion of human rights and freedom of religion into government—a proud Iranian contention that has been supported by the UN, which translated the Persian king's Charter of Human Rights into all its official languages in 1971. The original charter had been prompted by the king's conquering of Babylon; it is most instructive to read today, particularly since what was Babylon in Cyrus's time is now Iraq.

the Athenians to flee their city, because the Persians would destroy it and burn their shrines. When the Athenians begged for a second and more positive opinion, the Pythia grudgingly replied that Zeus would grant his daughter Athína what she wished, but only to a limited degree. He would not withdraw his previous prediction that Athens would be destroyed. However, the all-seeing god now also offered a somewhat enigmatic ray of hope: that the Athenians would eventually be saved by "a wooden wall" when they faced the Persians at "divine Salamís," the island that sat just off Athens's port of Piráeus. This wooden wall, some Athenians believed, could perhaps be the formation of fighting ships within their relatively small but determined fleet. Thus, they would base their entire defense on what seemed to many—particularly the Spartans—an extremely flimsy prognostication by a god who had recently appeared too above-it-all to make much of a difference.

DIVINE INTERVENTIONS

In 480 B.C. the Persian war machine poured into Greece, its navy sailing southwest along the Greek coast toward Athens, its army marching down the mainland toward the twin objectives of the treasury at Delphí and the city of Athens, where the Persians hoped to rip the heart out of any remaining Greek resistance.

At the pass of Thermopylae, halfway down the coast, the Persian army was met by a small band of three hundred Spartans led by their king, Leonídas, who, remembering Zeus's warning at Delphí, decided to sacrifice himself and his men to save Sparta. In a storied battle, the Spartans and their king delayed the enemy advance long enough to allow the Greeks to evacuate Athens and regroup their navy in the Bay of Salamís.

Herodotus tells us that shortly afterward, as a division of the Persian army sent to loot the great treasury at Delphí was approaching the sanctuary, the god told the Delphians not to worry with defenses, that he was perfectly capable of taking care of the Persians himself. With that, he launched a salvo of thunderbolts at the advancing soldiers, striking the surrounding mountains and sending two huge crags from the top of Mt. Parnassus crashing down upon the troops, who promptly fled the scene in panicked disarray. Commentators on Herodotus say that there is no truth in any of this, that the Persians would not have attacked Delphí because its oracle was leaning toward the Persians and the area's soldiers had already joined Xerxes' forces, as had most of the country north of Athens. The commentators add that the story was probably cooked up later on to bring the always-important oracle back in line on the Greek side. On the other hand, Herodotus, who was writing his *Histories* some forty years later, said that he had gone to Delphí and seen the fallen rocks. But in those early days of rational, scientific research, what really mattered—for him and for the Greeks in general—was not so much the actual facts (which they knew could never be fully known) but what they were said to be by tradition, by the myths, legends, and other stories that had come down about a particular event. To them, this was what we call history.

Meanwhile—to continue Herodotus's delightful version of the story—the Persian fleet was meeting with similar catastrophes. As its ships arrived off the coast of Évia for an expected rendezvous with the badly delayed army, the winds that Zeus had instructed the Delphians to pray for suddenly arrived—a monstrous gale, brought by Boreás, the God of the North Wind, which smashed their ships upon the rocks and sank almost four hundred of them, nearly one third of the armada. Then, when the survivors thought they had found safe anchorage in a bay on the coast of Thessaly, Zeus deluged the terrified seamen with rain and a nightlong barrage of thunder and lightning sent down from the summit of nearby Mt. Pelion. In the morning, the sea was awash with corpses and the flotsam of another two hundred wrecked ships. "God," wrote Herodotus, "was indeed doing everything possible to reduce the superiority of the Persian fleet and bring it down to the size of the Greek." While Zeus's actions are part of the tradition that Herodotus believed in, it is also true that this and the subsequent, miraculous defeat of the Persians actually happened. As for the god's role in it all, that depended on which side you were on.

When the Persian army finally reached Athens, it was—as Delphí's oracle had predicted—easily able to sack the city and burn the temples on the Acropolis. But in the subsequent sea battle in the narrow straits of Salamís—presaged by an earthquake on the morning of the encounter—the Persians' lumbering triremes were deftly outmaneuvered by the "wooden wall" of smaller Greek vessels and completely destroyed. Within a year, the last of the Persian army had been withdrawn from the Greek mainland, leaving the Greeks—in particular, the mighty Athenian fleet—as undisputed masters of the entire Aegean.*

At the same time, the Greeks were happy to affirm that even though the heroic efforts of their soldiers, sailors, and generals had clearly defeated the Persians, it was the great hand of Zeus the Savior that had been behind every single victory. Eight years later, in 472 B.C., the Athenian playwright Aeschylus, who had been a soldier in the Persian Wars, would have a chorus of Persians lament their stunning defeat as follows:

---

* While Athens had been sacked, its army and fleet were left virtually unscathed. At the same time, the Spartans were perfectly content to withdraw to their comfortable redoubt in the Peloponnese, their cherished isolation and independence apparently preserved. However, for the Persians, it wasn't a defeat at all, but a great victory, and in their schools, it is still taught as such: The Persians had invaded Greece, annihilated the Spartans and their king at Thermopylae, looted and burned Athens, and enslaved the innumerable prisoners they took. Of course, there had been that little setback at Salamís, but by and large, they had done well. The empire was still dominant throughout the Middle East and would remain that way for another century and a half, while the Greeks' experiment in democracy would consume itself in about seventy-five years. Then, of course, there was the coming of that infernal Iskander, whom the Greeks called "Alexander the Great." But that is another story.

Thy hand, O Zeus our king, has swept from sight
The boastful pride of Persia's vast array,
And veiled the streets of Susa
In gloomy mists of mourning.

The Golden Age of Classical Greece had begun. And shortly after this, at Olympía, the first great mainland temple to Zeus—wonder of the world—would begin rising from the earth to embody and embrace the grandeur of it all.

22

THE WONDER OF THE WORLD

I belong to Zeus.

INSCRIPTION ON A VICTOR'S STATUE, C. 495 B.C.

Before this time, Zeus's all-encompassing magnificence had made it unthinkable to confine him within a man-made structure—even to a single place. Sacrifices were made to the god only on outdoor altars with no adjacent temples, and whenever a city-state held a festival in his honor, its authorities would be careful to stage the event outside the city limits. But both the magnitude of Zeus's contribution to the great victory over the Persians and a pressing need to once again bring all the Greeks—who were beginning to chafe under the supremacy of a growing Athenian empire—to a common celebratory table, made a grand temple to the god at Olympía seem a matter of divine will. Ironically—or fittingly, depending on your point of view—the temple would be funded at the expense of devotees of the Great Mother, the people of the neighboring city-state of Pisa, who had previously graced the sacred Altis with a shrine to Héra, its cult statue the goddess seated on her throne with a diminutive Zeus standing consortlike at her side. Pausanias tells us that when the city-state of Elis defeated Pisa to gain undisputed control of the area, it offered the spoils of Pisa's treasury to fund a shrine created solely for Zeus. It and its cult image were intended as the most magnificent tribute to a deity ever created.

The temple alone would take ten years to build. It was 95 feet wide, 230 feet long, and, at 68 feet, the height of a six-story building. The trunks of its thirty-four exterior columns were 7 feet in diameter at the base and 34 feet high—two and a half times those of Héra's temple across the way. Inside—in the inner sanctum, or *cella*, where the statue of the Olympian Zeus would eventually sit—were another eight columns. Although the stone out of which its columns and foundation had to be fashioned was a gray and undistinguished local conglomerate, a thin layer of stucco was used to make it appear marble. Meanwhile, the roof was weighted with the real thing, hauled all the way from the prestigious Athenian quarry on Mt. Pentéli. Also made of marble were its more than one hundred water spouts, each carved in the shape of open-mouthed lion's heads. A gilded figure of Níke, the Goddess of Victory, crowned the peak of the front, or east, pediment. Below this, sculpted in bas-relief, Zeus stood calmly and majestically between two former kings of the Peloponnese, Pélops and his predecessor, Inómaos, whom Pélops had murdered to take the throne.

But once the temple was completed, the god's devotees would then have to wait at least another thirteen years to see how the great Athenian sculptor Phidias would create an effigy of the god grand and fitting enough to fill its interior.

PHIDIAS

Phidias was already celebrated for helping Pericles rebuild Persian-ravaged Athens into the envy of the Mediterranean world. In 447–38 B.C., he had overseen the construction of all the major edifices on the Acropolis, including the Propyleum (entranceway) and Parthenon, and had himself designed and built the magnificent gold and ivory statue of Athína which now stood in the temple's interior.

If we are to believe Plutarch, Phidias's story ends at this point, before he can even create the statue of Zeus. It seems that rival politicians' fierce resentment of Pericles' prestige and power resulted in attacks on a number of his closest associates, Phidias included. Accused of stealing some of the gold used to make Athína's statue, Phidias was brought to trial. Even though he was exonerated when all the statue's gold was taken off and weighed, he was sent to prison, where, says Plutarch, he died.

This story was given complete credence until 1958, when the long-lost workshop of Phidias at Olympía (mentioned by Pausanias) was found beneath a fifth-century Byzantine church. Subsequent discoveries, including that of a cup labeled I AM OF [BELONG TO] PHIDIAS have established beyond a reasonable doubt that the sculptor was alive and well and at Olympía working on the statue of Zeus in about 435 B.C. One way or the other, either by fleeing Athens or by being allowed to go freely into exile, Phidias had made it to Olympía to create the masterwork of his own times and many another to come.

Like the construction of the temple, the fashioning of Zeus's statue would take a decade or more. The workshop was built in the exact dimensions of the temple's *cella** in order to allow Phidias to mold and assemble the statue's outer shell of gold and ivory upon an inner framework of wood before dismantling the colossus and carting it across to the temple, about 150 yards to the east.

The effigy was then reassembled at the far end of the sanctuary's 200-foot length. Zeus was 40 feet tall even when seated upon his throne of ebony, gold, and ivory; his head reached to within inches of the 43-foot ceiling, high as a four-story building; and his shoulders nearly touched the columns on either side, a spread of 21 feet. The final effect was of a force much too grand to be contained by a building even as immense as his sanctuary, as if he could at any moment

---

* The building's shape, unusual for a Byzantine church, was one of the clues that led to the workshop's discovery.

stand and shatter this puny attempt by his worshippers to pin their sovereign deity down to an actual place and time.

Zeus's head, limbs, and powerfully muscled torso were sculpted entirely of ivory. In his left hand, he grasped a jeweled scepter made of precious metals, on top of which was perched a golden eagle, symbol of his power. In the palm of his upturned right hand stood a gold and ivory figure of Níke. Across his loins lay a robe of beaten gold, fashioned to fall just above his ankles. His feet were shod with golden sandals and his brow crowned with finely wrought golden olive branches. Two golden lions sat at his feet, while before him lay a long, rectangular reflecting pool in which the god's image shimmered on a surface of glistening, flower-scented olive oil.

He was vibrant with divinity—a golden-haired, bearded giant in the prime of his life, who seemed to have left his violent, promiscuous, and all-too-human youth behind him to focus on grander, more godly concerns. As he sat on his throne, gaze fixed far above the heads of his supplicants, he appeared to be measuring matters that only a god as great as he could comprehend, alone in the realm of Absolute Power, embodied by his massive, awesome effigy.

It was said that when the exhausted Phidias stepped back to view what was clearly his life's crowning achievement, he prayed to the god for a sign to show whether he was pleased—whereupon Zeus sent a bolt of lightning crashing to the ground to signal his approval. The Greeks would later mark this most sacred spot with a bronze urn, which Pausanias testifies was still there centuries later.

The statue of the Olympian Zeus instantly became the focal point of veneration for the entire Greek world. Pilgrims journeyed year-round to this remote corner of the northwest Peloponnese to offer their homage, coming from as far away as the shores of Spain, North Africa, the Middle East, and the Black Sea. All who entered his temple—emperors, peasants, and even the most world-weary of travelers and skeptical of philosophers—were so awed by the grandeur of the god's presence that they ranked the Pyramids of Egypt and the Hanging Gardens of Babylon with the Olympian Zeus as what were then the world's three great wonders.

THE RITUALS

Once the temple was complete and the statue installed, the athletes marked their participation in the Games with two visits to the god. The first, scheduled on the morning after their arrival in Olympía, was a swearing-in ceremony which took place at dawn, not at the temple but in front of the open-air altar of Zeus Órkios, God of Oaths. On the altar lay the dismembered corpse of a wild boar, its entrails spilling out over the stone slab on which it had been butchered, body parts sliced open so that the communicants could take their vows with palms flat upon the glistening flesh. Pausanias tells us that the statue of the god behind the altar—much smaller than that of the Olympian Zeus—was calculated to be "the image of Zeus most likely to strike terror into the hearts of sinners." Bronze body rippling in the light of flames, silver thunderbolts poised in either hand, the Great Thunderer stood ready to incinerate anyone who dared violate his dictum of fair play in the Games.

The second visit to the god (and the first to his temple) took place on the fifth and final day of the festival, when the individual victors were brought before the Olympian Zeus, himself permanently crowned with a golden wreath of olive branches in recognition of his victory over Krónos. Here, the athletes received their own coronation with branches cut and woven from the sacred olive tree planted in the Altis so long before by Hérakles; they were then showered with leaves and flowers by the spectators ringing the gallery. Thus, in this most solemn and joyous of ceremonies, the victors offered up their triumphs to the all-conquering god and, in return, received his triumphal blessings.

FUN AND GAMES

As the festival's popularity grew, however, and its scope expanded, the proceedings inevitably became much more about fun, games, and profit than about thanking Zeus for his divine protection and bounty. As we have seen, the central act of the first Olympic festivals had been the ritual sacrifice of one hundred oxen to the god, a feast which was said to have been attended by Zeus himself. But in the Games' heyday of the sixth to fourth centuries B.C., when an estimated forty thousand hungry revelers crowded the sanctuary, it is doubtful that the Great Thunderer would have made an appearance. Not in the foul and raucous mess the festival had become, packed with sweaty, odorous bodies jousting for every bit of flesh they could grab on to, human and/or animal, muddying the ground with their reeking wastes, and shattering Olympía's sacred peace with their incessant celebratory din of song and dance dedicated to the miracle of being Greek.

Nor would the god have been likely to attend the much more exclusive round of parties given to fete the Games' victors on the festival's final evening. Here, the winners hobnobbed as near equals with the aristocratic elite, discussing the rewards they would be given back home—the statues, stipends, and advancements toward new careers in politics or business or even the priesthood. Amid such earthly concerns, chances were that the Great Father of gods and men might have been completely overlooked. In the old days, everything had been dedicated to the god, with even the statues of the victors that were set up in the Altis inscribed, I BELONG TO ZEUS. Later, as these effigies became more realistic, more about the actual person than the god to whom he was supposed to owe obeisance, all such pretenses were dropped along with the inscription.

But Zeus still had his temple, the most magnificent in the world. That, they couldn't take away from him.

Not yet, anyway.

23

THE DYING FALL

What was scattered
Gathers,
What was gathered
Blows apart.

HERACLITUS, *Fragment 40*

The demise of Zeus's two-thousand-year reign was, in its final, violent, and often bizarre centuries, most poignantly played out at Olympía and Delphí. Even as Phidias was assembling his colossal tribute to the Olympian Zeus, and the Games were expanding to three other venues; even as other magnificent monuments to man and the gods were being raised throughout Greece and achievements in the arts and sciences were guaranteeing immortality for their creators; and even as Zeus was being hailed as Greece's Savior, the Greek mainland was becoming increasingly ravaged by internal conflicts. The worst of these were the two catastrophic Peloponnesian Wars between Athens and Sparta, which raged off and on from 460 to 404 B.C. and would eventually suck in nearly all the Greek city-states as well as some of their colonies and, in its final throes, even Persia.

Historians, including the original recorder of the wars' history, the

Athenian general Thucydides, agree that the hostilities had been provoked by Athens's attempts to impose its will on as much of Greece as it possibly could. So blatant was Athens's arrogance in this regard, and so brutal were its suppressions of dissent among its allies that even Zeus was moved to side with the Spartans. Through the voice of his oracle at Delphí, he promised that "victory would be theirs . . . and that He himself would be with them, whether invoked or uninvoked."

Although Sparta finally did prevail, the furies spawned during the wars would continue to suck the lifeblood out of both sides. In 399, Athens's storied experiment in democracy would come to an end with the death of the seventy-year-old philosopher Socrates in an Athenian dungeon, drinking a poisonous brew of the herb hemlock as ordered by a jury of 501 of his fellow citizens. He had been condemned for claiming that he had been privy to the word of the god through what he called his *daímon,* giving him directives that could be neither ignored nor denied.

However, in contrast to the destruction that Zeus had visited upon the Mycenaean Empire after Troy, this time the cause was clearly not the gods but man and his confused graspings for power. As a result, the now-completed colossus of the Olympian Zeus—already surreal with its radiant ivory flesh and golden locks—would increasingly be seen more as a spiritual force than a physical one—rising ever higher into the heavenly realms of eternal truths and universal laws, where his near-monotheistic sovereignty seemed to offer the best and perhaps only hope for peace and justice, as this fourth-century-B.C. hymn to Zeus makes poignantly clear:

Zeus, ruler of nature, that governest all things with law . . .
Thou dost harmonize into One, all good and evil things,
That there should be one everlasting Reason of them all . . .
O Zeus, the All-giver, dweller in darkness of cloud,
Lord of thunder, save Thou men from their unhappy folly.

In substance and supremacy, Zeus was, in fact, beginning to bear a remarkable resemblance to his contemporary in Judea, an ineffable Jewish god whom some called Jehovah.

At the same time, the more worldly pronouncements from his oracle at Delphí were sounding less like the Word of God than muffled echoes from a tomb—an acknowledgment, perhaps, of what the god knew was coming. Over the next eight hundred years, there would follow, in fits and starts, the long, slow destruction of the rest of the glories that had been Greece, torn to pieces in a series of natural and man-made disasters that would end, in A.D. 395, with the literal dismemberment of the great Olympian himself.

THE MACEDONIANS

In 373 B.C., Delphí's magnificent Temple of Apóllon was leveled by an earthquake, rockfalls, fire, and flood. Eventually, it would be rebuilt, but by that time, two lengthy wars had been fought between various city-states trying to gain control of its riches. When the dust finally settled, in 337 B.C., the victors were upstart interlopers from the savage wilds north of Mt. Ólympus: a one-eyed Macedonian king named Philip II and his eighteen-year-old scion, Alexander. Although these "Macedons" were said by Hesiod to have been fathered by Zeus and spoke a rough brand of Greek, they were still regarded by the Greeks of the more sophisticated south as more than a bit beyond the pale. In the face of such snobbery, the victorious Philip and Alexander populated Olympía's Sacred Precinct with statues of the Macedonian royal line, fashioning them all, most tellingly, of gold and ivory—just like that of the Olympian Zeus across the way—while also raising a large, circular edifice nearby ostensibly as a votive offering to the Father of Gods and Men. But it was called, naturally, the Philippaeum.

A year later, Philip was assassinated, and three years after that, in 334 B.C., Alexander set out on his long, fatal march to conquer Asia.

The campaign would last twelve years. During its course, Alexander visited Zeus's oracle at Ammon in the Libyan desert. From here, he would send forth the word (and have it announced at Olympía) that he had learned from the oracle that he was, in fact, not a son of Philip at all, but instead, the son of Zeus, the last of the Great Thunderer's long line of illustrious offspring.

In 323 B.C., after torching the Persian capital of Persepolis, penetrating the thickets of India, and attempting to make his own soldiers prostrate themselves before him as sign of his divinity, the thirty-two-year-old Alexander came to his mortal end in Babylon, between the two rivers of what is today the graveyard of Iraq.

THE GOD'S LAST STAND

From 323 to 280 B.C., the wars fought between Alexander's generals, the Diádochi (Successors), for control of his conquered territories resulted in widespread anarchy in mainland Greece and attempts at plundering both Olympía and Delphí. In 279 B.C., the barbarian Gauls, taking advantage of this disarray, invaded from the north with an army of about two hundred thousand men and marched straight down the Greek mainland to plunder Delphí's Sacred Precinct. The Delphians, in a state of panic, consulted their oracle, but—just as he had during the Persian invasion—the god told them not to worry, that he would deal with the barbarians himself. Shortly afterward, the earth began to shudder in a daylong series of violent quakes. These were accompanied by an incessant barrage of thunder and lightning, the latter striking groups of Gauls, setting them and their shields on fire. As night fell, so, too, did rocks and entire crags from the surrounding mountains, crushing scores of soldiers as they huddled by the cliff against a fierce blizzard that had come roaring down from the heights. By morning, this relentless terror had driven the invaders completely insane. Mistaking each other for the enemy, they attacked their comrades in an orgy of mutual slaughter, killing, Pausanias tells us, more than sixteen thousand of their number. After their commander committed suicide, the rest withdrew, pursued by the Greek forces. Along the route, many more died of hunger, and in the end, not a single Gaul survived the retreat.

While this was an actual, historical event, it also seems to have been a final earthly visitation by the god, his last stand, as it were. Never again would Zeus be said to have summoned up such a vigorous defense of his homeland, nor put his powers so spectacularly on display. The Romans were coming, and as their forces gradually crushed all of Greece into submission, even Zeus seemed to give up hope of stopping them. But he would never abandon his patriotism.

THE ROMANS

In 80 B.C., the Roman general and dictator Sulla made the mistake of trying to transfer the Olympic Games permanently to Rome, but before he could complete the change, he was struck down by a burst abscess. Later, the mad emperor Caligula (A.D. 12–41) entertained similarly misguided ideas. Having previously ordered his own head placed upon the statues of various gods and goddesses throughout the empire, he attempted to install an effigy of himself as Zeus in the inner sanctum of the Jewish temple in Jerusalem. When this failed due to massive local resistance, Caligula instead ordered Zeus's colossal statue at Olympía to be dismantled and transported to Rome, where he intended to place it before the Forum with, as usual, his own head on top. However, as workmen were at Olympía preparing to dismantle the statue, the Great Thunderer "suddenly uttered such a peal of laughter that the scaffolding collapsed and the workmen took to their heels." Sometime afterward, two Roman colonels, shouting the god's name,* were among the group of assassins who knifed the emperor to death as he walked through the Forum.

The next imperial ruler to try his luck at Olympía and Delphí was Nero (A.D. 37–68), purportedly as insane as Caligula, although guided by different priorities. Nero fancied himself a great singer and lyre player, and when he had (literally and figuratively) exhausted his audience in Rome, he announced that "only the Greeks have an ear for music and are alone worthy of my efforts." Whereupon, he boarded a ship and headed for the promised land. At Olympía, Nero broke tradition by inserting a series of artistic events into the heretofore athletics-only competitions. Worse, he entered every single song contest. Inasmuch as none of the spectators were allowed to leave during his excruciating and interminable performances, it was said that during their enforced attendance, several women gave birth while other members of the audience feigned sudden death in order to be carried away. Nero also fancied himself a charioteer and was, of course, ruled the winner of the sole race he entered, even though he fell off his vehicle and failed to finish. Afterward, he had all the statues and busts of the previous victors in the event removed and tossed into the public cesspool. As a parting gift, however, he favored the judges with large sums of money and granted the entire province Roman citizenship.

During this visit to Greece, Nero also starred at Delphí's Pythian Games and, in the process, looted some five hundred of the sanctuary's best statues to send to his palace in Rome. It was also said, perhaps apocryphally, that when the Pythia refused to admit him to her Inner Sanctum because he had murdered his mother, the insulted emperor retaliated by having the sacred fissure stuffed with dead bodies.

Inevitably, Nero got his comeuppance. In A.D. 68, after the Roman Senate declared him an enemy of the state and condemned him to death by torture, he was driven to commit suicide by sticking a sword in his own throat—with, it should be noted, his private secretary's zealous

* That is, "Jupiter!"

assistance. But these pollutions of Zeus's sites by foreign despots had done their damage. By the middle of the second century A.D., the god's reputation was so sullied that the Greek satirist Lucian had no qualms at all about writing: "Oh, Zeus . . . where are your crackling lightning and your roaring thunder now? . . . Your much vaunted, far-ranging and ever-ready weapon has—I know not how—lost its fire and grown cold and possesses now not even a tiny spark of anger against evil-doers . . . nobody sacrifices to you now and nobody crowns you save perhaps an occasional victor at the Olympics . . . In short, they will soon depose you, most noble god, and cast you in the role of [castrated] Cronus."

24

FIRES FROM HEAVEN

To Olympus, which they say is the everlasting home of the gods.
Here no wind beats roughly, and neither rain nor snow can fall;
but it abides in everlasting sunshine and in a great peacefulness of light,
wherein the blessed gods are illumined for ever and ever.

HOMER, *Odyssey*

By the time Fárzaneh and I reached Litóhoro, the base-village of Mt. Ólympus, the streetlamps were being switched on even though it was only six p.m. The weather, which is always perverse around the mountain, looked more like winter than April. A heavy mist had moistened the asphalt so that it gleamed with reflected rivulets of the white, red, green, and blue lights from the neon signs in a horde of shops, cafés, restaurants, discos, and hotels crowding the town center. But the sidewalks were almost empty. This was the halfway season, the lull between Easter and the coming flood of summer tourists. Behind and above the town, a necklace of streetlamps curved upward, then faded into grayish, low-hanging clouds. Beyond all of this, the mountain loomed in darkness, its presence more felt than seen, visible only as something thicker and blacker than the evening sky.

Nearly three weeks had passed since we had chanced upon Pericles' travel agency in Athens. Now we were making the final pilgrimage of our journey, a visit to the home of the gods, to see not only the mountain but, more important, a second-century-B.C. statue of Zeus recently unearthed at the nearby archaeological site of Dion. The find had been trumpeted in the press as a highly significant discovery, the first ever found that was dedicated to "Zeus the Highest," which is to say, to Zeus worshipped as a monotheistic god some two centuries before the birth of Christ. In a way, it was the missing link between the Olympian gods and the Christian trinity.

The hotel that Pericles had sent us to turned out to be not, as he had said, in Litóhoro but some five miles eastward, toward the coast and one hundred yards or so inland from the chilly waters of the Thermäikos Gulf. It was a modest, three-story edifice whose acre or so of property was marked off from a series of as-yet-undeveloped plots by a low, cinder-block wall topped with chicken wire. At the base of the wall were piles of paint-spattered planks and pieces of scaffolding. In the tiny lobby, a tang of fresh whitewash lingered in the air, like a harbinger of spring. Behind the reception desk was a mural of Mt. Ólympus, painted with a childlike, god's-eye perspective from a few miles out above the Aegean. In the artist's rendering, the sky was a bright baby-blue. Fluffy white cumulus clouds gathered over the light frosting of snow that covered the massif's peaks, while squiggly ribbons of a few red and white lines festooned its apple-green slopes, marking the trails and road upward and making the mountain look as festive and harmless as a birthday cake.

Later, I would learn that the hotel's aging owner—whom I shall call Aléxandros—had once made a business of guiding mountain climbers to its several summits. So even though Pericles may have stuck us in these out-of-the-way lodgings miles from the mountain, he had fortuitously placed us right in the lap of someone who knew just about everything there was to know concerning Ólympus. Since Pericles had never mentioned this important fact, it is doubtful he was aware of it. The Fates, however, most certainly had been.

On our first morning at the hotel, Aléxandros introduced himself as we were breakfasting in the otherwise deserted dining room. "*Morgen!*" he boomed in German, marching toward us from the lobby. Everything about him, including his shock of pure white hair, was thick, gnarled, and sturdy, like the trunk of an ancient olive tree. He was eighty-two, he would proudly announce, and had spent his entire life on and around Ólympus. His eyes were a Nordic blue, like many Macedonians of ancient stock, and his skin permanently ruddy from years of weathering. When you shook his hand, it was like grasping a warm chunk of rock. He apologized for the scaffolding lying around outside. We were the first visitors of the season. His daughter and her husband ran the place, he said. He was just an old man now, with nothing much to do, which was why he had come to talk to us. He liked to speak with strangers, to learn about the outside world.

When I explained, first, that we were American, not German, and, second, that we were there researching a book about Zeus, Aléxandros was delighted. He knew all about the mountain, he said, and he had a nephew, Kóstas, who had been working for years on the excavations at Dion and could tell us everything we wanted to know. And if we wanted, he continued, he could find someone to take us to the summit of Ólympus.

The latter, I hastily assured him, wouldn't be necessary. First, we hadn't brought the right clothes or shoes. Second, we didn't have time for what would have to be an overnight trek. And third, all I needed, anyway, was a little information. What I failed to mention, on the other hand, was the somewhat embarrassing fact that I had already attempted the ascent years before but had turned back in a sweaty-palmed panic at the very first refuge stop, having spent most of the eleven-mile drive up to that point desperately hugging the inside cliff face of the mountain's narrow dirt-and-gravel road, the outside edge of which skirted a sheer drop of perhaps a thousand feet, with no shoulder, no guardrail, not even a bush or two to stop you from being sucked out into the beckoning vacuum. So on this particular morning, when Fárzaneh and I had awoken to find the weather even worse than the day before, with thick, gray clouds now hanging more than halfway down the mountain and the lowlands sopping wet with mist, I couldn't have been happier. Now I would be able to honestly tell my agent and my editor that even though I had intended to make the trip to the summit of Ólympus, to what was called the "Throne of Zeus," the weather had made it completely impossible.

I motioned to Aléxandros to pull up a chair and asked him if there were any artifacts near the summit—cult items similar to ones found atop other mountains throughout Greece. "Any temples to Zeus, altars, statues—those kinds of things?"

He peered at me for a moment, carefully, as if judging my worthiness to hear what he was about to reveal. Then he leaned forward, motioning for us to do the same, even though there was no one within earshot. "There were many things up there," he said. "Many things—temples, golden statues, many treasures." He paused, then lowered his voice even further, to a guttural whisper. "But they took them all away."

"The archaeologists?" I asked. "The government?"

Aléxandros shook his head.

"Who, then?"

He smiled. And stuck his thick index finger straight up toward the sky.

"*They* did."

"The . . . gods?"

He sat back, arched a knowing Greek eyebrow, and shrugged. "Who are we to say? They came down from the sky thousands of years ago and landed up there"—he pointed in the direction of Ólympus—"on a *kosmodrómio*, an airfield for ships from other planets." He leaned forward again, eyes glittering. "Who else do you think built the pyramids and the big walls at Mycenae, Tíryns, and the Acropolis? The Cyclops? Ordinary human beings like us? Bah!" Then he settled back in his chair, knowing he had us hooked. "So they stayed for a while," he said, "had children with some of us—demigods, we called them, like Achilles and Hérakles—and then, when they left, they took all the gold statues that were on top of Ólympus with them. To their galaxy."

There was an enormous silence as he studied our reaction, Fárzaneh and I sitting with what we hoped was a look of respectful astonishment, not daring to even glance at each other. Abruptly, Aléxandros clapped a thick palm on the tabletop and stood up. "But let me call my nephew," he said with a satisfied grin. "He knows more than me."

Northern Greece has always been fertile soil for any number of mysterious religious persuasions. Bordered by the Ólympus massif in the south, the Balkans in the north, and Turkey to the east, it is very much a place apart: brooded over by the thickly forested mountains, ridden with bears and boars, and pocketed with enclaves of peoples—such as the nomadic Sarakatsáns and the few Muslims remaining from the Ottoman occupation—who prefer to keep to themselves. In the old days of Philip and Alexander, the area was known for the ferocity of its warriors, both the Macedonians and the Thracians, with the latter considered particularly barbarous. Gray-eyed and red-haired, they not only tattooed themselves and offered human sacrifices, but ate—of all things foreign to this olive-saturated country—butter.

The region has three holy mountains—Ólympus, Áthos, and Fengári—each of which early on attracted worshippers who gathered in cults around its base. Mt. Fengári, on the island of Samothrace, had the sanctuary of the powerful and demonic Kabíri, ancient deities whose rites, perhaps the oldest in all Greece, were conducted in a strange, non-Greek tongue, with gods that had no names.* The mountain peninsula of Áthos, in turn, was said to have been the home of Zeus and Apóllon before they moved to Ólympus. Later, it was believed to have been visited by the Virgin Mary, blown there in A.D. 49 by a storm as she was sailing from Joppa to Cyprus with St. John the Evangelist to visit Lazarus. The Virgin was so taken by Áthos's beauties that she asked her son to grant it to her. He immediately complied, giving it to her as her garden, "a haven of salvation for those wanting to be saved." Which is why it now hosts twenty monasteries and a number of individual hermitages, while forbidding the presence (except for the Virgin) of any and all females, including chickens.

Northern Greece was also the birthplace of the sainted minstrel Orpheus, who would return here after having failed to bring his beloved Eurydice back from the Underworld. And it was through here that Diónysos made his triumphant return from Asia, on his way south with his wild, wine- and blood-soaked orgies to upset the rational applecart of Greece's Archaic and Classical ages. When the king of Thrace, Lykúrgos, refused to acknowledge his divinity, Diónysos had the man's subjects take him into the mountains and feed him to wild horses. It was even said that some of Diónysos's female followers, the maenads, so lusted after quiet, gentle Orpheus that they tore him to pieces in a frustrated amorous frenzy, then nailed his severed head to a lyre and tossed both into a river, where the head floated down to the sea, still singing.

Afterward, Diónysos would continue on to his birthplace of Thebes, where he would subject its king, Pentheus, to a similar dismemberment. This time the maenads were joined by the king's maddened aunts,

---

* Prométheus was a Kabíri, and Zeus was said to have mated here with Eléktra, the daughter of Atlas, to sire both Dárdanos, the ancestor of the Trojans, and Harmonía, who would later marry Kadmos on the same island. Among its members were Philip and Olympías, Alexander the Great's father and mother, who were said to have fallen under each other's spell at the ceremonies and may have conceived their godlike son that very night. Hadrian also made a pilgrimage here, as did the Apostle Paul, who stopped by in A.D. 49 on his first visit to Greece.

who played catch with chunks of his flesh while Pentheus's equally batty mother proudly paraded her son's severed head stuck atop a pole.*

Nowadays, the region hosts the strange rituals of the Fire Dancers of Thrace, famous for the trancelike state that enables them to dance barefoot over a wide bed of white-hot coals without being burned. As part of their observances, the celebrants slit the throat of a black bull or goat and let its blood pour down into a basin set into the ground outside the local church. Watching this, one can easily understand how deeply rooted these rites are in the region's pre-Christian past, perhaps going even farther back than Zeus himself.

At the same time, Mt. Ólympus continues to attract its share of sects: a commune of Jehovah's Witnesses from Boston has settled in the area, and every summer, an annual gathering of modern-day Zeus worshippers comes to the mountain's base to honor not only the twelve Olympian gods but also, most specifically, Prométheus for his having brought fire down the mountain to mankind. So our hotel owner's belief in godlike aliens landing on Ólympus was not at all that far off the region's already well-beaten path to otherworldly powers.

Aléxandros's nephew met us at the entrance to Dion's archaeological site. Kóstas was a hefty, shaggy dog of a man in his early thirties, with a bushy black mustache and a prematurely balding pate. His eyes, behind a pair of thick, horn-rimmed glasses, were warm, brown, and intensely focused, as if he was afraid that at any second he might miss something of great importance. He was a native of the village of Dion, he would tell us later, the son of a farmer. He had started off as a teenager doing odd jobs in the digs and had now graduated to a position of some

* The "pole" was the sacred *thyrsus*—a giant, ivy-covered staff of fennel often tipped with a metal point.

authority. Exactly what, I was never able to determine, but he certainly seemed to know his way around. And he spoke excellent English.

"Sorry," he said, "but I could not arrange for the museum to open early for you to see the statue. So we must wait an hour. Perhaps you would like to walk around the site first." He gestured toward the lush, green, tree-dotted landscape before us. "I can show you where Zeus's original sanctuary was, where we found his statue."

Dion, whose name means "City of God," is saturated, literally and figuratively, with Zeus's divinity. The springs of his daughters, the Nine Muses, fed by underground runoffs from the mountain, bubble up around the area, and the river that borders its eastern edge was said to have flowed with the blood of his grandson Orpheus, the Muses having buried his body parts somewhere in the area.* Here, in 2003, workmen digging to broaden the river and diminish the danger of floods accidentally stumbled upon Zeus's statue and temple, hidden beneath its hardened silt for some 2,200 years.

At the time of our visit, the river, only a few yards across, was running high, and the pillowy-green expanse of the entire one-hundred-acre site was so waterlogged in parts that we often had to cross on planks and the stones of earthquake-toppled walls to make our way from one shrine to another. The grounds, originally and solely sacred to the Great Mother, had been officially dedicated to Zeus in c. 413 B.C. by the Macedonian king Archelous I. Afterward, it became the spiritual center of the mighty Macedonian Empire of Philip II and his son, Alexander, and it was from here that Alexander and his army embarked, with Zeus's blessings, on their conquest and demolition of Persia. It was also here that Alexander was planning, as stated in his

* The river which carried Orpheus's head down to the sea is the Évros, on the border between Thrace and Turkey.

will, to build a grand temple in honor of the Great Thunderer, who had, by that time, been revealed as his true father.

Today, there are only crumbled vestiges of the relatively tiny temple that was eventually built to Zeus a century or so after Alexander's death. At the same time, however, Dion's size and importance continued to grow, as public and private buildings proliferated, well-fortified walls surrounded its perimeters, and sanctuaries sprang up everywhere: to Deméter, Ártemis, Aphrodite, Eros, and Asklepiós, the God of Healing, as well as to Isis, Sarapis, and Anubis, brought to Dion as a result of Alexander's conquests of Egypt. Diónysos, too, is here in the form of a splendid floor mosaic depicting him naked aboard his panther-drawn chariot, wineglass in hand, speeding across the sea.

Although the city was razed by invaders in the second century B.C., it was rebuilt and its sanctity treated with great respect by the all-conquering Romans. Awareness of the area's holiness continued even unto Christian times, when it became the seat of the local diocese and site of at least two basilicas. It was only in the fifth century A.D. that earthquakes and floods finally forced the locals to abandon the area for safer grounds.

Now, although much of the glory is gone (as is the coastline, which is so far to the east that it cannot even be sensed, much less seen), the continuing excavations are slowly but surely turning it into the most important archaeological dig in the country—as evidenced by the large amount of press coverage given the discovery of Zeus's statue in the year 2003.

On our way back to the village and its museum, we passed Dion's great Hellenistic theater. Kóstas told us that it was probably on this very spot, in an earlier construction, that the seventy-eight-year-old Euripides had sat for the first performance of his masterpiece, *The Bacchae*, which vividly recounted the horrible details of Pentheus's dismemberment. Kóstas turned to me. "Do you know the play?"

I nodded.

He asked if I remembered the part where Diónysos, who has appeared amid the Thebans disguised as a man, suddenly vanishes. Then, as his disembodied voice calls for revenge upon Pentheus, who has mocked him, the god sets a pillar of sacred fire burning between the heavens and the earth.

"A little like flames shooting down from the tail of a spaceship, maybe?" I said with a smile—fully expecting, now that the subject was on the table, that Kóstas would join me in making gentle fun of his uncle's imaginings.

But he barely blinked. "Exactly." He glanced up at cloud-shrouded Ólympus and then back at Fárzaneh and me, fixing us with a look of utmost seriousness. "The ancient peoples thought they were gods and called their spaceships 'chariots.'" He shifted his gaze to me. "You must know the books by von Däniken."

This was another surprise. I had thought that Aléxandros was voicing beliefs born out of local superstitions. Instead, uncle and nephew (and who knew how many others in the area) seemed to be drawing their information from the writings of a man, Erich von Däniken, whose *Chariots of the Gods* and other books have been widely discredited—ridiculed, in fact—by everyone in the scientific community for suggesting that visitors from outer space were the "gods" responsible for all the unexplained phenomena on the planet, from the Egyptian and Aztec pyramids to Stonehenge and Easter Island, not to mention many of ancient Greece's monumental structures.

On the other hand, I must admit that I have numerous, well-educated friends in America and England who swear by von Däniken's books. So here we mortals are, still longing for whatever evidence we can get, however flimsy, of Promethean fire power (and godly salvation) having once come down to us from the mountain and translating what we don't understand into the magic of our time, in this case, interplanetary rocket ships. Well, as the great Danish physicist Niels Bohr said about a horseshoe hanging on the wall of his den, "You never know."

Fortunately, before I could answer Kóstas's query about knowing von Däniken, I was saved by a church bell tolling the hour from somewhere within the village.

He glanced at his watch. "Come," he said, "the museum will be open. Time for you to meet our Zeus."

The god's statue took pride of place in the entranceway to the museum's main room, its marble surface gleaming a soft, pale, pinkish beige under the several spotlights that illuminated it from above. As at Olympía, Zeus was seated upon a high-backed throne, upper torso bared, a beautifully sculpted robe draped across his legs and falling to just above his sandaled feet, one foot set slightly forward. But compared to the colossus at Olympía—or even to petite, five-foot-tall Fárzaneh, for that matter—Dion's Zeus was disappointingly small, a bit less than lifesize, so that when you approached, you were looking down on him—as if at a child.

Moreover, he was headless.

"You see what is written," said Kóstas, pointing to letters carved into the statue's base:

ΙΕΡΟ ΥΠΣΙΣΤΟΥ ΔΙΟΣ

"This tells us that he was the highest of the gods," continued Kóstas. "Worshipped as the single god in Heaven, above all others. Almost monotheistic. This statue is a very important discovery. A clear transition between the Olympian religion of the Twelve Gods and the monotheism of the Jews and Christians."

Again, I looked down at Zeus's effigy. So puny, so broken, and such a far cry from all the earlier glory.

"We believe," Kóstas continued, "that he had a lightning bolt in one hand and a scepter in the other."

"What about his head?" I asked, pitilessly.

Kóstas shrugged. "We are still looking for it. They almost certainly carried it off and threw it where no one would ever find it. Probably, with a god as powerful as Zeus, into the sea. So there would be no danger that the head would be found and reattached, the god made whole again. They did that with all the statues they could get their hands on. Beheaded every one."

"Who?" I said.

"You don't know?"

I glanced up at the sky. "Them?"

He smiled.

"No. The aliens tried to preserve things, took what they could away for safekeeping."

"So who did the beheading?"

He seemed somewhat surprised.

"Why, the Christians. Of course."

25

THE FINAL METAMORPHOSIS

"Lord . . . ," I cried, "averter of woe,
Ever a lord thou hast been, and behold, in dust thou art low."
But at night, with a smile on his lips, the god stood by me sublime,
And said, "A god though I be, I serve, and my master is Time."

PALLADAS OF ALEXANDRIA (c. A.D. 319–400)

It had been a long time in coming, this ascent of the Christians to not only the top of the mountain but a position of such absolute power within the Roman Empire that they were able to dictate which faiths could be worshipped and which were to be thrown on the trash heap. Although legitimized by Constantine the Great and his coemperor, Licinius, in 313, the cult of Jesus was initially allowed only a single stall in the crowded marketplace of the empire's religions, with some 90 percent of the populace still favoring a whole panoply of deities, from the pre-Roman hearth goddess Vesta in the West to the bull-slaying Persian god Mithras in the East. This in spite of the fact that Constantine's mother, a devout Christian, had brought the True Cross (and its nails) back from Jerusalem, and that the emperor himself not only had been inspired by a sky-borne sign of the cross to conquer his rivals for the throne, but was baptized into the faith on his deathbed in 337.

While Constantine's sons and successors had done the best they could to weaken worship of what they called the "pagan" religions, issuing numerous edicts shutting down temples and prohibiting such practices as the reading of entrails, they were much too engrossed in killing off the rest of their family (and finally, each other) to keep a check on the pent-up fanaticisms that they had let out of the catacombs. As a result, infighting among Christian sects for supremacy in interpreting Christ's nature and Good News seriously escalated, their battles often making the excesses of the barbarians to the north look delicate by comparison. Riots in Alexandria, Rome, and Constantinople left thousands dead, while unspeakable tortures were visited upon those who refused to convert to their captors' beliefs, with "the mouths of the communicants," according to the great English historian Edward Gibbon, author of *The Decline and Fall of the Roman Empire*, "held open by a wooden engine while the consecrated bread was forced down their throat; the breasts of tender virgins were either burnt with red-hot eggshells, or inhumanly compressed between sharp and heavy boards."

These and similar abominations turned many a potential Christian back into the comforting arms of paganism and its all-embracing deities, while the Caesar of the West, Julian, was emboldened to march his army on Constantinople and restore the empire's glory by putting the old gods and goddesses firmly back on their pedestals. Although Julian was able to push through significant legislation reopening the old temples and guaranteeing freedom of religion, he quickly discovered that the meek, having inherited the earth (and the empire's bureaucracy), were not about to so easily give it up. Within a year, Julian was forced to move his court out of Constantinople to the pagan stronghold of Antioch, in northern Syria. Here, while sacrificing to Zeus on a mountaintop near the city, he claimed that he had encountered the Great Thunderer himself. But not even Zeus could change what the Fates had written, nor what the Delphic oracle had foretold. A year and a half before, when Julian's army was approaching Constantinople, he had dispatched an emissary to obtain the Pythia's blessings on his efforts. The message he received in return was chillingly to the point.

Tell him that Delphí's fair-wrought house has fallen,
No shelter has Apóllon, nor sacred laurel leaves;
The fountains now are silent; the voice is stilled.

In March 363, Julian was killed while campaigning against the Persians in the East. There were even rumors that the spear that did him in was Roman, and that his murderer had been a Christian from within his own ranks.

Seventeen tumultuous years later, in 380, after much infighting among a succession of rulers, the Christian faithful at last had someone of their own fervent persuasions ensconced on Constantinople's throne. A Spaniard by birth and inquisitional temperament, he was called Theodosius (God's Gift), and his first act as emperor was to have himself baptized a Christian. His second was to proclaim his half of the empire Christian as well. And his third, after a period of relative tolerance, was to order the extermination of every remaining sign of pagan worship within his sphere of influence. As a result, over the next fifteen years, his increasingly rabid followers would roam the east, Greece included, looting and destroying all the temples that Julian had reopened, burning a lot of them down and decapitating every pagan statue they could lay their hands on, that of Zeus at Dion among them.

Up to this point, the sanctuaries of the three ancient oracles at Dodóna, Olympía, and Delphí had remained sacrosanct, having stayed open even when the edicts of Constantine's sons were closing down the rest. Nevertheless—as the oracle's reply to Julian had made poignantly clear—the sanctuaries had by now fallen on hard times, depleted of most of their riches and much of their faith.

Dodóna, far off in the northwest, had remained relatively unscathed. Olympía, on the other hand, had suffered considerable damage during the barbarian invasions of the mid-third century

A.D., not only to its surroundings but to its reputation. In addition, the Games had become increasingly secular, now having so little to do with honoring Zeus that when a third stadium was built in about 350 B.C., it was the first to be laid outside the Altis, the god's Sacred Precinct and site of all Olympía's sacrificial altars and temples, including that of the Olympian Zeus. Moreover, since the advent of the Romans, the contests were no longer restricted to those of Greek birth and the Greek faith. Numerous foreign victors were listed during the Games' final years. In fact, the last recorded triumph, in A.D. 385, belonged to a boxer from, of all places, Persia.

Meanwhile, Delphí, after suffering the indignities of Nero, had had a brief renaissance during Hadrian's reign and the residence of Plutarch as its high priest. But by the time Pausanias visited, c. A.D. 160, the sanctuary's most valuable artifacts had been either melted down for money or looted, and its oracle was virtually moribund. At the time, therefore, that Julian had sent his entreaty to Delphí, the Sacred Precinct and its Pythia were, for the most part, little more than curiosities for visiting tourists.

As a result, when Theodosius finally went after these last, oracular bastions of the old faiths, there was little resistance—from either the people or the gods.

At Dodóna, the god's sacred, prophetic oak was uprooted and a huge hole dug underneath, both to search out treasure rumored to be beneath its roots and, more important, to eliminate any chance of the tree's resurrecting itself. At Olympía, the cult of Zeus was banned, and, in 393, the Games, their nudity deemed offensive, were closed down. Subsequently, the temples there and at Delphí were plundered, put to the torch, and reduced to rubble. At the same time, Theodosius ordered Zeus's colossal Olympian statue, the Great Wonder of the World, to be taken apart and carted off to Constantinople, where it would be disposed of at his whim, most likely consigned to the fire, its gold melted down for the royal treasury, and the rest pulverized beyond any possibility of a future restoration.

As it happened (or as the still-operative Fates may have had it), when the statue arrived at Constantinople, Theodosius, who was off in Rome concluding a power grab of the western throne, abruptly reached what Gibbon called "his speedy dissolution," his body swollen with dropsy, most likely the result of congestive heart failure.

While Theodosius's death may have let Zeus's statue off the hook, at least temporarily, it did not spare the god's homeland. A year later, Theodosius's successors ceded Greece to Alaric and his Goths, and in short order, all that remained of the country's Olympian grandeur was buried in barbarian oblivion, as silent as the Pythia herself.

As far as Zeus's statue was concerned, its dismembered pieces seem to have continued to lie in whatever storeroom they had been placed on their arrival from Olympía, dust-laden and nearly forgotten, the god's immense head most probably lolling idiot-like in a corner while rats rustled through the hollows of his limbs and torso.

But the once-great Thunderer would have had at least one visitor that we know of: the lord chamberlain of the emperor, a eunuch named Laúsos. We can assume that Laúsos, unmanned as he was, would have sympathized more than most with the emasculation of this once-mighty deity, now consigned to such humiliation, neglected by the powers that be while they incessantly schemed against each other for dominance in the post-Theodosian empire.

During this period, it must have sometimes seemed to Laúsos that he alone cared about what happened to Zeus and the other magnificent works of pagan art that the empire had in its possession. Perhaps—when Laúsos had been a young and impetuous lower-level member of the court—he had even obtained permission to care for the captive deity by occasionally visiting to bathe its ivory skin with olive oil to protect it against the city's pervasive damp rot. It is entirely possible, in fact, that while he was kneeling beside Zeus, gently caressing his face, torso, and limbs, that the future lord chamberlain had felt the Great Thunderer's presence there in the room with him, hovering around its sacred effigy, just as the ancient Greeks had believed it could. And perhaps this brought the beardless, baby-faced eunuch to experience more reverence for the god than was officially permissible.

In those days, it was dangerous to openly profess fealty for anything pagan. Even speaking the names of the pagan gods was forbidden. In fact, within the court, the only safe stance you could take on the old religions was one of clearly stated contempt. This was especially true if you were lord chamberlain. But Laúsos seems to have been a most pragmatic individual who kept his profile low; he was only rarely mentioned in the annals of the times; when he was, it was his devout Christianity that was pointedly played up, most particularly in his patronage of a book of inspirational stories mostly about the Desert Fathers, which extols him as a "Noble and Christ-beloved servant of God . . . guardian of our holy and revered empire."

No one knows exactly when Laúsos made his move to resurrect the Greek god of gods. What is certain is that sometime in the first decades of the fifth century, Zeus's statue was brought up out of its entombment and reassembled in the portico of the lord chamberlain's palace. There Laúsos would have it hold court in one of the greatest displays of pagan art ever amassed in the 1,200-year history of the Byzantine Empire, one which would include such works as the fourth-century-B.C. statue of Aphrodite by Praxiteles, a Héra of Samos, an Athína from Lindos, a sculpture of Eros from Myndos, and such exotic animal and mythological figures as tigers, giraffes, unicorns, and centaurs.

While Constantine the Great had made a point of adorning his capital with pagan trophies, this had been when Christianity was only a minor cult among many flourishing in the empire.* Laúsos's exhibition, taking place during the most puritanical of Christian regimes, was guaranteed to be not only breathtaking but even scandalous.

* Among Constantine's treasures were the statue of Zeus from Dodóna and the sacred bronze tripods from Delphí.

What seems to have made it permissible was a decision to display the collection not *inside* the palace but *outside* in its portico, right on the Mese, Constantinople's busiest east-west thoroughfare. Here, in the harsh, noisy, dusty daylight of the city, the statues would have been robbed of their mystery, desacralized, and seemingly, like prisoners of war, put on display for public humiliation.

There were also, however, other, deeper factors involved. Recently, cracks had been opening in the uncompromising monotheism that the first Theodosius had imposed upon the region. Civil wars between the ruling factions of the East and West had badly weakened the empire. At the same time, hordes of foreign armies—Persians, Visigoths, Ostrogoths, Vandals, and Huns—were pressing upon the borders from all sides, scavenging for bits and pieces and, increasingly, bloody chunks torn from what they saw as a dying animal.

In addition, the Church, once so pristine in its devotions, was catering more and more to the superstitious needs of its congregations, whose Christian faith had flowered not far from pagan roots. Churches were now becoming lush with gleaming, silver- and gold-plated trappings: icons, incense burners, candelabras, and reliquaries, their air thick with the intoxicating scent of burning wax and incense, and their walls sinuous with frescoes and crowded with dangling stamped-metal images of eyes, hands, feet, legs, and entire bodies, all in need of a miraculous cure from what used to be called a god or goddess but was now known as a saint.

In short, fresh green tendrils of the old faiths were winding their persistent way back into the light even as the walls of Christianity's empire were seen to be crumbling. So the Laúsos collection would have been a further concession to this popularity, ostensibly presented as an homage to the artistic achievements of the empire's rich classical heritage. How visitors privately responded to these images was another matter altogether. There is no question that Laúsos's daring collection, with its naked bodies and other forbidden pagan fruits, would have allowed a huge breath of fresh, illicit air to breeze through the cloistered confines of an empire now controlled by the sworn virgin-in-Christ Pulcheria, older sister of the young and malleable Theodosius II.*

Of course, by that time, Zeus's effigy wasn't in the best of shape. Even if Laúsos or someone else had cared for it all those years, the ivory on its once-immaculate body would by now have been cracked and yellowed, the precious stones plucked out over the centuries. It had even—some scholars speculate—been shorn of its golden accessories: the sandals, robe, crown of olive branches, magnificent beard, and splendid locks, perhaps leaving the god as bald and creaky as the old Greek philosophers. Nevertheless, there was certainly enough life left in the Great Thunderer to inspire someone high up in the Byzantine court—perhaps even one of the emperors who followed Pulcheria—to order the most extraordinary metamorphosis in all the two thousand years of the god's storied, shape-shifting existence: what would be, in effect, his assumption into the highest level of the Christian firmament.

The name of the artist chosen to effect this transmutation is unknown. Doubtless, he was one of many anonymous craftsmen regularly working for the glory of the empire. In making his preliminary sketches, he would have probably gone to Laúsos's palace when the portico was closed to the public, perhaps at night, limning the god by torchlight as the glow from the flames flickered fiery-red and orange across his mighty visage, abolishing all signs of age and deterioration. While we cannot know for sure what the original rendering looked like, what the artist most certainly came away with was a picture of Zeus as the most ancient of the Greeks had feared and adored him, as majestic as in Homer's fearsome vision, "bowing his dark brows, the ambrosial locks swaying on his immortal head, shaking vast Olympus to its core."

* Pulcheria was later made a saint by both the Eastern Orthodox and Roman Catholic churches.

* * *

Byzantine churches are models of the sacred universe. To stand within one is to be overwhelmed by the awesome majesty and beauty of God's creation. Around you, closest to the ground, the walls are filled with frescoes and mosaics of God's earthly aides: the saints, the martyrs, and prophets of the Church. Above them are the archangels, and above these, directly overhead, the Twelve Apostles, who encircle the base of the great dome of Heaven. In the center of this dome, gazing down in all his stern and fatherly grandeur, is Christ Pantocrator, Lord of the Universe.

However, as scholars know, the prototype for this majestic image of Jesus is none other than the Great Thunderer himself, transfigured by the inspired order of an ancient, fifth-century Byzantine emperor into Christianity's absolute ruler of Heaven and Earth, the appellation "Pantocrator" (All-powerful) being the Greek approximation of the Hebrew *El Shaddai*, literally "God of the Mountain."

Unfortunately, we have only imperfect ideas of what the originals of both the Olympian Zeus and the Pantocrator looked like. In fifth and sixth centuries, a series of terrible fires raged through Constantinople, one of which lasted five days and burned down half the city, including the central church of Ághia Sophía, where Zeus's image had most probably first been painted. Also consumed in these fires were Laúsos's palace and its great art treasures, among them Zeus's magnificent effigy. Although there are innumerable subsequent renderings of the Pantocrator, none are more powerful than the one that peers out from the dome of the eleventh-century Church of the Virgin at the monastery of Dáphni outside Athens. As with the magnificent chryselephantine statue of the Olympian Zeus, the piercing gaze of this new Lord of the Universe is clearly measuring concerns that only one as high and mighty as he can comprehend, brow creased, heavy beard turning down the corners of his mouth, dark lines shadowing his eyes. But instead of staring straight ahead, the god is looking warily to his left, as if seeing or hearing something in the distance, something threatening—coming toward him, perhaps, out of the ever-dangerous East.

Zeus, however, has continued to live on in countless other ways, most vividly in the portrayals of him by Nikos Kazantzákis, the renowned twentieth-century Greek writer. Born, like the Great Thunderer, on Crete, Kazantzákis grew up with the god as a near-tangible presence in the daily life of the island, as real to most Cretans as Christ himself. Among the best of his many vivid renderings of Zeus's divinity, Kazantzákis has bequeathed to us the following:

> From yonder, from Africa, came the Notus, the warm south wind which swells out the trees, the vines, and the breasts of Crete. The whole island, as it lay in the water, came to life beneath the warm breath of this wind which makes the sap begin to rise. Zeus, Zorba and the south wind mingled together, and in the night I distinctly saw a great male face, with black beard and oily hair, bending down and pressing red hot lips on Dame Hortense, the Earth.

Αμήν.

ACKNOWLEDGMENTS

To my editors at Bloomsbury, Nick Trautwein and Panio Gianopoulos, first, for their astute understanding of what I wanted to achieve, and second, for contributing mightily, through their most discerning notes and unflagging enthusiasm, to its realization. To my copy editor, Vicki Haire, for the prodigious, painstaking work she did in sorting her way through the labyrinth of Greek names, reference notes, dates, places, and assignations and making sure not only that I got it right but that the readers would, too. And to the managing editor, Greg Villepique, for his much-appreciated patience in allowing me the time to do all that had to be done.

To my agent, Liza Dawson, who suggested that I combine my twin passions for Greek mythology and history with my love of traveling to get up out of my armchair and start on the three-year odyssey of researching and writing this book. And to her and her husband, Havis, for guiding me along the way with not only their editorial expertise but also their precious friendship.

To the masterful Greek archaeologist Iánnis Sakellarákis, for having so graciously offered me his hospitality and deep insights on Greek religion during a long and rainy April afternoon at his Athens apartment; to his former assistants and my former students at Anatolia College in Greece, Michalis Sifakis, now a journalist and filmmaker, and Vangelis Kyriakídis, currently a lecturer in Aegean prehistory at the University of Kent in England, for reappearing in my life just in time to get my researches properly in gear; and to Michalis's wife, Chryssa, and her mother, Zambia, for inviting my wife and me to a sumptuous Easter feast at their Cretan village, which happened to be just a mile down the road from the very spot where, some 4,500 years before, Zeus had ravished the abducted Asian princess, Evrópi. Many thanks, too, to Dimitrios Pandermalis, professor of archaeology at the University of Thessaloniki, a family friend and supervisor of the archaeological site of Dion, who has, over the years, generously offered me his time and much important information about its history and discoveries.

To my children, Samantha and Oliver, for their enduring love and for their belief in my work, even in the darkest of times. To Fárzaneh for more things that have to do with love than I can possibly put in writing, and, in addition, for the many invaluable contributions to this book made by her unique Persian perspective.

To Hal and Judy Prince, whose enthusiasm for things Greek equals mine, for having nevertheless followed the dictates of the Fates in bringing me back again to these shores so that I could do this work. To Sydny Miner, my editor at Simon & Schuster, for the lift-off given me by her faith in *The Summer of My Greek Tavérna*. And to my good friend, the novelist Dick Wimmer, for supporting every step of my efforts with a wise combination of constructive criticism and unabashed jubilation.

NOTES

ABBREVIATIONS USED IN THE NOTES

AOG	The Ancient Olympic Games
ART	Art and Religion in Thera
BOS	The Battle of Salamis
CW	Catalogue of Women
CWH	Fragments: The Collected Wisdom of Heraclitus
DP	Digging for the Past
EB	Encyclopedia Britannica
EBA	The End of the Bronze Age
EGM	Early Greek Myth
ETG	The Earth, the Temple, and the Gods
FFH	The First Fossil Hunters
GAG	God Against the Gods
GBWW	Great Books of the Western World
GG	The Greeks and Their Gods
GGM	The Genealogy of Greek Mythology
GGOE	The Goddesses and Gods of Old Europe
GI	The Greeks and the Irrational
GITM	Greece in the Making
GM	The Greek Myths
GR	Greek Religion
GTG	Guide to Greece
HGM	A Handbook of Greek Mythology
HLRE	History of the Later Roman Empire
HT	Helen of Troy

IH	Immortal Helen
ISTW	In Search of the Trojan War
MCH	The Marriage of Cadmus and Harmony
MG	The Myth of the Goddess
MGR	Myths of the Greeks and Romans
MMR	The Minoan-Mycenaean Religion
NO	The Naked Olympics
NYRB	The New York Review of Books
OCD	Oxford Classical Dictionary
PA	Poetica Astronomica
PH	The Poems of Hesiod
PW	The Peloponnesian Wars
TC	The Twelve Caesars
TH	Troy and Homer
WWCM	Who's Who in Classical Mythology
ZG	Zorba the Greek

2. THE COMING OF THE GREEKS

7 "*Soft countries . . . good soldiers too*" Cyrus the Great, quoted in Herodotus, *Histories*, IX.122.

8 *Dyaus* Cook, *Zeus*, vol. 1, chap. 1 *passim*; Burkert, *GR*, pp. 125–26. The original Greeks were part of a group of peoples who have come to be called Proto-Indo-Europeans. What little is known about them has been determined by studies of how their hypothetical language spread from the Caucasus southeast to Iran and India (the latter as Sanskrit) and west into most of Europe, where its roots now appear in languages as diverse as Greek and Celtic, not to mention English. Their vocabulary suggests that they were patrilineal (tracing their kinship through the males), that their tribes had kings, and that their chief deity was a god of the sky. They also knew snow, had carts, and developed from nomads into farmers. In about 2500 B.C., they began spreading out into Europe and Asia, a process which would continue throughout the next two thousand years.

10 *Recent discoveries* See Robert Drews, *The Coming of the Greeks*, who uses linguistic and archaeological evidence to prove, first, that the Greeks came out of the Caucasus and were skilled in both chariot warfare

and long-distance transportation of warriors by ship. Second, he believes, as I always have, that after their invasion, the Greeks would not have taken four hundred years to reach the Peloponnese but would have conquered the mainland as swiftly and brutally as possible, in a matter of months, not centuries.

11 *chariots . . . lightweight* Ibid., p. 84.

11 *long, bronze-hard swords,* Ibid., p. 86.

12 *The girl they chose* See Calasso, *MCH*, p. 295, referring to Plutarch. Many of the details in my narrative are informed, but fanciful, speculation. We don't know who told the Greeks of the Caucasus about a passage from the Black Sea to Greece. The episode of sacrificing the young girl to make rain is based on solid evidence of such practices (or simulations thereof) extending into the twentieth century. The mountain they would have used is now called Mt. Pelion, which rises directly behind the modern, extremely charming port city of Vólos in Thessaly. The sacrifice would have been to Zeus Acreaeus (Zeus of the Mountaintop), the Cloud Gatherer. It was a ritual that would eventually be practiced on the summits of the highest peaks in every region and island of Greece, most of them now named after the Prophet Elias, also a rainmaker. As time passed and it was learned that Zeus no longer approved of human sacrifice, a ram was substituted for the human victim. Later on, death and blood were eliminated altogether. In 1916, the *Annals of the British School in Athens* reported that a simulacrum of this ritual was still being performed atop that very mountain, Pelion, "where an old man in a black sheepskin mask is killed and brought to life again by his companions, who are dressed in white fleeces" (see Robert Graves, *GH*, 148.10).

15 *called themselves Pelasgians* Very little is known about the pre-Olympian religion of the Greeks. The meager details I provide about Helios and their earth goddess, the Broad One, were gleaned from Walter Burkert's superb and comprehensive survey, *Greek Religion* (I.1–2). Details about the natives' living conditions can be found in Emily Vermeule's excellent work on the period, *Greece in the Bronze Age*. Their creation myth is mostly taken from Graves's *The Greek Myths* (1–2). By Herodotus's time (c. 450 B.C.), the Pelasgians had become a near-mythical people who were said to be the country's original inhabitants.

15 *Great Island* Iánnis Sakellarákis, *DP*, p. 81.

3. THE MINOANS

17 "*Crete is something else . . . has been performed*" Henry Miller, *The Colossus of Maroussi*, p. 153.

18 *Idaían Dactyls* Diodorus Siculus, *Library of History*, vol. 5, 64.1–65, as quoted in De Bakker, *Across Crete*, pp. 229–30.

21 *in about 1640 B.C.* The dating of the event is currently the subject of a great debate that, as the Dartmouth Web site puts it, "has been raging since 1987 . . . As a result, absolute dates within the first two-thirds of the second millennium B.C. (ca. 2000–1350 B.C.) are presently in an unusually active state of flux" (Dartmouth College, *The Prehistoric Archaeology of the Aegean*, Chronology and Terminology, p. 3, http://projectsx.darmouth.edu/history/bronze_age/). Some scientists have recently fixed the explosion as happening sometime between 1644 and 1636 B.C. This date was arrived at through the study of deposits of sulfuric acid gathered from Greenland ice cores, where layers of precipitation going back thousands of years have been preserved. This would place the eruption just before or during the invasion of the mainland by Greek forces from the Caucasus. See also "New Evidence," *New York Times*, May 3, 2006.

4. FEARSOME ECHOES

23 "*There have been . . . agencies of fire and water*" Plato, *Timaeus*, 22.

23 *a thick, heavy darkness* Meanwhile, winds high in the atmosphere picked up the lighter particles and swirled them several times around the globe, producing, for months and years afterward, a worldwide series of spectacular (and somewhat unnerving) sunsets. One of these sunsets was witnessed by a Norwegian artist named Edvard Munch, who described the experience this way: "I was tired and ill—I stood looking out across the fjord [in his hometown of Oslo, Norway]—the sun was setting—the clouds were colored red—like blood—I felt as though a scream went through nature—I thought I heard a scream—I painted this picture—painted the clouds like real blood. The colors were screaming." On one of his four attempts to turn this experience into art, Munch scrawled: "Can only have been painted by a madman."

He called his effort *The Scream.* (See Robert Hughes, *The Shock of the New* (New York: Alfred A. Knopf, 1982), p. 285.)

27 *Sodom and Gomorrah* Genesis 19:24.

28 "*There came a sound . . . With fearsome echoes*" Euripides, *Hippolytus*, lines 1201–16. See also Mavor, *Voyage to Atlantis*, pp. 86–87, and Pellegrino, *Unearthing Atlantis*, pp. 93–95.

28 "*Zeus, the god of gods . . . spake as follows*" Plato, *Critias, 121* (Jowett translation, GBWW, vol. 7, p. 485). Plato's fourth-hand account of the Atlantis legend is our only source for it. He was (he said) told the story by one Critias, who got it from his grandfather, also named Critias, whose father, Dropides, told it to him. Dropides had gotten the story from his relative, the famous Athenian lawmaker Solon, who had, in turn, heard it from the Egyptian priests of the city of Saïs. Plato's description of the citizens of Atlantis seems to apply perfectly to the citizens of Crete and their Minoan Empire: "They were not to take up arms against one another, and they were all to come to the rescue if any one in any of their cities attempted to overthrow the royal house . . . for they possessed true and in every way great spirits, uniting gentleness with wisdom . . . Nor did wealth deprive them of their self-control; but they were sober, and saw clearly that all these goods are increased by virtue and friendship with one another. But then, Plato tells us, "*there occurred violent earthquakes and floods; and in a single day and night of misfortune . . . the island of Atlantis . . . disappeared in the depths of the sea.*" (*Timaeus, 25*, Jowett translation, GBWW.)

30 *15,000 to 100,000 inhabitants* Vassilakis, *Knossos*, p. 32.

31 *the double ax—the sacred implement* Nilsson says, "Of all the religious symbols and emblems that appear in the Minoan civilization the double axe is the most conspicuous, the real sign of Minoan religion and as present as a cross in Christianity and the Crescent in Islam" (Nilsson, *MMR*, p. 194). The Cretan goddess is often pictured with butterfly wings (see Baring and Cashford, *MG*, fig. 10b and 10c, p. 113). Baring and Cashford also state that Marija Gimbutas, in her groundbreaking *The Goddesses and Gods of Old Europe*, "suggests that the double blades of the axe evolved from the Neolithic butterfly . . . The butterfly is still in many lands an image of the soul, and in Greek, the word for butterfly and the soul were the same—*psyche.*" Both the ax and the butterfly, Gimbutas adds, are "images of the goddess" (Gimbutas, *GGOE*, p. 186).

32 *sculpted, stuccoed, clay horns* The foremost modern authority on Greek religion, Walter Burkert, writes, "The finds from the Neolithic town of Çatal Hüyük now make it almost impossible to doubt that the horned symbol which [Sir Arthur] Evans called 'horns of consecration' does indeed derive from real bulls' horns. The serried ranks of genuine bulls' horns discovered in the house shrines at Çatal Hüyük are hunting trophies won from the then still wild bull and set up in the precinct of the goddess; in the background lies the hunter's custom of partial restoration, the symbolic restitution of the animal killed" (Burkert, *GR*, p. 37).

32 *lábrys* Scholars believe that Crete's original settlers must have picked up this word in their migrations from Mesopotamia through the western shores of Asia Minor (see Nilsson, *MMR*, pp. 223–25).

32 *a shrine to the goddess* As Nanno Marinatos points out in writing about the Mesopotamian city-state (source of the Minoan people and religion), "The temple was primarily the dwelling of the god. It was also a ceremonial center, a treasury, a town hall, a storehouse, a commercial center. In addition, it housed the priestly personnel and the temple workers. Thus, it resembled a medieval monastery more than a Greek temple or a Christian church" (Marinatos, *ART*, p. 24).

33 *this new tsunami* Indications that there was a tsunami at this time (c.1400–1500 B.C.) is provided by two far-flung pieces of evidence. One was found during the excavation of a Minoan seaside villa at Amnisos, the port of Knossós. Here, the excavator, Spyridon Marinatos, the Greek archaeologist who would later uncover Akrotíri, noted that the massive walls of the villa had collapsed not *inward*, as is usual in an earthquake, but *outward*, as if a huge wave had crashed down upon the villa and then, in its backwash, pulled the great stone blocks toward the sea, one piece some three hundred feet away from its other half. (See Mavor, *Voyage to Atlantis*, pp. 52–53, and Pellegrino, *Unearthing Atlantis*, pp. 51–52.)

The second indication that a tsunami occurred at this time comes from Egypt. That the wave may also have reached Egyptian shores is a possibility that has been long speculated upon by a bevy of responsible scientists, who also theorize that its approach might have caused the "Red Sea" (or whatever body of water it was) to part—just as the receding of the sea before the Christmas 2004 tsunami struck left fish exposed on the shores of Jakarta—which allowed the

Israelites to escape before the wave inundated the pharaoh's pursuing troops, as a similar one would later engulf the poor Indonesian children who went out to get those fish.

34 *the aftermath of the 1883 Krakatoa eruption* For the Krakatoa rebellions, see Winchester, *Krakatoa*, pp. 317–38.

34 *Greek anger at the Cretans' intransigency* At the same time, many of the wealthier Minoans fled the island. Eventually, some of them settled on the coast of what is now Israel, where they became known as Philistines. But they were no longer the joyous people and artists who had built Knossós. They had, instead, become merchants and were particularly known for their insensitivity to intellectual and creative pursuits. Later Greek writers called their country Philistia. Under the Romans, this became Palaestina.

5. CRADLE TO GRAVE

37 "*Come, let us begin . . . that were aforetime*" Hesiod, *Theogony*, lines 36–38 (translated by Hugh Evelyn-White, my adaptation).

38 *ever obeisant* See Baring and Cashford, *MG*, figs. 41, 42, p. 133.

38 *sacrificed as a bull* See Harrison, *Prolegomena*, pp. 481–82.

38 *hundreds of bees* See the *Penguin Dictionary of Symbols*, p. 511. Also Nilsson, *MMR*, p. 542–50, and Baring and Cashford, *MG*, pp. 118–20, including a fascinating passage (p. 120) on the connecting etymology of honey, heart, death, fate, and wax.

38 *funerary jars* When the temperature falls below about fifty-seven degrees Fahrenheit (fourteen degrees Centigrade), the bees cease flying, form a tight cluster to conserve heat, and await the return of warm weather. They can survive for several weeks in temperatures of minus-fifty degrees Fahrenheit.

42 *set ablaze* Kerényi, *Dionysos*, p. 34.

43 *ichor* In the *Iliad*, Aphrodite herself is wounded by a Greek mortal, Diomédes, causing this immortal blood to flow (Homer, *Iliad*, V.340). See also Kerényi (*Dionysos*, p. 34), who describes *ichor* as "not red blood but a paler liquid resembling buttermilk or whey . . . Aristotle [uses it] describing the amniotic fluid (*Historia animalium*, 586b 32)."

43 *an enormous stone* This stone was shaped exactly like the end of a bullet or the nose cone of a space capsule. It measured about thirty

inches from base to tip. We know the size, because later, after Zeus and Rhéa had tricked Krónos into regurgitating it, Zeus would deposit this sacred memento of his survival at the sanctuary of Delphí, whose first priests, not coincidentally, were wandering, shipwrecked Cretans. Although the original stone (called the *ómphalos*, or navel, stone) has since mysteriously disappeared, copies were made and remain on view. You can see them, as Fárzaneh and I did, when you visit this stupendously beautiful site. One is in its museum, the other on the grounds along the Sacred Way, just down the road, in fact, from the very spot where the sanctuary's first oracle, Ge (i.e., Gaía,) uttered her cryptic prophecies.

43 *the Koúrites* Harrison, *Thémis*, p. 12.

43 *magical white clay* Gypsum, which is found in volcanic regions where it has been precipitated out of the action of sulfuric acid on seawater and limestone.

43 *delightful toys* Harrison, *Thémis*, pp. 14–15; Kerényi, *Dionysos*, p. 269. It was also said that the child was given a mirror, so that he would be diverted by his own image, which he had never seen before. If this is true, if a mirror was among the gifts, then the killers would have ensured the infant's resurrection, because a mirror captures the soul so that it can later be brought back to life. (Kerényi, *Dionysos*, p. 265.)

44 *quivering with divinity* Stories about the existence of a tomb of Zeus on Crete had been circulating throughout the ancient world for centuries, as had the contrary belief that the people of Crete were near-pathological liars. The quote from Kallímachus is just one example of the latter. Some four hundred years later, after St. Paul was shipwrecked on Crete in A.D. 46 while on his way to Rome and wrote to Titus about his experiences, this opinion became gospel truth. In his letter to Titus, Paul says of the Cretans, "One of themselves, even a prophet of their own, said, 'The Cretians [*sic*] are alway [*sic*] liars, evil beasts, slow bellies' " (*Titus* 1:12). By the first century B.C., the presence of Zeus's tomb on Crete had became an accepted fact. Local tradition—one strain of which held that Zeus had been a prince gored to death by a wild boar—placed his grave not in the Idaían Cave, but on Mt. Yoúktas, just south of Knossós. (See Cook, *Zeus*, vol. 1, pp. 157–63.) Stories of the mountain also persisted because people had begun to notice that when they looked at it from due north—particularly when approaching the harbor of Iráklion by sea—they

could (as you can today) discern the unmistakable silhouette of Zeus's huge, recumbent head on its summit, the pointed end of his beard jutting skyward on the western side.

45 *after the birth of Jesus* Julian was the apostate Byzantine emperor who tried to restore pagan religion. His successor, Theodosius I, then expunged such wicked tolerance from the empire once and for all (see below, chapter 25).

45 *Sakellarákis* Sakellarákis, *DP*, p. 171. Also based on a private conversation I had with Sakellarákis at the end of our journey. He was a most gracious and affable host. Much of what he told me has been incorporated into these chapters on Crete. His beautifully crafted book, *Digging for the Past*, contains a fund of information about both Crete and archaeology. None of the objects that Sakellarákis found in the cave were as striking, however, as two that had been uncovered in the first major excavation of the cave made nearly a hundred years earlier by the Italian archaeologist Federico Halbherr. For centuries prior to this, it had been thought that another cave on Crete, the so-called Díktaian Cave at Psychró in the mountains east of Iráklion, was Zeus's legendary birthplace. But Halbherr found a clay tablet whose inscription firmly identified the nearly forgotten cave on Mt. Ida as the true site of the worshipping of the Cretan-born Zeus. Equally if not more impressive was the discovery of a number of bronze votive shields and large, shieldlike cymbals, or *tympana*. On one of the cymbals, the Koúrites dance and beat drums around a young Zeus, who sports a false, Gilgamesh-like beard and stands upon a bull while ripping apart a lion held above his head. See Vasilakis, *Herakleion Archeological Museum Visitors Guide*, p. 228. These items can be viewed in Room XIX of the museum. See also Cook, *Zeus*, vol. 1, p. 645. Although these offerings were made relatively late in the cave's history (i.e., c. 700 B.C.) and show a definite Eastern influence, they clearly demonstrate a belief in Zeus's birth and youth in the Idaían Cave of Crete.

45 *a shepherd's knife* Sakellarákis, *DP*, p. 172.

45 *a flock of sheep* Ibid., p. 199. Photo on same page.

47 *a willow* Graves, *GM*, 7.c.; Cook, *Zeus*, vol. 1, pp. 529 and 530 n. The tree is no longer there. Of course.

47 *aigís* Pronounced "ay-GHEES" in Greek. Often confusingly spelled "aegis" in English, it is pronounced either "EE-jis" or "AY-jis." H. L. Rose states that the word *aigís* meant "goatskin" (Rose, HGM, p. 48).

The *OCD* supplies detailed information about its various manifestations, including Herodotus's assertion that Athéna's *aigís* copied the goatskin dresses worn by Libyan women (*OCD* under *aegis*).

47 *symbol of his lordly power* One of Amálthia's nourishing horns, accidentally broken off by the rambunctious Zeus as he was playing with her as a child, was also granted immortality by the god. It is otherwise known as the famous *cornu copiea*, the Horn of Plenty, which remains forever overflowing with whatever its possessor desires (Grant and Hazel, WWCM, p. 25; *Dictionary of Symbols*, p. 516). Interestingly, the earliest depiction we have of such a symbol—created some twenty thousand years before Zeus's birth—was found carved out of a limestone block in another sacred cave, at Laussel in France. In the bas-relief, the Great Goddess holds the horn in her right hand as the left hand rests upon her most voluptuous belly, transferring the horn's fruitfulness into her womb. (Fig. 42, Baring and Cashford, *MG*, 44.) Thus does the goddess continue to spread her tendrils throughout creation, in spite of the still unflagging efforts of the gods who followed to eliminate her influence in every way possible.

47 *especially amorous* Grant and Hazel, WWCM, p. 233.

6. THE ROAD TO POWER

49 "*War, father of all things . . . king*" Haxton's translation, *CWH*, p. 28.

52 *as enormous as their name implies* "Titans" was the appellation given to them by their father, Ouranós, after their complicity in castrating him. Etymologically, *titan* does not mean "giant." As Hesiod himself points out, it means "one who strains." It is also connected with the word for "vengeance," which is what all the Titans would suffer because of their terrible deed. (See the *Theogony*, lines 206–10; also R. M. Frazer's *PH*, p. 38.) That said, the ancient Greeks, too, regarded these creatures as gigantic. Hence, the later, and current, connotation. (Grant and Hazel, *WWCM*, p. 332.)

52 *The grateful Cyclopes* Graves, *GM*, 7.e.

53 *flaming lightning bolts* This whole passage is taken from Hesiod (*Theogony*, lines 692–710).

54 *at the mercy of his sons* Graves, *GM*, 7.e. His sources, in turn, include a bevy of ancient authorities, ranging from Hesiod to Plutarch.

54 *what Plutarch says* Plutarch, *De defect. orac.*, 420A. Cited by Rose, HGM, p. 45.

55 *an enormous number of posts to fill* A recently published genealogical chart of Greek mythology took a Manhattan judge, his son, and various assistants nearly forty years to untangle and compile. It covers twenty generations and has an index which includes 3,673 proper names. (Jon O. Newman, *A Genealogical Chart of Greek Mythology* [Chapel Hill: University of North Carolina Press, 2003].) Another, less cumbersome version is Vanessa James's *The Genealogy of Greek Mythology*, but it, too, is often frustrating in its labyrinthine convolutions.

55 *throughout the cosmos* In ancient Greek, the term *kosmos* meant not only "world" but "order." See Plato: "And philosophers tell us, Kallikles, that communion and friendship and orderliness and temperance and justice bind together heaven and earth and gods and men, and that this universe is therefore called Cosmos or order, not disorder or misrule, my friend." Plato, *Gorgias*, 508 (translation by J. Harward, GBWW, vol. 7, p. 284).

56 *Changing into a snake himself* Graves, *GM,* 13.a; Cook, *Zeus*, vol. 1, p. 398. This knot of double serpents, said to be nearly impossible to disentangle, was immortalized in the winged and snake-entwined staff, or caduceus, of Hermes, the messenger of the gods. As such, the caduceus was thought to confer immunity on Greek diplomats and other messengers and was carried by them on their various missions.

56 *Lust for Héra wrapped Zeus's loins* See Homer, *Iliad* XIV.294 and 346–352 for the Greek poet's description in full of my somewhat truncated translation.

57 *cuckoo bird* The cuckoo and its myth are described by Pausanias when telling of his visit to Mycenae and environs. There, in the great temple of Héra, an effigy of the goddess grasped a scepter, on top of which sat a cuckoo, the source of the story (Pausanias, *Description of Greece*, II.17.4). Inasmuch as Pausanias doesn't tell us what kind of cuckoo it is, I have taken the liberty of imagining it not as the rather common ash gray and white *Cuculus canorus* found in Europe and Asia, but rather, the male *Chrysococcyx cupreus* that is native to tropical Africa. I think that, for Zeus, assuming the latter's resplendent finery would not have been all that much of a stretch. Farther south from the temple, there were sanctuaries to Héra and Zeus on the tops of their separate mountains: on Pron for Héra and for Zeus atop Mt.

Cuckoo (Kokkugioi), supposedly the site of his transformation into this seductive feathered gem (Pausanias, ibid., II.36.1).

58 *One authority* Guthrie, *GG*, p. 68.

58 *the grandest of all Greek temples* Herodotus, *Histories*, III.60. This observation was made in about 440 B.C., just before the Parthenon was completed and the Temple of Zeus at Olympía begun.

59 *enveloped by her lips* Calasso, *MCH*, p. 24; Burkert, *GR*, note 23, section III.2.2. Calasso remarks that such an image would never have been allowed within the shrines of any of the other goddesses, even Aphrodite's. Burkert calls the image "quite enigmatic." Unfortunately, whatever we know of it is only through hearsay.

60 *Héstia or Deméter . . . a much better choice?* Deméter would become the reluctant bride of her other brother, Hádes. The neglected Héstia would remain forever a virgin, best known by her Latin name Vesta, whose priestesses, the Vestal Virgins, were famous in Roman times. They were also much desired by the male members of their congregation, even though it was well known that if a vestal was caught breaking her vow of virginity, she would be punished by being buried alive.

60 *older than Zeus* Homer, *Iliad*, IV.59–60.

7. SPREADING THE FAITH

65 "*Longings for love . . . the wedding bower*" Ovid, *Metamorphoses*, II.847–48 (my translation).

65 "*the everlasting home of the gods . . . for ever and ever*" Homer, *Odyssey*, VI.41–45 (translation by Samuel Butler).

66 *the nymph Dióni* Rose, *HGM*, p. 53.

67 *Delos* Delos would become a hugely important center of worship from Mycenaean to Roman times, c. 1500 B.C. to the first century A.D. Today it is accessible only by private craft or by the motor launches that leave on regularly scheduled tours from nearby Mykonos.

68 *happy being a virgin* The Parthenon—the name of her temple on the Acropolis in Athens—derives from the Greek for "virgin."

68 "*queen of clamorous combat*" Hesiod, *Theogony*, lines 924–26.

68 *Hephéstos* Ibid., 927–29; Grant and Hazel, WWCM, p. 157; *OCD*

under "Hephaestus." His name today—pronounced, as it was in ancient time, "EEphaistos"—means "volcano."

69 *Maía* Hesiod, *Theogony*, lines 938–39.

69 "*luck-bringing angel*" *Homeric Hymn* IV.3. The ancient Greek for "messenger" was *ángelon*.

70 *Hesiod and his followers tell us* See Hesiod, *Theogony*, lines 820–80. For the cave, see Pindar, *Pythian Ode I*, lines 15–17. It was known as the Corycian Cave.

70 *indescribable noises* Hesiod, *Theogony*, lines 830–35. Graves, *GM*, 36.a. Pindar, *Pythian Ode I*, lines 15–22.

71 *its worst political nightmares* That the proto-Persians were so infected is evidenced by the fact that their earliest surviving liturgies—written down in the "grisly minutiae" of their Antidemonic Law—were rites designed not to appease or praise the gods, but solely to keep the power of the Evil Ones at bay, as if this was what mattered most in life (A. T. Olmstead *History of the Persian Empire* [Chicago: University of Chicago Press, 1959], p. 18). Later, these ideas would be most notably developed by the great Persian prophets Zoroaster (c. 628–551 B.C.) and Mani (c. 216–276). The latter posited the highly influential doctrine of Manichaeism, in which the world is seen as dominated by a continual struggle between the forces of evil and good, of Darkness (led by Satan) and Light (led by God). St. Augustine (A.D. 354–430) was a follower of Manichaeism for nine years before finally converting to Christianity and thereafter assailing Mani's assumption that Satan had a power equal to God's.

71 *Socrates . . . greatest of all evils* Plato, *Gorgias*, 509 (my translation).

71 *human fallibilities* Burkert, *GR*, p. 180.

72 "*spawned monster serpents . . . and fish-men, and rams* Translation by L. W. King (1907). It and other versions can be found on various Internet sites, including http://www.sacred-texts.com and http://www.answer .com. See also the insightful commentary by Baring and Cashford, *MG*, p. 275–81. Also see Donald A. MacKenzie, *Myths of Babylonia and Assyria* (Whitefish, Mont: Kessinger Publishing, 2004), pp. 138–48, for a vivid recounting of the *Enumah Elish* story of the encounter between Tiamat and lightning-wielding Marduk. Subsequent Hittite myths transcribed in the fourteenth century B.C. would tell of the victory of their weather god over a dragon named Illuyankas, while a Canaanite inscription from northern Syria refers to the victory of the thunderbolt-

carrying Baal over a monstrously slimy, many-headed sea serpent which would variously be named Yamm, Lotan, and, finally, in Hebrew, Leviathan.

72 *one variant* Apollodorus, *Library*, I.vi.3.

73 *Mt. Etna* Hesiod, *Theogony*, line 860. Hesiod's name for the mountain is Aidna, which prompted later believers and mythographers, including Apollodorus (vi.3) to identify it as Etna, the great volcano in Sicily. This, however, is much disputed. Many believe Hesiod meant a location in Asia Minor. (See R. M. Frazer's comment, *PH*, p. 82.) Tiphón is also said to be the source of those deadly gale-force winds that plague the seas and oceans—as the word *typhoon* suggests, this being a melding of the Greek myth with the Chinese word for "great winds," *ta fâng*.

8. PROMÉTHEUS, PANDÓRA, AND OTHER MATTERS

74 "*Zeus is hard . . . ever pitiless*" Aeschylus, *Prométheus Bound*, line 35 (translation by G. M. Cookson).

75 *a near Christ-like figure* Prométheus also served as a model for Milton's Satan and Melville's Ahab—monumentally flawed beings whose futile flailings against the great inequity of it all turn them into tragic and sympathetic antiheroes.

76 *differing opinions* In Hesiod, Zeus is said to have been aware of what was happening and played along with the game in order to be able to inflict the punishments that followed. But this is believed to have been a later insertion into Hesiod's poem. See R. M. Frazer's comments, *PH*, p. 67. Also Rose, *HGM*, p. 55, fn. 57.

77 *their creator* See the story in Rose, *HGM*, p. 54. His references are a fragment of Hesiod (no. 268), the fables of Hyginus (line 142), and Pausanias, *GTG* I.x.4.3. In the latter, Pausanias claims that he saw, outside a shrine at Chaeronea in Viotía (just north of Athens), two large, clay-colored lumps which were said to have been left over from the stock out of which Prométheus fashioned the human race. Pausanias testifies that these lumps smelled like human flesh. The scholar Peter Levi, whose notes for Pausanias are a constant and edifying delight, states that an eighteenth-century (A.D.) visitor found clay exactly this odorous but that the eminent early nineteenth-century

traveler Colonel Leake found only the clay, but not the smell (ibid., p. 411, n. 19). How humans managed to propagate before this time is never explained, save, perhaps, under the notion that God often acts in mysterious ways. It should also be noted that Prométheus's reputation in this area is why Mary Shelley dubbed the creator of her monster "*Frankenstein; or, The Modern Prometheus.*"

78 *the same kind of humiliation* It would also, in a sense, give mankind custody of the godhead itself. Fire, as we saw earlier, was believed to embody the Great Goddess. Later, in the Persian religion of Zoroaster (628–551 B.C.), it was regarded as the son of the Great God, Azura Mazda, and was therefore the god's representative on earth (see Hinnells, *Persian Mythology*, p. 37). Fárzaneh says that today most Zoroastrians live in the city of Yazd, in central Iran, where this sacred flame has been kept burning for more than two thousand years. Meanwhile, of course, on Holy Saturday, a similar flame is shepherded all the way from Jerusalem to be passed out to Greece's Orthodox flock as the Resurrection is announced.

78 "*an evil . . . with a nature to do evil*" Hesiod, *Theogony*, lines 600–601 (translation by H. G. Evelyn-White).

78 "*the shamelessness . . . treachery of a thief,*" Ibid., lines 570–615; *Works and Days*, lines 60–83; Rose, *HGM*, p. 55.

78 *ignored Prométheus's warnings* Hesiod, *Works and Days*, lines 86–89. Robert Graves says, on the contrary, that Epimétheus did heed his brother's warning and wouldn't have anything to do with Pandóra. But that this caused an enraged Zeus to nail Prométheus to the mountaintop, which, in turn, prompted Epimétheus to hastily change his mind (Graves, GM, 39*j*).

79 *the sole resource . . . we mortals now have* Hesiod, *Theogony*, lines 565–612; *Works and Days*, lines 42–105. Many authorities believe that this dire portrait of Pandóra was inserted into the myth by the notorious misogynist Hesiod himself, who was, in addition, a farmer and prone to justified complaints about the endless toil required by his profession. Interestingly, he was writing his diatribe blaming women for all the evils in the world at just about the same time that the story of Eve was being composed for the Book of Genesis. (*NIV Study Bible*, p. 2.)

When Erasmus changed the jar to a box, he also had Zeus send it to Prométheus via Pandóra—in effect making the god the guilty party (Panofsky and Panofsky, *Pandora's Box*, pp. 14–17). The Panofskys also note that it was Plutarch who made the latter connection when commenting on Homer's *Iliad* and the two great jars which the poet describes as sitting on the floor of Zeus's halls—one to distribute good to mankind, the other ill fortune (*Iliad*, XXIV.527). Since Erasmus, the box has proved to be impossible to dislodge from the public mind. In one of its more recent, highly dramatic appearances, it is opened by a helplessly curious, film noir blonde at the end of the classic movie *Kiss Me Deadly*, when the horrific white light emanating from within seemingly annihilates the world in a nuclear holocaust. And then, of course, there is the equally persistent equation of "box" with the female genitalia, and the troubles these too can purportedly unleash for the majority of men.

79 *into the rockface* Aeschylus, *Prométheus Bound*, lines 64–65. His descriptions of the vicious manner in which Prométheus is bound to the rock are still searing in their vividness and seem to be a powerfully accurate reflection of the violent, brutish behavior of the Greeks and their gods in those distant Bronze Age times.

79 *Homer tells us* Homer, *Iliad*, I.399–406. Some scholars believe that this incident was entirely fabricated by the poet. See the note I.470–83 in Robert Fagles's translation.

79 *eleven other Olympian deities* The others were Aphrodite, Áres, Ártemis, Deméter, Hephéstos, Hermes, and Héstia. Diónysos had not yet been born, and when he was, Héstia would step aside to give him her place.

80 *Graves, citing a scholiast* Graves, *GM*, 13.*c*, note 5.

80 "*when I hung you aloft . . . helpless to help you*" Homer, *Iliad*, XV.19–22 (my translation).

9. DIVINE RIGHTS

83 "*We boast . . . this parent earth*" Aeschylus, *The Suppliant Maidens*, lines 535–37.

83 *sleek warships* Strauss, *The Trojan War*, p. 40.

83 *from near the very beginnings of the cosmos* This was also the time when Zeus, able to be everywhere at once, was also inserting his seeds into several

other royal lines. These included those of Hellen, ancestor of the Hellenes (i.e., the Greeks), whom he may have fathered with Pyrrha, son of Pandóra and Epimétheus; Macedonia (through Thyia, a daughter of Hellen); of Endymion, the king of Elis; Troy (through Zeus's liaison with one Eléktra [not *that* one], a daughter of the Titan Atlas); Pelasgus, ancestor of the Pelasgians, and Argus, king of Argos, both of the last through a fling that Zeus had with Niobe, another of the numerous first mortal women he ever loved. Interestingly, however, the Great Thunderer had nothing to do with the relatively late royal line of Athens—which is to say, of course, that apparently, they did not see fit to claim him, in those later, more enlightened times (perhaps), as an ancestor. (All the above is traced in James, *GGM*, *passim.*)

84 "*Zeus' desires . . . hurls humans down to doom*" Aeschylus, *The Suppliant Maidens*, line 669. Neither Ínachos nor his father, Okeanós, were punished by Zeus, the latter having refused to take the Titans' part during the war.

85 *drew a cloud around them* Ovid, *Metamorphoses*, I.612–13.

85 *himself as a bull* Aeschylus, *The Suppliant Maidens*, line 301.

86 *pressed her velvet snout into his hand* Ovid, *Metamorphoses*, I.569–747 (Melville translation).

87 *son even mightier than* himself Aeschylus's *Prométheus Bound* is part of what seems to have been a trilogy. Only fragments remain of the other two plays, *Prométheus the Fire-Bringer* and *Prométheus Unbound.*

87 "*how unjustly I suffer*" Aeschylus, *Prométheus Bound*, lines 849–75.

88 *at the mouth of the Nile* For a more detailed description of her journey, see Aeschylus, *Prométheus Bound*, lines 790–816, and *The Suppliant Maidens*, lines 540–64. See also Graves, *GM*, 56.*b* for its modern geography.

88 *bigger than a bull* Diodorus Siculus, *Library of History*, I.35; Herodotus, *Histories*, II.65–77. *Crocodile* means "pebbled lizard" in Greek, while *hippopotamus* can be translated as "river horse," *hippo* meaning "horse" and *potamós* meaning "river." The historian Nonnos says *Nile* comes from the *new slime* (*néa ilís*) that is deposited on the earth with the annual flooding of the river (Nonnos, *Dionysiaca*, III, lines 275–78).

88 *in the temple of the Sun* Herodotus, *Histories*, II.69–73.

89 *Diodorus Siculus . . . the gods came from that country* Diodorus Siculus, *LH*, I.10.2–7; Herodotus, *Histories*, II.50.

89 "*Zeus's sacred garden*" Aeschylus, *The Suppliant Maidens*, line 556.

10. THE CRETAN SAGA

91 "*The virgin did . . . contend with Jove?*" Ovid, *Metamorphoses*, II.445–48 (translations by Garth, Dryden, Addison, Pope, etc., 1717).

92 *falling . . . in love* Hesiod, *CW*, no. 19; Apollodorus, *Library*, III.1.1; Graves, *GM*, 58 *passim*; Calasso, *MCH*, pp. 3–9. Also Ovid, whose much later and highly voluptuous version has Hermes doing the spadework (Ovid, *Metamorphoses*, II.833–75; III.1–6).

95 *serendipity* Originally from a Persian tale called "The Three Princes of Sernedip," in which these princes were always coming across things they had not been in search of.

101 "*her passion . . . madness inflicted on her by Poseidon*" Frazer, note 3 to Apollodorus, *Library*, III.1.3–4 (Loeb edition, p. 305).

102 *regularly counseled by Zeus* Homer, *Odyssey*, XIX.179.

104 *he wanted Aegeus's son, Theseus, to be first* Plutarch, *Lives*, GBWW, vol. 14, p. 6. Some sources used by Plutarch say that Theseus was shamed into volunteering, but not until the third trip. On the matter of Minos making the demand, Plutarch tells us that this version comes from the great and authoritative scholar Hellanicus, who wrote his account three hundred years earlier than Apollodorus, sometime near the beginning of the fifth century B.C.

105 *the constellation Corona Borealis* Hyginus, *Poet. Astr.*, II.5 (see Rose, *HGM*, p. 265).

106 *which he named Athens* Plutarch, *Theseus*, XXIV.1.

106 *The tomb . . . has never been found* See Pausanias, *Description of Greece*, I.17, as well as Peter Levi's note 91, bk. 1.

107 "*Zeus's glorious son . . . judgments upon the dead*" Homer, *Odyssey*, XI.568–71 (my translation).

108 *Kazantzákis . . . six years old* Kazantzákis, *Report to Greco*, p. 89 (translation by P. A. Bien).

109 "*For the first time . . . the skull*" Ibid., p. 87.

109 *recast as historical facts* Indeed, it seems to have been a regular practice of the Mycenaeans to raid the coast of Asia Minor for female slaves

and their children, while killing off the men in the process (see Wood, *ISTW*, pp. 159–61).

109 *the great Greek historian Herodotus* Herodotus (c. 484–425 B.C.) was the first Greek historian to travel around what was thought of as "the inhabited world" (*oikouméni*) and attempt a comprehensive picture of its past and present. He was born in Halicarnassus (present-day Bodrum on the western coast of Turkey), which was then controlled by Persia, and was forced into exile by the Persians for conspiring against their rule. He then sojourned throughout the region before settling in Athens and then southern Italy to complete his massive opus.

109 "*the great and marvelous deeds . . . to make war on one another*" Herodotus, *Histories* I.1. (my translation). The appellation "barbarian" was a common name given to anyone who didn't speak Greek, because to the Greeks, all foreign languages sounded like a lot of "bar-bar-bar-bar . . ."

110 *that she-devil from Sparta, Helen* She had already been kidnapped once before, when she was twelve, to be the bride of the Greek king Theseus, and almost certainly was despoiled before her brothers could steal her back.

110 *the Greeks . . . should stay out of it* Herodotus, *Histories*, I.4.

111 *still call Evrópi* There are numerous speculations about how Europe got its name, but none have proven definitive. Herodotus said that no one knew where the name came from, unless it was from the princess Evrópi. But he didn't think this was probable, since she had never gone to the area (Herodotus, *Histories*, IV.45.1). But her brother, Kadmos, had, and since it is a known fact that for the ancient Greeks, the name Evrópi designated all of Greece outside of the Peloponnese (see the *Homeric Hymn to the Pythian Apollo*, lines 250 and 290), it might be that Kadmos's search for his sister in that region gave it its name. Eventually, the appellation was extended to include all the territory to the north, i.e., present-day Europe (see the entry "Europe" in the *OCD*).

11. THEBES: THE ILL-FATED MARRIAGE OF KADMOS AND HARMONÍA

112 *"Two great urns . . . neither gods nor men"* Homer, *Iliad,* XXIV.527–33. (my translation).

113 *perfect for a fortified acropolis* Thebes was apparently first settled by Mycenaeans in the fifteenth century B.C. and by the mid-fourteenth century was a major Mycenaean center (see the *OCD* under "Thebes"). Mesopotamia cylinder seals discovered in 1964 give some credence to the legend that Kadmos introduced writing to Greece. (See the *EB* under "Thebes.")

114 *sliced off its head* For a wonderfully grisly description of this encounter, see Nonnos's *Dionysiaca,* IV.356–419. See also Euripides' vivid account in his *Phoenician Maidens,* lines 659–76.

114 *first called Kadmía and later Thebes* It was apparently not called Thebes after the Egyptian city of the same name. In Egypt, that city was known as "the City" or "the city of the god Ammon." It is speculated that the appellation Thebes came from the way the Greeks Hellenized one of the Egyptian names, "the Most-Select of Places," for the city's temple of Karnak. The name for the Greek city comes from a local nymph, Thebe, the wife of Zethus, who ruled the city with his twin brother, Amphion. Their mother, Antiópi, had been the daughter of the regent of Kadmia when she attracted the eye of Zeus, who impregnated her while in the form of a goatlike satyr. (Grant and Hazel, *WWCM,* pp. 26, 35.)

115 *Muses sang their golden songs* Pindar, *Pythian Odes,* III.94. Pausanias says the Muses sang within the citadel, and that its citizens still pointed out the spot in his time, also showing him exactly where the wandering heifer finally lay down (Pausanias, *GTG,* IX.12.3 and 12.1).

115 *his rough affection* Apollodorus, *Library,* III.4.3. Later, the necklace and golden wedding robe would bring disaster and the pursuit of the Furies on their subsequent owners, a trail of vengeance that was ended only when the two wedding gifts were deposited with the oracle at Delphí for safekeeping.

115 *mingling* The verb was a favorite euphemism for sexual intercourse. See Hesiod's description of Zeus making love to Seméli (*Theogony,* lines

940–41). I am indebted to Roberto Calasso for his insights into the relationship of gods and man in *The Marriage of Cadmus and Harmony*, his profound meditation on the Greek myths. See particularly pp. 52–54 and 387.

117 *an appellation whose meaning* Early authorities suggested that his name indicated a double birth, but this theory has now been thoroughly discredited, with no convincing alternatives having been proposed (see Burkert, *GR*, pp. 162–63; Rose, *HGM*, pp. 149–50).

118 "*a charlatan and sorcerer . . . with his disease*" Euripides, *The Bacchae*, lines 233–38, 353–54.

118 *both the vine and the theater* Diónysos was credited with bringing both wine and drama to ancient Greece. The theater is believed to have originated in choral songs (dithyrambs) honoring Diónysos, and all the superb plays of Greece's Classical Age were performed in Athens at the Great Dionysia, a yearly drama festival honoring the god.

118 *a girl and a goat* Apollodorus, *Library*, III.4.3; Diodorus Siculus, *Library of History*, III.62.6; Kerényi, *Dionysos*, p. 246; Graves, *GM*, 27.*a*. (See also Frazer's footnote 4 in Apollodorus, *Library*, III.4.3, pp. 320–21.) A goat was the principal sacrificial animal at Dionysian rites, at which it was torn apart and eaten raw. A sixth-century Orphic writer recounts an alternate story that the Titans tore the infant Diónysos to pieces and boiled him up to eat, but that Rhéa saved him and took him to Inó. (See Graves, *GM*, 27.1; Kerényi, *Dionysos*, pp. 243–61; G. S. Kirk, *The Bacchae* [Cambridge: Cambridge University Press, 1979], p. 6.)

119 *madly wandering the world* Graves, *GM*, 27 passim.

119 *wine, the drink of immortality* Nonnos, *Dionysiaca*, XII.293–362. See also Kerényi, *Dionysos*, pp. 57–68.

120 *the Blessed Isles, or Elysian Fields* See Apollodorus, *Library*, III.5.4; Euripides, *Bacchae*, 1530 ff. See also Homer's description in his *Odyssey* (IV.563–64). These have tentatively been identified as the Canaries (*OCD* "Islands of the Blest").

12. THE HEROES OF THE ARGOLID—I: PERSEUS

121 *"And Zeus the Father made . . . human heroes god-born"* Hesiod, *Works and Days*, lines 158–59 (my translation).

121 *by his uncle Bílos* For the full account of both branches, see Apollodorus, *Library*, II.1.4 to II.8.5 (which details Bílos's branch through the labors of Hérakles) and III.1.1 to III.4.3 (which follows Agínor's branch to the birth of Diónysos).

122 *iróon: "heroes"* Hesiod, *Works and Days*, lines 159–60 (my translation). Burkert, *GR*, note 2 to IV, 4. This is what Hesiod in his *Works and Days* posits as the Five Ages of Man which followed the birth of gods and men from their common mother, Gaía. The first was a Golden Age under Krónos when all men lived in toil-free harmony with nature and the gods. This was followed by a Silver Age in which men's impiety and hubris caused Zeus to bury them beneath the earth and create, in their stead, the men of the Bronze Age. The Age of Heroes then followed. Hesiod tells us he lived in the Age of Iron, one of evil, hatred, and pain. But this, too, he assures his audience, Zeus will also one day destroy. (Hesiod, *Works and Days*, lines 106–201; see also West's commentary, pp. 172–204.)

124 *a "fair-cheeked" woman* Pindar, *Odes*, Pythian 12, line 17.

124 *This so infuriated Athína* Ovid, *Metamorphoses*, lines 793–803; Grant and Hazel, *WWCM*, p. 266; Garber and Vickers, *The Medusa Reader*, pp. 1–2.

124 *her name means "ruler" or "queen"* Grant and Hazel, *WWCM*, p. 146.

124 *a faraway place* Many mythographers identify this as north Africa, most likely present-day Morocco. (See Garber and Vickers, *The Medusa Reader*, p. 40, for example.)

125 *Apollodorus tells us* Apollodorus, *Library*, IV.3. The word he uses is ασπίδι, that is, *shield.*

125 *"Over her shoulders . . . a sign of aigís-bearing Zeus"* Homer, *Iliad*, V.739–40 (my translation).

126 *to their very beginnings* Apollodorus, *Library*, II.4.4; Herodotus, *Histories*, VII.61.

13. THE HEROES OF THE ARGOLID—II: HÉRAKLES

127 "*So let that noble wife . . . Who would pray to such a goddess?*" Euripides, *Heracles Mad,* lines 1302–8 (translation by Edward P. Coleridge), GBWW, vol. 5, p. 376.

127 *impregnated her again* Apollodorus, *Library*, III.4.8.; Diodorus Siculus, *Library of History*, IV.9.2–4.

128 *to blind even all-knowing Zeus* See the *OCD* under "Ate." See also Homer, *Iliad*, XIX.90–94. Dodds, GI, pp. 2–8, 17–18, 37–41.

128 "*On this day . . . the land around him*" Homer, *Iliad*, XIX.101–5. The phrase "born of my blood" also meant, in Hérakles' case, directly of Zeus. See Homer, *Iliad*, XIX.115–16.

129 *Thus did . . . Evristhéfs receive the kingly power* Grant and Hazel, *WWCM*, p. 160; Rose, *HGM*, p. 205.

129 *grabbing Áte by her greasy locks* Ibid., 112–125.

129 *tricked the Goddess of Childbirth* Ovid tells us that Eilíthia had been all the while sitting at an altar outside the bedroom door, her legs crossed and fingers locked to close off the canal. So when the maid burst happily through the door to falsely announce the births, a surprised Eilíthia opened her legs and fingers, thus allowing the process to continue. Ovid informs us that for her pains, the maid was changed into a weasel. (Ovid, *Metamorphoses*, IX, lines 283–326.) Others say that her metamorphosis was into the little lizard that can be seen even today furtively slipping in and around Greek country houses (Rose, *HGM*, p. 207). Pausanias writes that the Thebans of his time said that Alkmíni's delivery had been held up by witches, and that it had been Tiresías's daughter who had tricked them into believing that the baby had been born anyway (Pausanias, *Description of Greece*, IX.11.2).

129 "*Hérakles*" *meaning "Héra's Glory"* Pronounced "EEraklees" by the Greeks and later transliterated by the Romans into its most well-known form, "Hercules." Also see Grant and Hazel, *WWCM*, p. 160; Rose, *HGM*, p. 205. Hérakles' much weaker fraternal twin was named Iphiklés.

130 *the Milky Way* Diodorus Siculus, *Library of History* IV.9. Hyginus (*PA* II.43). says that the Milky Way was formed after Hermes had brought the infant Hérakles to nurse on Héra's breast while she was sleeping, and that when she awoke and discovered this, she violently

pushed him away, causing him to spew out the milk into the sky. The unspoken corollary of this, of course, is that the galaxy (from the Greek word for milk: *gála*) in which we live is Héra's milk.

130 *several strapping sons* Apollodorus says that Hérakles was four cubits tall—exactly six feet—or, according to the historian Herodotus, four cubits plus one foot (see Apollodorus, *Library*, II.4.9, especially footnote 4 by Frazer).

131 *all fifty daughters* Ibid., II.4.10.

131 "*hero-god*" Pindar, *Nemean Ode*, 3.22.

131 *Kérberos* Hesiod, *Theogony*, lines 310–12, 769–74. Kérberos, variously described as having anywhere from three to fifty heads, with writhing serpents growing out of his back, and the tail of a dragon, was posted outside Hades' grim palace, graciously greeting new entrants to the Underworld with a welcoming wag of that tail but ruthlessly devouring any who might attempt to escape. Héra, in advising Evristhéfs to send Hérakles on such a mission, clearly never expected to be bothered by his hulkish heroics again.

132 *Some time after this* Hyginus quotes Aeschylus as saying that the original sentence was for thirty thousand years (*PA*, II.15; see also *Fabulae*, 54 and 144).

132 *to gnaw at Prométheus's ever-regenerating liver* Aeschylus has the eagle come every other day, allowing one full day in between for the liver to reconstitute itself. In M. L. West's fascinating commentary on Prométheus's bondage, he notes that the liver was, from at least as early as the fifth century B.C., considered the seat of the passions, particularly of lust (West, *Theogony*, pp. 313–14). It still is in present-day Iran. One of the first expressions I learned in Farsi was "*Jigaret bokhoram*," which literally means "I eat your liver," but can be figuratively translated as "I love you." Because this expression is frowned upon in polite company, I suspect that "I lust for you" would be more like it. When I asked Fárzaneh why not *heart* instead of *liver*, she replied, "Well, which is tastier?"

132 *downfall that Prométheus had foreseen* Aeschylus, *Prometheus Bound*, lines 916–26.

132 *adding to Hérakles' glory* Hesiod, *Theogony*, lines 528–34.

132 "*deceive or go beyond the will of Zeus*" Ibid., line 613.

133 *a basic plot* The trilogy consists of *Prométheus the Fire-Bringer*, *Prométheus Bound*, and *Prométheus Unbound*. Some scholars suggest that the first

mentioned may have been the last to be performed—as an upbeat, evening-ending satyr play. Carl Kerényi, the noted Hungarian classicist, argues most persuasively that logic dictates the order in which I have listed them. I am also using the reconstruction laid out in Kerényi's *Prométheus.*

133 *stealing . . . the Golden Apples* Kerényi, *Prométheus*, pp. 119–20.

133 *the Hydra* A many-headed, serpentine monstrosity sired by Tiphón (and raised by Héra) which he had slain as the goal of his Second Labor. See Apollodorus, *Library*, II.5.2, including note 3 by Frazer.

133 *take his place in . . . Tártarus*, Ibid., lines 1026–29.

133 *expired in Prométheus's stead* Apollodorus, *Library*, II.5.4

134 *humiliating dethronement* Hyginus, *Fabulae*, 54. See also Kerényi, *Prométheus*, pp. 123–28. It was later said that Zeus took pity on Híron, released him from Tártarus, and enshrined him in the night sky as the constellation Centaurus (Hyginus, *Poetica Astronomica*, II.38). For a modern version of Híron's story, see John Updike's fascinating early novel *The Centaur*. For more on the possible origins of the Prométheus story, see M. L. West's commentary on Hesiod's *Theogony* (lines 523–33, pp. 313–15) in which he tells of an old legend that the frequent earthquakes in the Caucasus are caused by a giant imprisoned for his sins in the mountains, where a vulture pecks at his liver. If, as is now believed, the Greeks originated in the area, this legend could have been around a lot longer than even West suspected when he wrote his commentary back in 1966.

134 *an . . . arrogant race* The adjective he uses can also mean "reckless" or "presumptuous."

134 *Hesiod . . . pictures the Giants* See Hesiod, *Theogony*, line 185; Homer, *Odyssey*, VII.59–61; West, *Theogony*, commentary on lines 185–86 (pp. 220–21).

134 *enormous, fossilized bones* Adrienne Major's *The First Fossil Hunters* provides a riveting and detailed account of these discoveries, especially in chapters 2, 3, and 5. The latter deals with the Gigantomáchy (pp. 195–202); see also John Boardman, *The Archeology of Nostalgia*, pp. 33–43, who acknowledges his debt to Major.

134 *famous rendering* The depiction is on a Corinthian vase from the sixth century B.C. and can be seen in the Boston Museum of Fine Arts. (See also Major, *FFH*, pp. 157–65.) Homer mentions it in the *Iliad*, XX.145.

135 *saving the feared Héra from certain rape* Apollodorus tells us that Zeus "inspired" the giant with lust for Héra and then stunned him with a thunderbolt, allowing Hérakles to kill him. If so, this may have been part of far-seeing Zeus's clever plan to eventually reconcile Héra with Hérakles.

136 *a particularly horrific revenge* While none of the other mythographers dare to name Héra as the cause, it seems, first, highly uncharacteristic of her *not* to have contributed to this final agony, and, second, she had, after all, raised the Hydra whose poisonous blood led to his death. Finally, the viciousness of the method has her modus operandi written all over it.

137 *a constellation* Apollodorus, *Library*, II.7.7; Grant and Hazel, *WWCM*, p. 171; Sophocles, *The Women of Trachis;* Ovid, *Metamorphoses*, IX, 270–72.

137 *so the Christians claimed* Acts 1:9. There are other interesting similarities, too, in Hérakles' harrowing of Hell and his raising of Alcestis from the grave. See Grant, *MGR*, pp. 222–40 and Euripides' *Alcestis*. Throughout the Greek world at this time, there was a whole passel of would-be heroes coming to the fore, all straining to burst through the boundaries separating man from his deities by attempting godlike feats of daring and/or overleaping the traps laid out for them by the Fates. Athens had Theseus; Corinth, Bellerophón (badly lamed in his failed attempt to ride the winged horse Pegasus to the top of Mt. Ólympus); Thessaly, Jason and his Argonauts, and Thebes and Mycenae, their entire royal houses, most notoriously, those of Oedipus and Átreus. Some of these were genuinely heroic and others much too arrogant for their own good. All but one, however, would tragically overreach themselves—the exception being Hérakles.

137 *gouged out its eyes* Apollodorus, *Library*, II.8.1. See also Frazer's note 1 on p. 278 for less juicy versions.

14. THE HOUSE OF ÁTREUS—I: THE BEGINNINGS

139 "*This house . . . from the open mouth of a grave*" Aeschylus, *Agamemnon*, lines 1309–11, spoken by the captured Trojan princess Cassandra, cursed with the gift of prophecy. My translation.

140 *on actual events* Nothing has been established one way or the other, although as one scholar points out, traditions linking them so strongly with Mycenae may be proof enough and "chronologically sound" (Deuel, *Memoirs of Heinrich Schliemann*, p. 231).

140 *the convoluted story* For a thorough breakdown of all the variants on the House of Átreus, see Gantz, *EGM*, pp. 533–56. Also Grant and Hazel, *WWCM*, p. 261; 309, Graves, *GM*, 108, and Rose, *HGM*, p. 81.

140 *Lydia* Today, what was Lydia is that area of Turkey east of the Turkish mainland port of Izmir (in Greek, Smyrna).

141 *an eternity in Tártarus* Odysseus sees him there: Homer, *Odyssey* XI.583; see also Apollodorus, *Library*, Epitome II.1; Hyginus, *Fabulae*, 82–83. It was sometimes said that Zeus also suspended a huge rock over his head, which was rigged to fall and crush him should he reach the food or water.

144 *Pausanias . . . tells us* Pausanias, GTG, V.13.1. (Translation by W. H. Jones in Drees, *Olympía*, pp. 17–18.)

144 *bring his giant ivory shoulder blade to Troy* Pausanias, *Description of Greece*, V.13.1–7.

144 *Scholars now believe* For more, see Major, *FFH*, pp. 104–10, which also includes a photograph of a similar bone. As for Pélops as a real person, see Thucydides, *PW*, I.9.

15. THE HOUSE OF ÁTREUS—II: MYCENAE

149 "*At Mycenae . . . beyond all conjecture*" Miller, *The Colossus of Maroussi*, p. 86.

150 *the Great Mother herself had created the spot* For more on this, see Vincent Scully's wonderful exegesis on the site in his *The Earth, the Temple, and the Gods*, pp. 37–38. He compares the two hills to both the sacred horns of the bull and the raised arms of the goddess that are found in so many representations of her. He also emphasizes the particular holiness of conical-shaped hills and mountains, such as that of Mt. Yúktas rising south of Knossós. And then, of course, there are volcanoes . . .

151 "*This is the great shining bulge . . . bottomless pit*" Miller, *The Colossus of Maroussi*, p. 88.

153 *the dead are raised* Constantinidou-Partheniadou, *A Travelogue in Greece*, pp. 170–73, 175–77.

153 *previously* appeared *to him* Deuel, *Memoirs of Heinrich Schliemann*, p. 228.

154 *atop her Holy Mountain* Baring and Cashford, *MG*, pp. 122–23; Hughes, *HT*, pp. 102–3.

155 *the guiding lights* See Hughes, *HT*, p. 101.

16. A TERRIBLE BEAUTY

156 *A Terrible Beauty* The chapter title is from Robert Fagles's superb translation of the *Iliad*: "Ah [exclaim the old men of Troy as they watch Helen walking the ramparts] no wonder / the men of Troy and Argives under arms have suffered / years of agony all for her, for such a woman. Beauty, terrible beauty!" (*Iliad*, III.185–89.) This, in turn, was echoed by Yeats in his poem "Easter 1916" when writing of the bloody fruits of the Irish Easter Rebellion.

157 *the terrible goddess Némesis* Hesiod, *Theogony*, lines 223–24. See also Grant and Hazel, *WWCM*, p. 228.

158 *pure Pelasgian goddess-worship* See Nilsson, *The Mycenaean Origin of Greek Mythology*, pp. 73–76. He states that Helen "always was a goddess at Sparta," a pre-Greek vegetation goddess who had strong links with Persephóni, abducted and raped by Hádes to become the queen of the Underworld.

159 *born inside an egg* Pausanias, *GTG*, III.16.1. Unfortunately, the egg has since disappeared.

159 *the Tree of Life* Nilsson, *MMR*, p. 530. The poet was Theokritus, who lived in the Hellenistic age of uncertainty and declining faith that followed the death (323 B.C.) of Alexander the Great. See also the fascinating exegesis of Professor M. L. West in which he connects the egg and the tree to Indo-European myths of the Daughter of the Sun, to ancient springtime festivities, and even to the Christian practice of hanging of fragile, egglike globes to Christmas trees (West, *IH*, pp. 12–13).

159 *the Diós Koúri* Gantz, *EGM*, pp. 323–28.

160 *Helen's twin brothers* It would seem from this that the twins were older than Helen, as it would later seem that Clytemnéstra, too, had a few years on her in being the first to marry. Perhaps Helen

took a while longer than we mortals can possibly imagine to hatch out of that egg.

160 *pushed him off a cliff* Apollodorus, *Library*, Epitome 1.24; Pausanias, *GTG*, I.17.6; Plutarch, *Theseus*, 32.

160 *on the marriage block* See Hughes, *HT*, p. 62.

160 "*at the prompting of Zeus*" Hesiod, *CW*, line 75 (Loeb edition, p. 199).

161 *just married . . . Clytemnéstra* Apollodorus, *Library*, Epitome 2.15. See Frazer's note.

161 *take Helen by force* Hesiod, *CW*, lines 89–95. The fragments describing the wooing of Helen can be found in Hesiod's *Eoiae* fragments, Loeb edition, pp. 193–98.

161 "*the greatest gifts*" Hesiod, *CW*, fragment 68 (Loeb edition, pp. 193–99).

17. REMEMBERED PAIN

162 "*Zeus rightly leads mortals . . . the decks of their power*" Aeschylus, *Agamemnon,* lines 176–83 (my translation).

162 *the last Athenian play . . . by Euripides* The play was *Orestes.* Euripides then went into exile in Macedonia, where he wrote his masterpiece, *The Bacchae*, in his final years.

162 *historical events* For the latest discoveries and conjectures, see Joaquim Latacz's fascinating *Troy and Homer* as well as various Web sites on the subject. See also Bettany Hughes's *Helen of Troy*, which relies a lot on Latacz's evidence, and Barry Strauss's recent *The Trojan War*, which covers all the various theories while telling the tale with compelling style.

163 *the tales of these happenings* As previously noted, the Greeks' first recorded remembrances of these events were the magnificent creations of Homer and Hesiod, written in the mid eighth century B.C. Over the next two hundred years, a series of lesser epics filled in those parts of the story not covered by the earlier masterpieces. While none of the later poems has survived intact, there are enough fragments and summaries left for us to at least sketch out their contents. Collectively, they were called the "Epic Cycle." Contained within this larger group was the "Trojan Cycle," which included the *Iliad* and *Odyssey*. The poems in this latter cycle were:

• *The Kypria*, which dealt with the preludes to and the beginnings of the siege of Troy. This includes the judgment of Paris and the abduction of Helen.

• Homer's *Iliad*, which covered a seven-week period in the ninth year of the war.

• *The Aethiopis*, which told of the death of Achilles.

• *The Little Iliad*, whose main event was the introduction of the wooden horse into Troy.

• *The Ilíu Pérsis*, which gave us the stories of Laocoön and the Greeks' sacking of Troy and departure for home.

• *The Nostoi*, or "Homecoming," dealing with the return of the Greek heroes and including the stories of Agamemnon's assassination and Orestes' revenge as well as the return to Sparta of Menélaos and Helen.

• Homer's *Odyssey*, recounting the homecoming of Odysseus.

• And finally: The *Telegoneia*, in which Odysseus renewed his wanderings and was killed by Telegonus, his son by Circe.

The complete "Epic Cycle" also includes a series of works dealing with the creation, the war with Giants, the Oedipus cycle, the wars of the Seven against Thebes, and the subsequent victory of their sons, the Epigoni, against the descendants of Kadmos. (See the *OCD* under "Epic Cycle.") All the existing fragments can be found translated in the Loeb Library edition of Hesiod (vol. 57).

164 *His name was Aléxandros* The most detailed version of this story, called the "Judgment of Paris," was compiled very late in the canon of Greek myths, by Hyginus (*Fabulae*, 92), but references in Homer (*Diad*, XXIV.27–30) show that it was known even before Homer's time.

In 1924, with the decipherment of Hittite cuneiform, a most startling document came to light. It is a treaty from c. 1280 B.C. between the Hittite king of the time and a personage called Aleksandu of Wilusa (Ilios, in Greek). Its contents provide for mutual protection in time of war and seem to indicate that there had been trouble brewing for Wilusa. Scholars believe that this not only shores up arguments for the historicity of the Trojan War but also suggests that Paris (i.e., Aleksandu) might have been real as well. See Latacz, *TH*, pp. 75–76; Peter Green, "Finding Ithaca," (*NYRB*, November 30, 2006, p. 64.), and Peter Strauss's *The Trojan War.*

164 *protectorate of the powerful Hittite Empire* See Latacz, *TH*, pp. 79–81.

164 *one by one to make her case* The most complete version of this part of the story is again a late one, that of Hyginus (*Fabulae*, 92). In the *Iliad*, Homer makes a brief reference to it, saying that Paris's judgment took place in a courtyard (*Iliad*, XXIV.28–30), but Hyginus and most later pictorial accounts place it in the countryside (Gantz, *EGM*, pp. 568–70).

165 *famed for her heart-stopping beauty* Hyginus, *Fabulae*, 92; Euripides, *The Trojans*, lines 924–37. See also Gantz, *EGM*, pp. 570–71, for numerous alternate versions.

165 "*Her lips . . . suck forth my soul—see where it flies!*" The complete passage famously reads as follows: "Was this the face that launched a thousand ships, / And burnt the topless towers of Ilium? / Sweet Helen, make me immortal with a kiss./ Her lips suck forth my soul—see where it flies!" Marlowe, *Doctor Faustus*, act V, scene 1, lines 98–101 (circa 1590).

165 *Sometime afterward* There had to have been time, for example, for Achilles to have reached adolescence.

166 *Aphrodite's Disease* Homer, *Odyssey*, VIII.266–366; Hesiod, *Theogony*, lines 933–37. For the disease, see Hughes, *HT*, p. 150.

167 *Odysseus feigned madness* *Kypria* fragment; Apollodorus, *Library*, Epitome 3.7; Hyginus, *Fabulae*, 95.

167 *the fifteen-year-old Achilles* Apollodorus, *Library*, Epitome 3.16. Like Diónysos, Achilles had been disguised as a girl.

167 *butchered Iphigénia* Certain sources, including the *Kypria*, said that at the last moment, Ártemis substituted a deer for the unfortunate girl and transported Iphigénia to her temple in the Black Sea area of Taurus, today the Crimea, where she became a priestess. This is also recounted by Euripides in *Iphigénia Among the Taurians* and *Iphigénia in Aulis*. As usual, Euripides' interpretations of the events are very much his own and highly controversial.

168 "*Many a stalwart warrior's soul! . . . to fulfill the will of Zeus*" Homer, *Iliad*, I.3–5 (my translation).

168 "*Oh, the two of us! . . . a killing doom within us both!*" Ibid., VI.422–23 (translation by Robert Fagles).

18. THE KILLING DOOM

169 "*That it is Zeus . . . there is also shame*" Quoted in Hesiod, "The Cypria, 20" (Loeb edition), from Plato, *Euthyphro*, 12a.

169 *Greeks bearing gifts* The story of Achilles' death was first told in the *Aethiopis* (Loeb edition of *Hesiod*, pp. 507–8) and later elaborated on by Apollodorus (*Epitome*, V.3), Hyginus (*Fabulae*, 107), and Virgil (*Aeneid*, VI.56–58). The death of Paris was recounted in *The Little Iliad* (Loeb edition of Hesiod, p. 511) and Apollodorus (*Epitome*, V.8). The tale of the wooden horse is in the *Odyssey* (IV.242–64 and VIII.499–510), the *Ilíu Pérsis*, which gives us the stories of Laocoön and the Greeks' sacking of Troy and departure for home (Loeb edition of Hesiod, pp. 511 and 521), and most famously in book II of the *Aeneid*, the account of how Laocoön, having warned the Trojans to beware of Greeks bearing gifts, is throttled, along with his two sons, by a pair of huge serpents (sent by Apóllon) which roar at him out of the sea (*Aeneid*, II.40–56, 199–233).

170 *killed or sent into slavery* This recent estimate of Troy's population comes from Latacz (*TH*, p. 24). If half the population had been males, this would have totaled some three thousand corpses, not counting those allies from the outlying villages and towns who were caught in the attack. It was the custom in those days to summarily execute all the males and send the women and children into slavery. This continued even under the enlightened rule of Classical Athens. Thucydides, in writing about the Second Peloponnesian War, cites several instances of Athenian reprisals against cities resisting their rule. This included the execution of one thousand males on the island of Mytilene (Thucydides, *PW*, III.50) and, subsequently, all the men of the town of Scion (ibid., V.32) and the island of Melos (ibid., V.116). In fairness to Athens, Sparta wasn't any better. But then, it didn't pretend to be.

Of all the Trojans, only Aphrodite's son, Aeneas, had listened to the warnings about the wooden horse. He had heard Cassandra and then Laocoön rant about what a mistake it had been to bring that thing into Troy. So, when those horrible serpents came out of the sea to wrap Laocoön and his two little boys in their terrible, coiling clutches, Aeneas put his father on his back and led his followers out into the safety of the mountains, back to the slopes of Mt. Ida, where he had been given birth by the goddess Aphrodite. From there, they would make their way west to found what would become the mighty Roman Empire, whose troops would finally enact the Trojans' (and the goddess's) revenge in 146 B.C. by making Greece a Roman province. (See Scully, *ETG*, p. 22.)

170 *making their way back to Greece* For the individual specifics, see Nestor's account in Homer, *Odyssey*, III.130–36, 276–302, and that of the Trojan Cycle, "The Returns," Loeb edition of Hesiod, pp. 525–26. Also Gantz, *EGM*, pp. 662–63.

170 *the Spartan king cast aside his sword* Loeb edition of Hesiod, *The Little Iliad*, p. 519. It should be noted that, at this point, Helen clearly still had her charms, even though she was in her forties and, by the standards of the times, an old woman. On average, Mycenaean women were giving birth at twelve and dead at about age twenty-eight (Hughes, *HT*, p. 41).

171 *like golden-spindled Ártemis* Homer, *Iliad*, IV.122–24. This is not a casual comparison used to give a bit of glamour to the scene. As every Greek would have known, Ártemis was, first of all, the goddess whom Agamemnon had so offended at Aulis that he had had to sacrifice his daughter Iphigénia in penance and, as a result, would himself be slaughtered by Helen's sister, Clytemnéstra. Moreover, Ártemis came from that same hotbed of evil that Tántalos did, Lydia, and she was one of a long line of surrogates of the Great Mother (including Kybele and Anahita) who had made their way across the Aegean to take root in Greece. She is so terrible in some of her aspects that she is pictured with the Gorgon's serpent-haired head, and when sacrificed to, she often demanded human blood. Although the Goddess of the Hunt, she is also a protector of all things wild and weak, including animals and children. (Burkert, *GR*, pp. 149–52.) So when Homer pictures Helen in this way, it is to give her an aura not simply of danger but of motherly comfort as well.

171 *a single tear in grief* A quote taken directly from Homer's *Odyssey*, IV.219–34 (my translation). It was most likely opium, which, when mixed with alcohol, becomes the powerfully soothing narcotic called laudanum. Opium was treated with great respect by the Greeks, who viewed it as a sacred gift of the goddess. It was probably handled and prepared only by priestesses in rites of communion with the Great Mother's powers. See Hughes, *HT*, pp. 103–5, 233.

171 *no one raised a hint of recrimination* Helen casually tells Telémachos of her encounter with Odysseus the night he snuck into Troy disguised as a beggar, when she seems to have seduced him, "bathing and anointing his body with oil," to worm from him the secret plans of the Achaíans (*Odyssey*, IV.242–64) before letting him escape back to camp. Menélaos jovially follows this with his own story of how Helen subsequently tormented him and the others hiding in the wooden horse by coming to view it on the arm of her latest paramour, Prince Deïphobos, who had married her after his brother Paris's death. She circled the horse three times, caressing its sides and calling out the names of those within in the voices of the wives, trying, to no avail, to trick them into revealing their presence. "You must have been possessed by some *daímon* seeking glory for the Trojans," says the amiable, drug-addled Menélaos, apologizing for her. (*Odyssey*, IV.271–89.)

171 *worship Helen as the goddess* Homer, *Odyssey*, XV.160–80.

173 *blaming Zeus, Fate, and the Furies* Homer, *Iliad*, XIX.85–90.

174 "*like an ox at its trough*" Homer, *Odyssey*, XI.411 (my translation).

174 "*She turned her back on me . . . the whore*" Ibid., XI.404–26.

174 *the port of Mycenae* Ibid., III.309–12, IV.431–569; and Apollodorus, *Epitome*, VI.1. See also Gantz, EGM, pp. 662–64, 676.

175 *Oréstes married their beautiful daughter, Hermione* In the *Odyssey*, the "ever-truthful" Old Man of the Sea prophesizes to Menélaos (IV.561–69) that because he is married to Zeus's daughter, he will not die but be transported by the gods to an idyllic afterlife in the Elysian Fields. Homer tells us nothing of Helen's end, only implying, because of Telémachos's promise, that she will be worshipped as a goddess. Early tradition had it that she lived a long and peaceful life at Sparta and may have joined Menélaos in paradise. The Greeks would not decide her ultimate fate until much later, at a time, in fact, c. 404 B.C., when her Spartans were about to finish off Athenian democracy for good (see below, chapter 21).

19. THE VOICES OF GOD

179 "*Over the centuries . . . God softened also*" Kazantzákis, *Report to Greco*, p. 263 (translation by P. A. Bien).

179 *drought and earthquakes* Early mythographers said this destruction was caused by the return of Hérakles' sons to finally take the power long denied them. These assaults may also have been another source for the myth of the Great Flood (see Apollodorus, *Library*, I.7.2.) in which all the human race was destroyed except for Prométheus and Pandóra's son, Deucalíon, and his wife, Pyrrha. Their children and grandchildren would repopulate the world. Especially their first son, Hellen, who would be thought of as the progenitor of the new Greek race or, as they still call themselves, "Hellenes" (see p. 233) with Hellen's sons, in turn, fathering the three great tribal branches of early Greece: Xouthos (the Achaíans and Iónians), Aeolus (the Aeolians), and Dorus (the Dorians).

Explanations by experts in the field include these various "Acts of God" as theories of invasions by iron-weaponed raiders such as the Dorians from the hinterlands and/or by the mysterious "Sea Peoples" mentioned in Egyptian inscriptions. The latest and most persuasive of these hypotheses comes from Robert Drews, who suggests that when the barbarians came down from the hills, they arrived with new battle tactics (massive assaults by foot soldiers) and new weapons, among them, cast-iron swords. Within a forty- to fifty-year period (c. 1230–1185 B.C.), most of the above-mentioned empires were obliterated in wholesale orgies of destruction and plunder. (Drews, *EBA*, particularly chaps. 9–14.)

179 "*hastening to make an utter end . . . mortal man*" Hesiod, *CW*, p. 201 (Loeb edition, translation by H. G. Evelyn-White).

180 *Herodotus tells us* Herodotus, *Histories*, I.56–57.

180 *the old Mycenaean tales* About half the old gods listed on the Linear B tablets were "forgotten" (Burkert, *GR*, p. 48 and section I.3.6).

182 *the darkling plain* Interestingly, there is no indication in Homer, Hesiod, or the other ancient writers that there had been any such thing as a "Dark Age." On the contrary, Thucydides and other writers on the post–Trojan War period speak of "many changes and strife" and the sending out of settlements abroad, but in general, the impression is one of continuity rather than a deep disruption. (Thucydides, *PW*, I.12; Osborne, *GITM*, pp. 32–34.)

183 *magnificence of his being* For a detailed discourse on the site's effect, see Scully, *ETG*, pp. 136–37.

183 *Achilles prays* Homer, *Iliad,* XVI.233–48.

183 *saving Odysseus* Homer, *Odyssey*, XIV.327–30, XIX.296–99.

184 *in the bow of Jason's ship* Apollonius, *Argonautika*, line 520.

184 *the opening scene* Aeschylus, *The Eumenides*, lines 1–5.

185 *the goddess's sacred fumes* Whether or not there actually were fumes has been a matter of considerable controversy. Although the crevice and its inspirational vapors were later attested to by authorities as reputable as Diodorus, Pausanias, and the biographer Plutarch (who served an extended term as Delphí's high priest), when the French excavated the temple at the turn of the twentieth century, they found no evidence of any such fissure nor of any geologic formation that might have permitted such gases to arise. Their arguments were so persuasive that almost all accounts of Delphí written since the 1920s have relegated the fumes to the realm of wishful thinking. However, reports of new findings by a team whose investigators included a geologist, archaeologist, geochemist, and toxicologist have apparently proved that Plutarch and the others were not telling tall tales, that the oracle was indeed inhaling a kind of gas—specifically, ethylene—that would have fired her mind with what would have seemed to be divine inspiration. Whether or not it actually did is, of course, still open to question. An utterly absorbing account of these investigations (and of a history of Delphí) is *The Oracle*, by William J. Broad.

186 *setting loose two eagles* The source of the story of the eagles is a scholiast's commentary on the presence at Delphí of the golden eagles of Zeus, mentioned in Pindar, *Pythian 4*, line 6. (For the exact quote of the scholiast, see Cook, *Zeus*, vol. 2, p. 179.) The story of the navel stone vomited up by Krónos and placed at Delphí is first mentioned by Hesiod (*Theogony*, lines 498–500). When Pausanias visited Delphí, he saw it sitting outside the temple of Apóllon. He said that the Delphians poured oil on it every day and, at festival time, draped it with strands of unspun wool. Presumably this was in imitation of the swaddling blanket with which Rhéa covered it to fool Krónos into swallowing it (Pausanias, *GTG,* X.24.5). It has since been established, however, that that stone was just a copy of the original, which was always inside the oracle's holy of holies.

The geographer Strabo (c. 63 B.C.–A.D. 24) informs us that Delphí happened to be "almost in the center of Greece taken as a whole . . . [and was] believed to be in the center of the inhabited world," making it a perfect place for the Greeks to begin the long and difficult process of bringing themselves together as a nation (Strabo, *Geography*, IX.3.5–7).

187 *the language of the natives* Drees, *Olympía*, p. 12.

187 *a lightning bolt* Ibid., p. 17. Such lightning-struck places were always considered sacred and afterward enclosed, as this later was, to mark them off from the surrounding land.

187 *Hérakles . . . founding the Olympic Games* Pausanias also offers the alternate theory that Zeus himself instituted the Games to celebrate his victory and that Apóllon beat Hermes in the first footrace and then thrashed Áres, the God of War, in boxing (*GTG*, V.7.9–10).

187 *many trees* Pindar tells the story of its origins in his *Olympian Ode 3* (lines 20–35) and *10* (lines 41–60). Pausanias also mentions it (*GTG*, V.7.7). Pausanias also recounts the story of Hérakles bringing the poplar to Olympía (ibid., V.14.2–3).

187 *Pausanias is said to have written* Perrottet, *NO*, p. 61. I have not, however, been able to find the exact quotation in my edition of Pausanias's works.

188 *Its spirit . . . in its trees* The most important of Hérakles' imports was the olive tree, one of which was planted outside Zeus's temple and used to crown the winners in the Games. Pindar relates the story of its origins in his *Olympian Ode 10* (lines 41–60). Pausanias also mentions it (*GTG*, V.7.7). In addition, Pausanias recounts the story of Hérakles bringing the white poplar to Olympía, where it was used exclusively in burning the thighs of animals sacrificed to Zeus (ibid., V.14.2–3).

20. HOLDING THE CENTER

189 "*Zeus is ether . . . higher than this!*" Aeschylus, *Fragment*, quoted in Burkert, *GR*, p. 131.

190 *incised on blocks of stone* See the *OCD* under "Alphabet, Greek" (p. 66) plus Bernard Knox's lively discussion of the subject in his introduction to the *Norton Book of Classical Literature* (pp. 23–28). In addition, it has been suggested that the concept of the city-state may also have originated with the Phoenicians (see the *OCD*, p. 650).

190 *the city-states grew in size* Scholars estimate the number of city-states at about 1,500. Some (particularly on the islands) were no larger than present-day villages and their environs. Only a few had populations over 10,000. (Grant, *The Rise of the Greeks*, p. 332, fn. 12.)

191 *call themselves Hellenes* See Gantz, *EGM*, pp. 167–69. Also Hesiod, *CW*, 1 (Loeb edition, p. 155).

191 *the first Olympic games* The traditional date of 776 B.C. was attested to in a fourth-century-A.D. edition of Eusebius's chronology of ancient history, which says that the first Olympiad was in 776, "405 years . . . from the capture of Troy." See Text 10 in Osborne, *GITM*, p. 100.

192 *The proposal* Pausanias, *GTG,* V.4.5–6 and V.8.1–5.

192 *solely a Peloponnesian affair* Drees, *Olympía*, p. 36.

192 *the god's altar* Ibid., p. 66. Over the centuries, the ashes from these sacrifices (mixed and packed down with water from the Alphiós) would create an immense, conical pile that, in Pausanias's time (c. A.D. 150, almost one thousand years later), had reached the height of a two-story building (about twenty-two feet), with flights of steps cut into the ash on either side to take the sacrificing priests and others (women not included) to the top (Pausanias, *Description of Greece*, V.13.9; also Drees, *Olympía*, p. 21).

The altar had a circumference of 125 feet at the bottom and 32 feet at the top. It was so sacred, says Pausanias, that kites and other scavenger birds would never dare to try and snatch a morsel from the offerings. Earlier, however, Hérakles had been so plagued by flies during his sacrifices that he instituted a special rite to get rid of them. This honored Zeus in a new manifestation as "Averter of Flies." It was so successful that it became standard practice at all subsequent Olympics. The Roman encyclopedist Pliny the Elder wrote that following the rite, the flies dropped—well, like flies—while another Roman naturalist, Aelian, claimed that they "voluntarily" stayed on the opposite side of the river until the Games were over. See Pausanias, *GTG,* V.14.1, and Perrottet, *NO*, p. 71.

192 *tyrants took over* The epithet *týrannos* (tyrant) was a non-Greek word first applied to Gyges of Lydia (680–648 B.C.). Nowadays, there is a difference of opinion as to whether or not the term originally had the same negative connotation that it does today. The fact that the Greeks did not have a word for the phenomenon in their own language is

thought to mean that they considered it something foreign and (therefore) bad. On the other hand, it was understood by a majority of the Greek people as being the kind of government established by strong individuals concerned with granting some rights and better civic conditions to the rising middle classes by overthrowing the ruling oligarchies. Whereas the latter were small groups of privileged aristocrats who limited the benefits of the polis to the lucky few, tyrants made a point of instituting programs of public works and other patriotic displays which made all the people feel proud of their participation, mostly imagined, in the fate of their body politic. Therefore, tyrants had widespread approval. At least in the beginning. Aesop (c. 620–560 B.C.), however, would say, in his fable *The Wolf and the Lamb,* "Any excuse will serve a tyrant." Later, both Plato and Aristotle would condemn tyrannies (and the dictatorships they became) as the worst of all forms of government.

193 *colonies were founded abroad* In 770 B.C., a small Greek tribe called the Graii joined Évia in colonizing a spot on the Italian coast near Naples. Subsequently, the Romans began to call everyone who came from Greece "Graíci"—that is, "Greeks"—while the Greeks, of course, continued to call themselves "Hellenes" (Élliness).

193 *three new festivals* The one at Delphí was called, after its oracle, the Pythian Games. Isthmía was on the Corinthian isthmus. Both were established in about 582 B.C. A decade later saw the inauguration of the third at Neméa in the Argolid, famous as the site of Hérakles' triumph over the great Nemean lion. Shortly afterward, Athens did them all one better by expanding its local Panathenaía (all-Athenian) festival to one so rich with artistic as well as athletic events that it would attract participants from all over the country, regardless of their polis of origin. (Osborne, *GITM*, pp. 243–44.)

193 *Man was . . . the measure of all things* In about 350 B.C., as we shall see, a new stadium was constructed at the foot of the eastern side of the Hill of Krónos, thus moving the games outside Zeus's Sacred Grove and fully into the realm of the secular (Swaddling, *AOG*, p. 29).

21. THEIR FINEST HOUR

194 *"Man is the measure . . . that it is not"* The quote is from Plato, *Theaetetus*, 152a (my translation). Whether or not Protagoras actually said this is not certain.

194 *its image of the gods* I have taken this observation about the *Iliad* from Osborne, *GITM*, p. 244.

194 *"The spear struck him . . . legs and knees"* Homer, *Iliad*, XIV.464–68 (my translation).

195 *slaves or corpses* See Simone Weil's "The *Iliad*, or The Poem of Force." This essay has recently been published as part of an edition which also includes Rachel Bespaloff's "On the Iliad." Both were written at almost the same time, in 1939, when their Jewish authors were going into exile in the United States and attempting to deal with the kind of war being forced upon humanity by the Nazis. For Weil's comment on turning people into things, see *War and the Iliad*, p. 3.

195 *the real truth about Helen* Pausanias, *GTG*, III.19.11. See also Peter Levi's most informative footnote (p. 71, no. 184) on the matter.

195 *"Not true these words . . . the walls of Troy"* Plato, *Phaedrus*, 243a (Stesíchorus fragment 32 Bergk; my translation). Plato refers to it twice, once in his *Phaedrus* (lines 242–43) and again in *The Republic* (IX.586). In the former, he cites Stesíchorus's blindness as an example of what can happen to you if you impugn a divinity (i.e., Helen), and in the latter, to speak of the Trojan War in terms of people's destructive fighting over shadows to satisfy "their ignorant, insatiable lusts."

195 *off course to Egypt* An alternate version has Zeus send Hermes to rescue his daughter from Paris's clutches and whisk her off to Egypt for safety, leaving Paris to return to Troy empty-handed.

In about 430 B.C., Herodotus wrote in his *Histories* that he had spoken to Egyptian priests who confirmed the story of Helen's spending the war in Egypt under the protection of their king, Proteus. He goes on to say, however, that the Achaíans' (i.e., Greeks') tragic refusal to accept the truth had been willed by Divine Providence so that "it might be made evident to all men that when great wrongs are done, the gods will surely visit them with great punishments." (Herodotus, *Histories*, II.113–20, Rawlinson translation, GBWW, vol. 6, pp. 71–73.)

Euripides took up both Herodotus's theme and Stesíchorus's recantation in two of his plays, *Eléktra* and *Helen*, the latter written in about 412 B.C., when Athens itself was in a state of siege and swallowing the bitter fruit of its attempts to impose its rule upon the rest of Greece. At the end of Euripides' third-to-last play, *Oréstes*, when Oréstes slays the Spartan queen as he has slain her sister, the playwright has Apóllon take Helen up to Ólympus to sit at Zeus's side. Not coincidentally, perhaps, this play was written in about 408 B.C., when Helen's Spartans were threatening to overwhelm Athens. Pausanias, on the other hand, tells us the much more romantic story that as Helen was dying, she was transported to an island in the Black Sea, where the great warrior Achilles had been waiting for her all those years, holding on to the vision he had once had of her outside the walls of Troy. Here, these two incomparable figures of Greece's Heroic Age would at last be joined in marriage and live in wedded bless, happily ever after. (Pausanias, *GTG*, VI.19.11.)

196 "*And we butchered ourselves . . . for a Helen*" Seferis, *Collected Poems*, pp. 354–61 (my translation).

196 *numerous temples, sanctuaries, and statues* For example: Pausanias, *Description of Greece*, II.20.6, II.31.6, III.23.10, IV.31.6, IV.34.6, V.5.1, VII.23.9, VIII.9.2, VIII.30.10 See also the online article by Francesca Jourdain, "The Lighthouse of Alexandria," http://www.ptahhotep.com/articles/lighthouse.html.

197 *Herodotus tells us* Herodotus, *Histories*, VI.44.

198 *some two million men* See ibid., VII.60, where he puts the number at 1.7 million men, not including the navy. Modern scholars estimate it at a more feasible 200,000 (Strauss, *BOS*, p. 42). Among Xerxes' more visible projects were the digging of a canal across the peninsula of Athos (a massive three-year effort whose filled-in, grass-tufted depression can still be seen today) so as to avoid the dangers of sailing around it and having his fleet wrecked by a storm, as had happened to his father in 493 (Herodotus, *Histories*, VI.44).

198 *the god advised the people of Delphí* Herodotus, *Histories*, VII.178.

198 *the Spartans were informed* Ibid., VII.220.

199 "*a wooden wall*" Ibid., VII.140–43.

199 *In a storied battle* Ibid., VII.219–34. The Persian king Xerxes, visiting the site afterward, ordered that Leonídas's head be cut off and impaled

above the battlefield upon a pole (Herodotus, *Histories*, VII.238). Today, a grand statue of the Spartan hero dominates the scene.

200 *in panicked disarray* Ibid., VIII.37.

200 *what they were said to be by tradition* See Paul Veyne's fascinating book-length essay on this, *Did the Greeks Believe in Their Myths?* (translation by Paula Wissing [Chicago: University of Chicago Press, 1988]). In a similar vein, J. M. Coetzee tells us that African thought generally agrees that "after the seventh generation we can no longer distinguish between history and myth" (J. M. Coetzee, "Diary of a Bad Year," an excerpt from the novel of the same name, *NYRB*, July 19, 2007, p. 20).

200 *the sea was awash* Herodotus, *Histories*, VIII.12–13; Strauss, *BOS*, p. 26.

200 *"God," wrote Herodotus . . . "The size of the Greek"* Herodotus, *Histories*, VIII.13 (translation by de Sélincourt).

201 *the last of the Persian army* Ibid., VIII.64.

202 "*Thy hand . . . In gloomy mists of mourning*" Aeschylus, *The Persians*, lines 533–36 (translation by Philip Vellacot). The play, incidentally, was funded by a wealthy, twenty-three-year-old son of an Athenian general—one of a series of astute political moves that would bring the young man, ten years later, to the leadership of Athens. His name was Pericles.

22. THE WONDER OF THE WORLD

203 "*I belong to Zeus*" Drees, *Olympía*, p. 105.

203 *whenever a city-state held a festival* At Athens, the ceremony for Zeus Soter was put on in Piráeus, and that of Zeus Meilichios was similarly set in a spot somewhere well out of town. An exception was the bizarre rite called the Bouphonia (Ox Murder) in honor of Zeus of the City, Zeus Dii Poliei. This was set around and upon the Acropolis in the last month of the year and involved the assumption of guilt on the part of all citizens for the slaying of the first of a herd of oxen that stopped to eat from the sacred grain spread upon the festival's altar. The ox's hide would then be resurrected (stuffed and yoked to a plow) and with this, the sin was absolved. Why? The reasons lie too far back in the primal past for scholars to be sure, but it seems to be

a sacrificial washing away of sins that is connected to the beginning of the new year—and thus "an affirmation of the city, in honor of Zeus, lord of the *polis*." (Burkert, *GR*, p. 231.)

203 *a shrine to Héra* See Drees, *Olympía*, pp. 114–15, in which he specifically equates the building of this temple with Zeus's winning "his long and arduous battle with the Mycenaean goddess [Héra]."

203 *the spoils of Pisa's treasury* Pausanias, *GTG*, V.10.2.

204 *the most magnificent tribute* Although there had been one previous edifice, the enormous temple of Zeus at Akragas on Sicily, completed in 510 B.C., it was so far off in the hinterlands as to be an event of little consequence in Greece itself. In addition, mention must also be made of the attempt by the Athenian tyrant Pisístratos, who decided in about 540 B.C. to honor his own dictatorial achievements in the city by housing Zeus there as well. Pisístratos died before the proposed temple could be completed, as would his two sons, the equally reviled Hipparchos and Hippias. Almost seven hundred years would pass before the Roman emperor Hadrian, that great lover of all things Greek, would have it finished (in A.D. 131). He called it the Olympieum. Today, its ruins and few remaining columns (at fifty-two feet, making it the tallest Greek temple ever built) are sad second cousins to the Acropolis, visible from there but visited by only a few wandering tourists, most of whom stumble upon it while walking out of the western end of Athens's luxuriant park, the Zappeion.

205 *If we are to believe Plutarch* Plutarch, "Pericles," chap. 31, 2–5.

205 *the long-lost workshop* Drees, *Olympía*, pp. 147–49. It is also a remarkable coincidence that the workshop where Zeus's statue had been created was being converted into a Byzantine church at the same time (mid-fifth century A.D.) that the statue (and Zeus himself) was at the Byzantine capital of Constantinople well on the road to being elevated into the Christian firmament—an event which we will recount at the very end of our story.

205 *mentioned by Pausanias* Pausanias, *GTG*, V.15.1.

206 *which Pausanias testifies* Ibid., V.11.9.

207 *after their arrival in Olympía* Before that, they had been housed for a month at the host city of Elis, competing to see who would be allowed to participate in the Games. Those chosen then had to march

two days over the Sacred Way to Olympía. It was an arduous, forty-mile trek in the hottest and driest time of summer, the period just before the harvest. But to endure it was yet another proof of the athletes' superior abilities.

207 *Pausanias tells us* Ibid., V.24.9. The quotation was taken from Swaddling, *AOG*, p. 39.

207 *his dictum of fair play* Pausanias, *GTG*, V.24.9–10. Swaddling, *AOG*, p. 39. Perrottet, *NO*, p. 84. This was not a mere formality. Using bribes, black magic, and countless other tricks of the trade to gain an edge had been common at Olympía since the day Pélops had switched the linchpins on Inómaos's chariot. Such practices were (and are) as natural to the highly competitive Greeks as breathing. So every means possible had to be used to curb them, including death threats from the Great Thunderer himself. Enormous fines were assessed, and certain cheaters were publicly whipped—a painful and particularly humiliating punishment normally employed only against slaves. (Swaddling, ibid., p. 39.)

Drees notes that these instances of bribery did not occur until the Peloponnesian War (431–404 B.C.) "sapped both the political and moral fiber of the Greek cosmos" (Drees, *Olympía*, p. 52). Whether or not these deterrents made much of a difference is impossible to know, although it may be safe to say that they were probably about as effective as current prohibitions against steroids.

208 *the ritual sacrifice of one hundred oxen* These one hundred oxen were a gift of the city of Elis. They were slaughtered one by one on a marble slab at the base of his Great Altar, the act accompanied by the high-pitched wail of flutes as the arterial blood spurted forth into a silver bowl. Only one of the beast's thighs was then carried to the top of the ever-growing pyre to be burned in Zeus's honor, the smoke rising to his abode in the heavens as a gift of sustenance from his worshippers. The rest of the animal was sent to the festival's butchers to be roasted over great pits and, that evening, distributed free to the Games' eager communicants. Afterward, the ashes were sprinkled with water from the Alphiós River and pressed down to become a permanent part of the ever-mounting altar (Perrottet, *NO*, p. 127). In addition to this particular rite, there were daily sacrifices to the god throughout the year. While most were simple offerings of incense, wine, and honey cakes, on special occasions, meat was also burned.

23. THE DYING FALL

209 "*What was scattered . . . Blows apart*" Heraclitus, *Fragments*, p. 27 (translated by Haxton).

210 "*victory would be theirs . . . whether invoked or uninvoked*" Thucydides, *PW*, I.118.2–3.

210 *the death of . . . Socrates* This version of events comes from a memoir of Socrates written by Xenophon, an Athenian military man and writer, who was part of Socrates' circle (Xenophon, *Conversations of Socrates*, "Socrates' Defense," 12). In Plato's version of the defense, Socrates famously claims that the Pythia said there was no one wiser than he because he knew that he knew nothing (Plato, *Apology*, 20e–21a).

210 *hymn to Zeus* Cleanthes (translation by T. W. Rolleston), http://www.geocities.com/westhollywood/heights/4617/stoic.html.

211 *two lengthy wars OCD* under "Sacred Wars," pp. 1343–44. Also Hoyle, *Delphi*, pp. 116–18.

211 *a large, circular edifice* Drees, *Olympía*, pp. 121–22. This building itself was known as the Phillipaeum. Outlines of its circular base can still be seen today in the Altis just west of Héra's temple.

212 *he had learned from the oracle* Whether Alexander actually believed this is still hotly debated. But he nevertheless used it to great effect, as attested to by coins showing him sporting the signature ram horns of Ammon. Ammon was also known as Amon-Ra, the father of the Egyptian gods who was considered to be Zeus under another name. This story is told in various versions by many ancient writers, among them Arrian, Diodorus Siculus, and Plutarch. For more modern views on Alexander, there are a slew of books. Among the most popular are those by Mary Renault, Robin Lane Fox, and Paul Cartledge. See also http://pothos.org for a fund of information about Alexander continually updated by devotees, amateur and professional.

212 *the graveyard of Iraq* Some fifty miles south of Baghdad, Babylon continued to lie in ruins until Saddam Hussein also tried and failed to reconstruct it. As of this writing, the site is now being used by U.S.-led forces as a military arms depot. The British newspaper the *Guardian* reports that U.S. and Polish forces, in the process of bulldozing and otherwise trampling the area underfoot, have done enormous damage to

its priceless archaeological remains ("Babylon Wrecked By War," *Guardian*, January 15, 2005, http://www.guardian.co.uk/Iraq/Story/0,2763,1391042,00.html).

212 *attempts at plundering both Olympía and Delphí* Drees, *Olympía*, p. 155.

212 *the barbarian Gauls* Pausanias, GTG, X.19.6.

213 *not a single Gaul survived* Ibid., X.23.1–7.

213 *The Romans were coming* In 191 B.C., Rome would take over Delphí and in 146 B.C., Olympía.

213 *a burst abscess* See Plutarch, *Lives*, under "Sulla."

213 *the Jewish temple in Jerusalem* Suetonius, *TC*, "Gaius (Caligula)," 22; Josephus, *Antiquities of the Jews*, XVII–XIX, Rolfe translation http://www.fordham.edu/HALSALL/ancient/suetonius-caligula.html). In his account, Josephus tells us that the prefect responsible for placing the images in the temples was Pontius Pilate (XVII.3.1). In Caligula's defense, it must be said that his was not the first despoliation of the Jewish temples. This had been accomplished by Alexander's successors, the Seleucids. In the process of completing a spectacularly large and ornate Great Altar to Zeus at Pergamon (in northwestern Turkey), the Seleucid king Antiochus IV went to war with Alexander's heir in Egypt, Ptolemy VI, and captured Jerusalem. He then proceeded to force the Jews to Hellenize, rededicating the Temple to Zeus (by chance, on December 25) and insisting that the Jews accept Zeus as Yahweh. This resulted in a revolt by the Hasidim (the "pious'), which led to the slaughter of many Jewish men, women, and children. After the death of Antiochus in 163, a full-fledged revolt followed, led by Judas Maccabee, the success of which is celebrated in the festival of Hanukkah (see the Apocrypha texts: 1 Maccabees and 2 Maccabees).

Finally, in the Book of Revelation, Pergamon, site of Zeus's Great Altar, is listed as the place "where Satan's seat is" (Rev. 2:12–13).

213 "*a peal of laughter*" Suetonius, *TC*, "Gaius (Caligula)," 57. It has been speculated that the "peal" or "roar" of laughter (depending on your translation) came from a sudden settling of the wooden scaffolding inside. Whatever, the statue would thereafter remain in situ for about another 350 years.

214 *knifed the emperor to death* He had stopped to watch a group of boys rehearsing, somewhat appropriately, a Trojan war dance. It was as if

the consequences of that fateful encounter were still reverberating down the ages (as it continues to do). Suetonius makes a point of telling us that Caligula was knifed some thirty times, "including sword thrusts through the genitals." He was twenty-nine and had ruled for less than four years. (Suetonius, *TC*, "Gaius (Caligula)," 57 (translation by Robert Graves.)

214 "*only the Greeks . . . worthy of my efforts*" Ibid., "Nero," 22. (my translation).

214 *granted the entire province Roman citizenship* Ibid., XXIII–XIV. Nero's atrocious lyre playing and singing also probably gave rise to the story that while Rome burned (A.D. 64) he fiddled—although the violin would not be invented for another 1,500 years or so. In fact, after the fire, he (or his advisers) seems to have opened his palace to house and feed refugees and launched an ambitious redevelopment program with spacious parks and avenues and a safe distance between houses. Rumors that Nero had started the fire led to his scapegoating of the tiny new religious sect known as Christians: "Covered with the skin of beasts, they were torn by dogs and perished, or were nailed to crosses, and were doomed to the flames and burnt, to serve as a nightly illumination, when the daylight had expired." Among those martyred were the apostles Peter and Paul. However, the Roman historian Tacitus (c. A.D. 55–117) tells us that this tactic backfired and generated sympathy for the Christians (Tacitus, *The Annals*, XV.44). In turn, the Christians would get their revenge some 350 years later when Theodosius sent them rampaging against the pagans and their artifacts.

214 *Nero also starred* Pausanias, *GTG*, X.7.1.

214 *the sacred fissure stuffed* Dio Cassius, *Roman History*, LXII.14.2. See also Hoyle, *Delphi*, pp. 136–37.

214 *his private secretary's earnest assistance* Suetonius, *TC*, XLIX.

215 "*Oh, Zeus . . . Cronus*" Lucian, *Works*, quoted in Drees, *Olympia*, pp. 152–53 (my insertion in brackets).

24. FIRES FROM HEAVEN

216 "*To Olympus . . . for ever and ever*" Homer, *Odyssey*, VI.41–45 (Butler translation).

219 *many treasures* Professor A. B. Cook tells us of "an anonymous Latin mythographer [who] records an actual cult of Zeus on Mt. Ólympus" and says that "sundry details concerning it are mentioned by Solinus, Plutarch, and Augustine." He adds that there was an altar to Zeus on the summit and that "it was believed that offerings left upon it would not be affected by wind or weather, but would be found again after a year's interval precisely as they had been left." This included "certain letters formed in the ashes on the occasion of their last visit." (Cook, *Zeus*, vol. 1, pp. 102–3.) Most of the other important mountains in Greece have at least traces—altars, pottery shards, thrones cut into the rock—to mark religious activity at their summits. Cook, for example, devotes a 120-page appendix to the mountain cults of Zeus, listing over one hundred sites in Greece and its environs where altars and temples were built and various sacrifices conducted. (Cook, ibid., vol. 2, part 2, pp. 868–987.) The great majority are now dedicated to the prophet Elías.

220 *gods that had no names* See Burkert, *GR*, pp. 281–85, and *Samothrace*, the superb guide to the excavations published by New York University's Institute of Fine Arts.

221 *feed him to wild horses* Apollodorus, *Library*, III.5.1.

221 *they tore him to pieces* See Ovid's *Metamorphoses*, book XI.

222 *the Fire Dancers of Thrace* The present ritual is said to have originated in the eastern Thracian village of Kostí (now a part of Turkey) in about A.D. 1250. According to local history, when the church of St. Constantine caught fire, the villagers rushed in to save the icons of Sts. Constantine and Eleni and emerged unharmed from the inferno, carrying the sacred images, which were not so much as singed. Today, a three-day ceremony commemorates the event on the saints' feast days (May 20–21), during which the celebrants work themselves into an ecstatic state with the help of the incessant beating of drums and then, their feet bare, dance themselves and their icons across the burning coals. Inevitably, a carnival atmosphere has grown up around the event, with merry-go-rounds, bumper cars, and hot dog stands set up in the vicinity, and TV and movie crews breathing down the necks of the already harassed devotees as they make their way through crowds of onlookers to the site of their fiery ordeal.

222 *Dion's archaeological site* The excavation of Dion, ongoing since 1973, has been undertaken by the University of Thessaloniki, under the

inspired direction of Professor Dimitrios Pandermalis. For more, see his excellent guide, *Dion.*

225 *a pillar of sacred fire* Euripides, *The Bacchae,* line 1082. Euripides would have watched this in 406 B.C.

225 *von Däniken* For particularly Greek subjects, see his *Odyssey of the Gods* (London: Vega, 2002).

227 *the Christians* As I write this, news has come of the discovery of a companion statue of Héra, of the same size and thick-grained marble as that of Zeus. Apparently, it had been used by the Christians as filling for a defensive rampart. It, too, is headless. (See the AP release "Greek Archeologists Find Hera Statue," March 2, 2007.)

25. THE FINAL METAMORPHOSIS

228 *"Lord . . . ," I cried . . . "my master is Time" Anthologia Palatina,* IX.441 (quoted in Bury, *HLRE,* vol. 1, pp. 374–75).

229 *the "pagan" religions* The Latin word *paganus* referred to "villagers" and, in military circles, to "civilians," that is, "noncombatants." To militant Christians fighting for their faith in God's army, this is then what pagan nonbelievers were: people who cut and run. (See Kirsch, *GAG,* pp. 14–15.)

229 "*the mouths of the communicants . . . sharp and heavy boards*" Gibbon, *Decline and Fall of the Roman Empire,* chap. 21.

229 *encountered the Great Thunderer himself* Fox, *Pagans and Christians,* p. 149. This was his second encounter with the god. He also claimed to have received a sign from Zeus in Paris when his troops had first proclaimed him emperor. Then he said he had seen the planet Jupiter glow in the sky (Julian, *Letter to the Athenians,* quoted in Kirsch, *GAG,* p. 234).

230 "*Tell him . . . the voice is stilled*" My adaptation of a passage quoted in Greek in William Smith's *Dictionary of Greek and Roman Antiquities* (London: John Murray, 1890), p. 43, from Cedrenus, *Historiarum compendium,* p. 304 (edition of 1647).

230 *Theodosius* For information about Theodosius I and life at the Byzantine court, there is no better source than Gibbon's delightfully readable masterpiece, *The Decline and Fall of the Roman Empire* (chaps. 27–28). Also very informative about this period are John Holland

Smith's *The Death of Classical Paganism*, Robin Lane Fox's *Pagans and Christians*, and the above-mentioned *God Against the Gods.*

231 *a boxer from . . . Persia* Drees, *Olympía*, pp. 156–58.

231 *the god's sacred, prophetic oak was uprooted* Dakaris, *Dodona*, p. 10.

231 *the Games . . . closed down* There are differing dates on this. A.D. 393 was recorded by Cedrenus in *Historia Comparativa* (326D–327A), written c. A.D. 1100. Another version dates the final Olympiad in c. 425, after which Theodosius's grandson, Theodosius II, ordered all pagan temples destroyed (see Drees, *Olympía*, p. 159).

232 *"his speedy dissolution"* Gibbon, *Decline and Fall of the Roman Empire*, chap. 27.

232 *rats rustled through the hollows* Lucian of Samosata spoke of the rats (see Swaddling, *AOG*, p. 20). The presence of Zeus's statue in Constantinople is attested to by the eleventh-century Byzantine historian Cedrenus in his *Historia Comparativa* (322 B.C.) as well as several other sources.

233 *speaking the names of the pagan gods was forbidden* Tertullian (c. A.D. 160–220), the first important Latin writer on church doctrine, speaks of "the Law [that] prohibits the naming of pagan gods" (*On Idolatry*, 20, quoted in Dowden, *Zeus*, p. 83).

233 *"Noble and Christ-beloved servant of God . . . revered empire"* *The Lausiac History*, a compilation by Palladius, quoted in Bassett, "Excellent Offerings," p. 11.

233 *most puritanical of Christian regimes* That of Theodosius II (401–450). See Gibbon, *Decline and Fall of the Roman Empire*, chap. 32 (GBWW, vol. 40, pp. 533–35).

234 *right on the Mese* Its location is disputed, but the only two possibilities offered are both within this area (Bassett, "Excellent Offerings," pp. 12–13).

234 *the statues would have been robbed of their mystery*, Ibid., pp. 19–20.

234 *now known as a saint* Gibbon, *Decline and Fall of the Roman Empire*, chap. 28, 4; Bury, *HLRE*, vol. 1, pp. 372–75.

235 *Homer's fearsome vision* Homer, *Iliad*, I.528–30 (adapted from the Samuel Butler translation).

236 *a series of terrible fires* Bassett, "Excellent Offerings," pp. 6–7, quoting two Byzantine chroniclers, George Kedrenos and John Zonaras, from the eleventh and twelfth centuries respectively.

236 *the monastery of Daphní outside Athens* Sherard, *Byzantium*, p. 110.

237 "*From yonder . . . Dame Hortense, the Earth*" Kazantzákis, *ZG*, pp. 219–20 (translation by Carl Wildman). It should also be noted that Zeus continues to gain fame, as well, in the nicknames of mighty American football players, bestselling computer games, travel companies, and, above all, the beagle Zeus, honored as such by my agent's daughter, Becky.

237 Αμήν Greek for "amen."

SELECTED BIBLIOGRAPHY

ANCIENT SOURCES

These sources are listed in their order of composition. The dates given are when the works were believed to have been written or brought to the public eye. The editions and translations that I used follow the original authors and titles.

Homer (c. 750–700 B.C.). *The Iliad* and *The Odyssey*. Translation by Robert Fagles. New York: Viking, 1990.

———. *The Iliad* and *The Odyssey*. Translation by Richard Lattimore. Chicago: University of Chicago Press, 1951.

Hesiod (c. 700 B.C.). *The Poems of Hesiod*. Translation by R. M. Fraser. Norman: University of Oklahoma Press, 1982.

———. *Theogony*. Edited by M. L. West. Oxford: Clarendon Press, 1966.

———. *Theogony* and *Works and Days*. Translation by H. G. Evelyn-White. Loeb Classical Library. Cambridge, Mass.: Harvard University Press, 1982.

———. *Works and Days*. Edited with prolegomena and commentary. Oxford: Oxford University Press, 1978.

The Homeric Hymns (c. 650 B.C. onward). Translation by H. G. Evelyn-White. Loeb Classical Library. Cambridge, Mass.: Harvard University Press, 1982. These thirty-three poems of various lengths were written to celebrate the feast of a particular deity. Their authorship is uncertain, although the ancient Greeks thought it was Homer.

Pindar (c. 498–446 B.C.). *The Odes*. Translation by G. S. Conway and Richard Stoneman. Rutland, Vt.: Everyman, 1997. Choral odes composed to celebrate the various victors at the Olympian, Pythian, Isthmian, and Nemean games. Most provide invaluable information about the victors' local mythical traditions.

Aeschylus (c. 499–456 B.C.). *The Complete Greek Tragedies.* Edited by David Greene and Richard Lattimore with various translators. Chicago: University of Chicago Press, 1960.

Sophocles (c. 468–413 B.C.). *The Complete Greek Tragedies.* Edited by David Greene and Richard Lattimore with various translators. Chicago: University of Chicago Press, 1960.

Herodotus (c. 450–420 B.C.). *The Histories.* Translation by Aubrey de Sélincourt. Revised and annotated by John Marincola. New York: Penguin, 1996.

Euripides (c. 441–406 B.C.). *The Complete Greek Tragedies.* Edited by David Greene and Richard Lattimore with various translators. Chicago: University of Chicago Press, 1960.

Aristophanes (c. 427–405 B.C.). *Archarnians, Lysistrata, Clouds.* Translation, introduction, and notes by Jeffrey Henderson. Newburyport, Vt.: Focus Classical Library, 1997.

Thucydides (c. 390 B.C.). *The Landmark Thucydides.* Translated by Richard Crawley. Edited by Robert B. Strassler. New York: Simon and Schuster, 1996. The date of Thucydides' composition is in considerable dispute. See Mark Munn, *The School of History.* Berkeley: University of California Press, 2000.

Plato (c. 399–347 B.C.). *Works.* Translated by Benjamin Jowett. Great Books of the Western World, vol. 7. Chicago: University of Chicago Press, 1952.

Apollodorus (first or second centuries B.C.). *The Library.* Translated by J. G. Frazer. Loeb Classical Library. Cambridge, Mass.: Harvard University Press, 1976. A summary of the known myths and heroic legends that had previously appeared in Greek literature.

Diodorus Siculus (c. 56–30 B.C.). *Library of History.* Translated by C. H. Oldfather. Loeb Classical Library. Cambridge, Mass.: Harvard University Press, 2004. A history of the world, the first five volumes detailing the mythology and paradoxology (wondrous occurrences) of the "inhabited world," making it a crucial source of the beliefs of the time.

Ovid (A.D. 1–8). *Metamorphoses.* Translated by A. D. Melville. Introduction and notes by E. J. Kenny. Oxford: Oxford University Press, 1986. Written in Latin. Retellings of the ancient myths so bewitching that many of his variations have become the accepted versions.

Pausanias (A.D. 143–176). *Guide to Greece.* 2 vols. Translated with introductions and notes by Peter Levi. New York: Penguin, 1985. A fascinating compendium of facts about the history of the region and its various religious customs, temples, and sculptures.

Plutarch (c. A.D. 98–120). *The Lives of the Noble Grecians and Romans.* Translated by John Dryden. Great Books of the Western World, vol. 14. Chicago: University of Chicago Press, 1952.

———. *Moralia*, vol. 5. Translated by Frank C. Babbitt. Loeb Classical Library. Cambridge, Mass.: Harvard University Press, 1936. Provides invaluable details about religious rituals and attendant matters.

Hyginus (second century A.D.). *The Myths of Hyginus.* Translated and edited by Mary Grant. Lawrence: University of Kansas Press, 1960. Contains his handbook of mythological genealogy, the *Fabulae*, and his *Poetica Astronomica*, both rich with wonderful tidbits often found nowhere else.

Suetonius (c. A.D. 117–138). *The Twelve Caesars.* Translated by Robert Graves, revised by Michael Grant. New York: Penguin, 2003.

Nonnus (c. A.D. 450–470). *Dionysiaca.* Books 1–15. Translated by W. H. D. Rouse. Loeb Classical Library. Cambridge, Mass.: Harvard University Press, 2004. Fascinating and wonderfully florid variations on the life of the god Diónysos as they had survived in the Christian world up to the time of the destruction of Zeus's Olympian statue.

The Scholiasts. This is a fifteenth-century-A.D. term for people in antiquity who left annotations in the margins of the texts they were reading. Their comments are often the only information we have on certain aspects of or variations on the standard myths, and many of these have been incorporated by later scholars, particularly those mentioned below, into the stories as fundamental to their telling.

Gibbon, Edward (1772–1787). *The Decline and Fall of the Roman Empire.* Great Books of the Western World, vols. 40 and 41. Chicago: University of Chicago Press, 1952.

OTHER WORKS

Baring, Anne, and Jules Cashford. *The Myth of the Goddess.* New York: Arkana, Penguin, 1993.

Bassett, Sarah Guberti. "'Excellent Offerings': The Lausos Collection in Constantinople." *Art Bulletin* 82, no. 1 (March 2000).

Boardman, John. *The Archeology of Nostalgia.* London: Thames and Hudson, 2002.

Broad, William J. *The Oracle.* New York: Penguin, 2006.

Burkert, Walter. *Babylon, Memphis, Persepolis.* Cambridge, Mass.: Harvard University Press, 2004.

———. *Greek Religion.* Translated by John Raffan. Cambridge, Mass.: Harvard University Press, 1985.

———. *Homo Necans.* Translated by Peter Bing. Berkeley: University of California Press, 1983.

Bury, J. B. *History of the Later Roman Empire.* Vol. 1. New York: Dover, 1958.

Calasso, Roberto. *The Marriage of Cadmus and Harmony.* London: Vintage, 1995.

Chadwick, John. *The Decipherment of Linear B.* New York: Random House, 1958.

———. *The Mycenaean World.* Cambridge: Cambridge University Press, 1976.

Constantinidou-Partheniadou, Sofia. *A Travelogue in Greece and A Folklore Calendar.* Translated by Michael Papapetrou. Athens: Sofia Partheniadou, 1992.

Cook, A. B. *Zeus,* 3 vols. New York: Biblo and Tannen, 1965.

Dakaris, Sotirios. *Dodona.* Athens: Ministry of Culture, 2000.

De Bakker, Johan. *Across Crete: Part One.* Amsterdam, the Netherlands: Logos Tekstproducties, 2001.

Deuel, Leo. *Memoirs of Heinrich Schliemann.* New York: Harper and Row, 1977.

Dodds, E. R. *Euripides' Bacchae.* Oxford: Oxford University Press, 1960.

———. *The Greeks and the Irrational.* Berkeley: University of California Press, 1951.

Dowden, Ken. *Zeus.* New York: Routledge, 2006.

Drees, Ludwig. *Olympía.* Translated by Gerald Onn. New York: Praeger, 1968.

Drews, Robert. *The Coming of the Greeks.* Princeton, N.J.: Princeton University Press, 1988.

———. *The End of the Bronze Age.* Princeton, N.J.: Princeton University Press, 1993.

Eliad, Mircea. *The Myth of the Eternal Return.* Translated by Williard R. Trask. Princeton, N.J.: Princeton University Press, 1991.

Fox, Robin Lane. *Pagans and Christians.* New York: Knopf, 1987.

Friedrich, Walter. *Fire in the Sea.* Translated by Alexander R. McBirney. Cambridge: Cambridge University Press, 1999.

Gantz, Timothy. *Early Greek Myth.* Baltimore: Johns Hopkins University Press, 1996.

Garber, Majorie, and Nancy J. Vickers, eds. *The Medusa Reader.* New York: Routledge, 2003.

Geldard, Richard G. *The Traveler's Key to Ancient Greece.* New York: Knopf, 1989.

Gimbutas, Marija. *The Goddesses and Gods of Old Europe.* London: Thames and Hudson, 1982.

Grant, Michael. *Ancient Mediterranean.* New York: History Book Club, 2002.

———. *Myths of the Greeks and Romans.* New York: Meridian, 1995.

———. *The Rise of the Greeks.* London: Phoenix Press, 2005.

Grant, Michael, and John Hazel. *Who's Who in Classical Mythology.* New York: Routledge, 2002.

Graves, Robert. *The Greek Myths.* Complete edition. London: Penguin, 1992.

Guthrie, W. K. C. *The Greeks and Their Gods.* Boston: Beacon, 1955.

Harrison, Jane. *Prolegomena to the Study of Greek Religion.* London: Merlin Press, 1980.

———. *Thémis.* London: Merlin Press, 1977.

Haxton, Brooks, trans. *Fragments: The Collected Wisdom of Heraclitus.* New York: Viking, 2001.

Hinnels, John R. *Persian Mythology.* London: Hamlyn, 1973.

Hoyle, Peter. *Delphi.* London: Cassell, 1967.

Hughes, Bettany. *Helen of Troy.* New York: Knopf, 2005.

James, Vanessa. *The Genealogy of Greek Mythology.* New York: Gotham Books, Penguin, 2003.

Kazantzakis, Nikos. *Report to Greco.* Translated by P. A. Bien. New York: Simon and Schuster, 1965.

———. *Zorba the Greek.* Translated by Carl Wildman. New York: Simon and Schuster, 1981.

Kerényi, Karl. *Dionysos.* Translated by Ralph Mannheim. Princeton, N.J.: Princeton University Press, 1996.

———. *Prométheus.* Translated by Ralph Mannheim. Princeton, N.J.: Princeton University Press, 1997.

King, Charles. *The Black Sea.* Oxford: Oxford University Press, 2004.

Kirsch, Jonathan. *God Against the Gods.* New York: Viking, 2004.

Knox, Bernard. Introduction to *The Norton Book of Classical Literature.* New York: Norton, 1993.

Latacz, Joaquim. *Troy and Homer.* Translated by Kevin Windle and Rosh Ireland. New York: Oxford University Press, 2004.

Lloyd-Jones, Hugh. *The Justice of Zeus*. Berkeley: University of California Press, 1971.

Mackenzie, Donald A. *Crete and Pre-Hellenic Myths and Legends*. London: Senate, Random House, 1996.

Major, Adrienne. *The First Fossil Hunters*. Princeton, N.J.: Princeton University Press, 2000.

Marinatos, Nanno. *Art and Religion in Thera*. Athens: I. Mathioulakis, 1984.

Mavor, James W. *Voyage to Atlantis*. Rochester, Vt.: Park Street Press, 1996.

Meagher, Robert Emmet. *Helen: Myth, Legend, and the Culture of Misogyny*. New York: Continuum, 1995.

Miller, Henry. *The Colossus of Maroussi*. New York: New Directions, 1958.

Nilsson, Martin P. *Greek Folk Region*. Philadelphia: University of Pennsylvania Press, 1972.

———. *The Minoan-Mycenaean Religion*. 2nd revised edition. New York: Biblo and Tannen, 1949.

———. *The Mycenaean Origin of Greek Mythology*. New York: Norton, 1963.

Osborne, Robin. *Greece in the Making, 1200–479 B.C.* New York: Routledge, 2005.

Otto, Walter F. *Dionysos*. Translated by Robert B. Palmer. Bloomington: Indiana University Press, 1965.

Pandermalis, Dimitrios. *Dion*. Athens: Adam Editions, 1997.

Panofsky, Dora, and Erwin Panofsky. *Pandora's Box*. Princeton, N.J.: Princeton University Press, 1962.

Pelligrino, Charles. *Unearthing Atlantis*. New York: Avon, 1991.

Perrottet, Tony. *The Naked Olympics*. New York: Random House, 2004.

Rose, H. J. *A Handbook of Greek Mythology*. New York: Dutton Everyman, 1959.

Sakellárakis, Iánnis. *Digging for the Past*, Athens: Ammos, 1996.

Sakellárakis, Iánnis, and E. Sapouna-Sakellárakis. *Arkhanes*. Athens: Ekdotike Athenon, 1991.

Scully, Vincent. *The Earth, the Temple, and the Gods*. New York: Praeger, 1969.

Seferis, Giorgos. *Collected Poems*. Translated by Edmund Keely and Philip Sherrard. Princeton, N.J.: Princeton University Press, 1981.

Sherard, Philip. *Byzantium*. New York: Time-Life Books, 1966.

Smith, John Holland. *The Death of Classical Paganism*. New York: Scribner's, 1976.

Strauss, Barry. *The Battle of Salamis*. New York: Simon and Schuster, 2004.

———. *The Trojan War*. New York: Simon and Schuster, 2006.

Swaddling, Judith. *The Ancient Olympic Games.* Austin: University of Texas Press, 1999.

Vassilakis, Antonis. *Herakleion Archeological Museum Visitors Guide.* Athens: Adam Editions.

———. *Knossos.* Athens: Adam Editions.

Vermeule, Emily. *Greece in the Bronze Age.* Chicago: University of Chicago Press, 1974.

Weil, Simone. "The Iliad, or the Poem of Force." In *War and the Iliad*, translated by Mary McCarthy. New York: New York Review of Books Classics, 2005.

West, M. L. *Hesiod's Theogony.* Edited by M. L. West. Oxford: Clarendon Press, 1966.

———. *Hesiod's Works and Days.* Edited with prolegomena and commentary. Oxford: Oxford University Press, 1978.

———. *Immortal Helen.* Inaugural lecture, Bedford College, University of London, 1975.

———. *Orestes* (Euripides). Edited with translation and commentary. Warminster, Wiltshire, England: Aris and Phillips, 1987.

Willetts, R. F. *The Civilization of Ancient Crete.* London: Phoenix, 1977.

Winchester, Simon. *Krakatoa.* HarperCollins, 2003.

Wood, Michael. *In Search of the Trojan War.* New York: Facts on File, 1985.

REFERENCE WORKS

Chevalier, Jean, and Alain Gheerbrant. *Dictionary of Symbols.* Translated by John Buchanan-Brown. London: Penguin, 1996.

Hornblower, Simon, and Antony Spawforth. *The Oxford Classical Dictionary. 3rd edition.* New York: Oxford University Press, 1996.

Barker, Kenneth, ed. *The NIV Study Bible.* Grand Rapids, Mich.: Zondervan, 1995.

INDEX

A NOTE ON THE AUTHOR

A philhellene who lived in Greece for twenty-two years, Tom Stone is the author of six previous books about Greece and its culture and language, including *The Summer of My Greek Tavérna*. He has written extensively on Greece and its history for various magazines and guidebooks. He lives in Los Angeles.

BOSTON PUBLIC LIBRARY
3 9999 06111 984 6